The Power
of Positive Coaching

The Jones and Bartlett Series in Health Sciences

AIDS Smartbook, Kopec

AIDS, Science and Society, Fan et al.

Anatomy and Physiology: An Easy Learner, Sloane

Aquatic Exercise, Sova

Aquatics: The Complete Reference Guide for Aquatic Fitness Professionals, Sova

Aquatics Activities Handbook, Sova

An Athlete's Guide to Agents, Ruxin

Basic Epidemiological Methods and Biostatistics, Page, et al.

Basic Law for the Allied Health Professions, Second Edition, Cowdrey/Drew

The Biology of AIDS, Third Edition, Fan, et al.

Bloodborne Pathogens, National Safety Council

A Challenge for Living: Dying, Death, and Bereavement, Corless, et al.

Concepts of Athletic Training, Pfeiffer/Mangus

CPR Manual, National Safety Council

Dawn Brown's Complete Guide to Step Aerobics, Brown

Drugs and Society, Fourth Edition, Hanson/Venturelli

Drug Use in America, Venturelli

Dying, Death, and Bereavement: Theoretical Perspectives and Other Ways of Knowing, Corless, et al.

Easy ACLS: Advanced Cardiac Life Support Preparatory Manual, Weinberg/Paturas

Easy ACLS Pocket Guide, Weinberg/Paturas

Emergency Encounters: EMTs and Their Work, Mannon

Essential Medical Terminology, Second Edition, Stanfield/Hui

Ethics Consultation: A Practical Guide, La Puma/Schiedermayer

First Aid, National Safety Council

First Aid and CPR, Second Edition, National Safety Council

First Aid and CPR, Infants and Children, National Safety Council

First Aid Handbook, National Safety Council

First Responder, American Association of Orthopaedic Surgeons, National Safety Council

Fitness and Health: Life-Style Strategies, Thygerson

Fostering Emotional Well-Being in the Classroom, Page/Page

Golf: Your Turn for Success, Fisher/Geertsen

Grant Application Writer's Handbook, Reif-Lehrer

A Guide to Bystander Care at a Roadside Emergency, AAA Foundation for Traffic Safety

Health and Wellness, Fifth Edition, Edlin/Golanty/McCormack Brown

Health Education: Creating Strategies for School and Community Health, Gilbert/Sawyer

Healthy Children 2000, U.S. Department of Health and Human Services

Healthy People 2000, U.S. Department of Health and Human Services

Healthy People 2000--Summary Report, U.S. Department of Health and Human Services

Human Aging and Chronic Disease, Kart, et al.

Human Anatomy and Physiology Coloring Workbook and Study Guide, Anderson

An Introduction to Epidemiology, Timmreck

Introduction to Human Disease, Third Edition, Crowley

Introduction to the Health Professions, Second Edition, Stanfield/Hui

Managing Stress: Principles and Strategies for Health and Wellbeing, Seaward

Mastering the New Medical Terminology: Through Self-Instructional Modules, Second Edition, Stanfield/Hui

Medical Terminology with Vikki Wetle, RN, MA, Video Series, Wetle

National Pool and Waterpark Lifeguard/CPR Training, Ellis & Associates

The Nation's Health, Fourth Edition, Lee/Estes

New Dimensions in Women's Health, Alexander/LaRosa

Omaha Orange: A Popular History of EMS in America, Post

Oxygen Administration, National Safety Council

Perspectives on Death and Dying, Fulton/Metress

Planning, Program Development, and Evaluation: A Handbook for Health Promotion, Aging, and Health Services, Timmreck

The Power of Positive Coaching, Nakamura

Primeros Auxilios y RCP, National Safety Council

Safety, Second Edition, Thygerson

Skill-Building Activities for Alcohol and Drug Education, Bates/Wigtil

Sports Equipment Management, Walker/Seidler

Sports Injury Care, Abdenour/Thygerson

Statistics: An Interactive Text for the Health and Life Sciences, Krishnamurty et al.

Stress Management, National Safety Council

Teaching Elementary Health Science, Third Edition, Bender/Sorochan

Weight Training for Strength and Fitness, Silvester

The Power
of Positive Coaching

Raymond M. Nakamura, Ph.D.
California Polytechnic State University
San Luis Obispo, California

Jones and Bartlett Publishers
Sudbury, Massachusetts

Boston   London   Singapore

Editorial, Sales, and Customer Service Offices
Jones and Bartlett Publishers
40 Tall Pine Drive
Sudbury, MA 01776
(508) 443-5000
(800) 832-0034

Jones and Bartlett Publishers International
Barb House, Barb Mews
London W6 7PA
UK

Library of Congress Cataloging-in-Publication Data
Nakamura, Raymond M.
The power of positive coaching/Raymond M. Nakamura.
     p. cm.
  Includes bibliographical references and index.
  ISBN 0-7637-0031-2
  1. Coaching (Athletics) 2. Coach-athlete relationships.
  I. Title.
  GV711.N36 1996
  796'.07'7—dc20   96-4186
                                                                             CIP

Acquisitions Editor: Joseph E. Burns
Associate Production Editor: Nadine Fitzwilliam
Manufacturing Buyer: Dana L. Cerrito
Editorial Production Service: Kathy Smith
Typesetting: LeGwin Associates
Cover Design: Marshall Henrichs
Printing and Binding: Malloy Lithographing, Inc.
Cover Printing: Coral Graphic Services, Inc.

Printed in the United States of America
00 99 98 97 96   10 9 8 7 6 5 4 3 2 1

To my wife Connie, who is my best friend and the most loving and gentle person I know. Without your love and insight, this book would not have been written. You continue to teach me simply by the way you live your life. Thank you for letting me be a part of it
and
to my son Kyle and my daughter Lindy whom I love so dearly.

Also,
to Leonard Jareczek, my high school track coach, who made me feel accepted, capable, and significant. Thanks coach, you were a terrific influence in my life
and
to the women of the DePaul University volleyball team that I was fortunate enough to coach.

Contents

PART I   **The Coach**   **1**

   CHAPTER 1   The Coach's Challenge   3

   CHAPTER 2   What Kind of Coach Are You?   19

PART II   **The Inner Athlete: Understanding Basic Needs**   **31**

   CHAPTER 3   Building Strong and Independent Athletes from the Inside Out   33

   CHAPTER 4   Emotional Affiliation: Acceptance and Belonging   49

   CHAPTER 5   Emotional Significance: Give Athletes a Sense of Purpose   59

   CHAPTER 6   The Capable Athlete: Structure for Success, Not Failure   69

   CHAPTER 7   The Capable Athlete: Encourage Success, Not Failure   83

   CHAPTER 8   The Need to Feel Safe   91

PART III   **Effective Communication**   **99**

   CHAPTER 9   Effective Communication: Listening to and Acknowledging the Athlete's Thoughts and Feelings   101

   CHAPTER 10   Sending Firm Messages and Establishing Team Rules and Procedures   113

   CHAPTER 11   Coaching Without Anger: Communicating Your Needs in Words   124

PART IV   **Establishing Responsible Behavior and Discipline**   **133**

   CHAPTER 12   Athletes in Conflict: The Mistaken Goals of Behavior   135

   CHAPTER 13   Coaching Responsible Behavior: Empowering Discipline   146

CHAPTER 14 Coaching toward Self-Discipline:
Using Natural and Logical Consequences   159

CHAPTER 15 Conflict Resolution   170

PART V **Putting It All Together**   **181**

CHAPTER 16 The Team Forum   183

REFERENCES   199

APPENDIX   203

INDEX   288

Preface

The Power of Positive Coaching is designed to help you with strategies and skills for building within each athlete the strength and ability to live a healthy, happy, and productive life on the athletic field. This book is not about teaching athletic skills. It is about understanding, meeting and supporting the athlete's emotional and social needs and teaching athletes about responsibility, self-discipline, social interaction, and self-reliance through athletics.

This book is about meeting the challenges of modern-day coaching so that you can learn to connect with your athletes in ways that will help them grow in the athletic arena. Its intention is to provide you with an understandable and usable way of approaching your wonderful, yet awesome task of coaching young people.

The Power of Positive Coaching is divided in the following way:

Part 1 consists of two chapters and focuses on the challenges that today's coaches face and the different leadership styles that they employ to meet them. Coach-player relationships have gone through significant transition and change, and today's coaches face new social challenges that they are not always prepared to meet.

Part 2 consists of six chapters and focuses on the athlete. This part gives you understandable and usable strategies to help you make positive connections with your athletes. These simple strategies are based on a foundation of mutual dignity and respect. The formula is simple: Give the athletes what they need, and the athletes will give you what you need. By making athletes feel accepted, significant, capable, and safe within the team setting, a coach will help athletes to develop positive perceptions of themselves. As a result, coaches will be setting the foundation to help athletes develop self-reliance, discipline, and responsibility.

Part 3 consists of three chapters and focuses on helping coaches to develop positive interpersonal relations through effective communication. Success will depend not only on how well you communicate your thoughts and feelings, but also on how well you listen. Communication skills are just as basic as driving a car. A person needs to know how to start and stop it. In between starting and stopping, one needs to know when to accelerate, when to put on the brakes, and how to keep the vehicle on course.

Part 4 consists of four chapters and focuses on helping you to develop a positive program of discipline that will help empower athletes to become self-reliant, self-disciplined, and responsible in their behavior. Knowing the primary goal of most behavior is the foundation for understanding most problems and knowing what kind of strategies to use in helping your athletes grow. Discipline that empowers athletes is based on treating them with dignity and respect rather than punishment and humiliation.

Part 5 consists of only one chapter but pulls together all the concepts of the book in a process called the team forum. This process is designed to help coaches and players make plans and decisions, provide encouragement, and solve problems. Team forums improve communications, cooperation, and responsibility and, most important, reflect how fortunate the athletes are to have each other. It is perhaps the most important chapter in the book.

A unique feature of each chapter is the section called "Time Out." There are two types of time outs. "Time Out: In the Coach's Corner" consists of vignettes, quizzes, written articles, and other activities to help illustrate the principles supported in the book. "Time Out: Self-Assessment" helps you assess the attitudes and behaviors that influence your coaching style. In addition, quotations have been placed in the margins of the pages to stress some of the major points in the text. Each chapter concludes with a question-and-answer section and a summary of major points.

Throughout this book I have tried to challenge some of the old ways of doing things and to offer strategies to help your athletes grow in healthy ways both on and off the athletic field. Carefully evaluate the suggestions in these pages, and try to determine what will work for you—after all, you know your athletes better than I do. Do only those things that feel right to you; otherwise, your athletes will see right through the strategies. Coaching and the art of developing positive relationships with your athletes are not easy. I don't believe that there is any one magical technique for all coaches. However, I do believe that whatever methods you choose, they must have a foundation based on mutual honesty, dignity, and respect.

I hope that in the end I have helped you to enhance your leadership skills, examine your coaching philosophy, and most important, connect with your athletes in positive ways.

The Coach

The Coach's Challenge

We live in a world that is sick socially, politically, and economically. It is for only one reason—lack of fair play and good sportsmanship in human relationships.

Avery Brundage
Former President of IOC [1948]

Today's coaches realize that despite the emphasis in the media, the most important objectives of sport participation are not just to win games or medals or to break records. In fact, Martens [1987] reported that fewer than 2 percent of coaches acknowledged that winning is their first priority and that most coaches genuinely subscribe to the American Coaching Effectiveness Program's (ACEP) philosophy "Athletes first, winning second." Consequently, the first priority of sports education should be to empower young athletes to reach their physical, emotional, and social potential through participation in sports.

Organizations like ACEP share similar philosophies. The Program for Athletic Coaches' Education (PACE) [Seefeldt and Brown, 1992], for example, includes some of the following emotional benefits that should be acquired through sports participation:

- developing a realistic and positive self-image;
- enhancing the likelihood of participation in physical activity throughout life;
- obtaining enjoyment and recreation;
- developing positive personal, social, and psychological skills (self-worth, self-discipline, teamwork, effective communication, goal setting, self-control); and
- denouncing drug use as the way to recreate, escape from reality, or enhance performance.

The National Youth Sports Coaches Association (NYSCA), as cited by Engh [1992], lists in its Coaches' Code of Ethics the following emotional goals:

I will place the emotional and physical well-being of my players ahead of any personal desire to win.

I will remember to treat each player as an individual, remembering the large spread of emotional and physical development for the same age group.

I will do my very best to provide a safe situation for my players.

I will lead, by example, in demonstrating fair play and sportsmanship to all my players.

I will remember that I am a youth coach, and that the game is for children and not adults.

To be prepared is half the victory.
CERVANTES

In essence, the goals of these organizations reflect the major goals of modern education. The California Task Force to Promote Self-Esteem and Personal and Social Responsibility [1990] supports the premise that education should include programs that help each individual raise his or her level of self-esteem by becoming more self-reliant, responsible, self-disciplined, and capable. Sports education is an extension of the classroom. Athletics is just one of many vehicles working together to help young people reach those potentials, and the coach is just one of the many drivers helping to fuel and guide each athlete to that end. By exposing the participants to the principles of fair play, good sportsmanship, achievement, and sport activity, the coach can encourage them to adopt these same principles both in the athletic arena and in other aspects of life. According to this philosophy, winning is not a state to arrive at, but a manner of traveling.

The Coach's Dilemma

Most coaches are competent in teaching the skills and knowledge required to play a sport. Most coaches have also participated in sports, and many have taken classes in teaching athletic skills. However, the art of nurturing an athlete's emotional and social health is left largely to chance. The discrepancy between valuing the athlete's emotional and social health and failing to give coaches specific training for that job comes from the assumption that if a person is an adult, he or she should already know how to nurture young athletes. But becoming a coach does not automatically confer on anyone the knowledge and skills required to do so. Without a better understanding of human nature and how to work with it, a coach does not have a complete game plan, and neither the coach nor the athletes will ever be complete winners.

This book is about the power of positive coaching. It is about the work and planning that come before, during, and after athletics. It is not about teaching athletic skills. It is about understanding, meeting, and supporting the athletes' emotional and social needs and teaching athletes about responsibility, self-discipline, social interaction, and self-reliance through athletics. It is about developing positive relationships through mutual dignity and respect.

Sports Education at the Crossroads

Education is an art, and an especially difficult one. . . . Every art is a dynamic trend toward an object to be achieved, which is the aim of this art. There is no art without ends, without stopping at any intermediary step.

Here we see from the outset the two most dangerous misconceptions against which education must guard itself. The first misconception is a lack of disregards of ends. If means are liked and cultivated for the sake of their own perfection, and not as means alone, to that very extent they cease to lead to an end, and art loses its practicality; its vital efficiency is replaced by a process of infinite multiplication, each means developing and spreading for its own sake. This supremacy of means over end and the consequence collapse of all sure purpose and real efficiency seem to be the main approach to contemporary education.

Jacques Maritain [1938]

The most pathetic person in the world is someone who has sight but has no vision.
HELEN KELLER

Sports education must also face the same challenge as education. Coaches must not allow sports to become the end. Sport is a means to the end: the development of self-reliant, self-disciplined, responsible, and capable young men and women.

TIME OUT: IN THE COACH'S CORNER

The Good and the Bad

When individuals choose to enter the coaching profession, many have preconceived notions of what to expect. However, each situation is unique, and most coaches face circumstances that require them to make adjustments. Sometimes situations require coaches to do things that were never listed in their job descriptions. The most honorable coaches try to teach their players right from wrong in both athletics and life. When coaches are at their best, they teach important lessons about teamwork, self-discipline, sacrifice and other virtues. It should

Leadership should be born out of the understanding of the needs of those who would be affected by it.
MARION ANDERSON

not be unreasonable to expect coaches to be honest, decent individuals who set positive standards by which their athletes are to perform. However, a few coaches do not always act in the best interest of their sport or their players.

The Good

The following story was reported on ESPN's *Cover Story* December 21, 1994. The description below are the words of the author, and not the words of the TV commentator.

> *Tonya Edwards holds the baby tightly in her left arm as she moves quickly along the sidelines of the basketball court at Northwestern High School in Flint, Michigan. Her eyes squint as she analyzes and directs the movement of the players. The intensity of her practice is increasing as her team is preparing for an upcoming game. Her right arm waves frantically as her finger points out directions, and her left arm readjusts to secure the baby's safety. She sometimes forgets and blows the whistle in the baby's ear. Suddenly, without warning, the baby burps up a small amount of fluid. Coach Edwards can only smile and then laugh as she calls for help and requests a towel to clean herself.*
>
> *Finally, Coach Edwards blows her whistle to give the players a break. Sweaty and tired, the baby's teenaged mother walks toward the sidelines to playfully cuddle her baby. She "coos" and "aahs," and the baby laughs.*
>
> *This scene, of course, is not from a typical high school basketball practice. But this scene has become all too familiar for coach Tonya Edwards whose team won the 1994 Michigan State High School Women's Basketball Championship. Coach Edwards had never thought that becoming a head coach would also require her to become a "head nanny." But during the past four years, four of her players had become mothers, and this year's squad was no different. Coach Edwards says with great compassion, "Just because she was a mother didn't mean that I was just going to drop her from the team and leave her on the outside."*
>
> *In addition, seven of her eleven players are from single-parent households, and Coach Edwards finds her role has expanded from coach to chauffeur (she drives many of the girls home after practice), laundry woman (she washes the team uniforms), diaper changer, and a mother for mothers.*
>
> *Even when the season ends, her responsibilities to*

What does it mean to be promoted into a leadership position? Frankly, it means we now have the authority to serve people in a special way.
UNKNOWN

her players don't. Her players still come to her for advice and help. One of her players commented , "I don't even talk to my mother about the things that I talk about with Coach."

The Bad

The following story is an Associated Press, 1994 release. Names and schools have been edited from the article.

Prep Player Takes Fight to Court

(Associated Press) — A high school soccer player who tore two ligaments during overtime play is suing the local school system, claiming he was kicked on purpose on a coach's orders.

The player, a senior co-captain on his high school soccer team, says he was kicked after the opposing coach yelled "Waste him! Waste him! Waste him!" in the final game of an Invitational Tournament.

The player alleges he was kicked after the opposing coach gave orders to his players. He is seeking more than $100,000 from the county school board.

Witnesses said one opposing player kicked him from behind while another opposing player slid at him with his cleats. The player who kicked from behind settled out of court for $25,000.

"I felt a contract was put out on that player," the referee told jurors. "There's no part in the game for that." The referee immediately awarded the victory to the violated team, which was favored to win. He handed a red flag — the most severe penalty in soccer — to the opposing coach.

The accused coach admitted in court Wednesday he used the phrase "waste him," but said it was not meant to be taken literally.

The civil lawsuit was expected to go to the jury today.

If you want to succeed you should strike out on new paths rather than travel the worn paths of accepted success.

J. ROCKEFELLER

Problems in Sports

Such problems as drug abuse, racism, sexism, lying, cheating, player abuse, and violence are increasing in both frequency and intensity among today's young athletes and coaches. Newspapers abound with stories of player rebellion and insurrection, coaches who physically and emotionally abuse their players, and disciplinary action against athletes and coaches who violate the rules of their program. In addition, a significant number of our young people are being exposed to athletic programs within educational institutions, which are entrusted with training our youth, that are neither fair nor honest. When a group of institutions of higher learning find it necessary to fine themselves hundreds of thousands of dollars or administer severe penalties for violating adopted codes, one can hardly expect the young athlete not to be confused about what is appropriate behavior.

Coaches, of course, are not responsible for all of the problems that have arisen within and outside of sport. However, coaches cannot allow these mounting problems to overwhelm them and become the excuse to give up and allow the problems to continue.

A man of character finds a special attractiveness in difficulty, since it is only by coming to grips with difficulty that he can realize his potentialities.
CHARLES DE GAULLE

Many coaches who want to encourage the positive emotional benefits of sport are unsure of what to do and where to go for help. If coaches have no direction and are not sure where they are going, they will surely end up someplace else. Regardless of all the enthusiasm and effort a coach has, it won't be enough if he or she has no real purpose or direction. Understanding some of the changing aspects of sports participation is the first step in changing this.

The Effect of Social Changes on Coaching

Coaches recognize that today's young athletes often have attitudes that are somewhat different from the attitudes that athletes once held. For example, it used to be unthinkable to question a coach's decision. Today, it is almost impossible to make a decision without question. Athletes today do not always respond to the old, demanding methods of coaching and discipline, and they cannot be treated as they were in the past.

Traditionally, coaches held a position of supreme dominance and authority. Not long ago, it was not only acceptable but unquestioned that coaches were superior to and had power over the players. But today's democratic society is moving toward social equality. This movement has led to new challenges that many people, including coaches, are not always prepared to meet.

In today's society, groups such as women and minorities are rightfully and finally beginning to receive equal treatment. Even within the workplace, management and labor have been moving toward a closer relationship of equals. Society is moving toward a system in which all people have the right to be treated as equals. Athletics is also experiencing these positive changes. Coach-player relationships have gone through significant transition and change, and today's coaches must not underestimate the impact of the changing society.

Should Players Have Equal Rights?

Some coaches are disturbed at the thought that their players are their social equals. It is true that coaches have more knowledge, experience, and skills than the athletes have, but these things don't confer automatic superiority. Equality means that each athlete, despite his or her individual differences and abilities, has an equal claim to dignity and respect. Neither coach nor player is superior or inferior. No individual ability or trait such as sex, age, color, wisdom, money, or position guarantees superiority or the right to dominate.

Equality in this context means that athletes are equal to coaches in terms of human worth and dignity. In a democracy, every athlete is entitled to respect and to self-determination within the limits prescribed by the social structure of the sport.

What coaches must realize is that today's athletes can no longer be forced into compliance. They must be stimulated and encouraged into voluntarily taking their part in the maintenance of order. Coaches can coach unconsciously by repeating the methods that their own coaches used, or they can make a conscious commitment to passing on only the values that society would like to see perpetuated. Doing it just the way their old coaches did it becomes an easy substitute for thinking. All coaches have the ability to rise above old, destructive patterns to create a healthy environment for themselves and their athletes. *The Power of Positive Coaching* is about replacing destructive patterns with positive strategies.

> *You cannot be friends upon any terms than upon terms of equality.*
> WOODROW WILSON

Today's Athletes Still Need Nurturing

Although society has changed and today's athletes think somewhat differently from the athletes of the past, they are still the same in many ways. Today's athletes still have basic physical and emotional needs that require fulfillment.

The teenagers who are at the greatest risk of abusing drugs, dropping out of school, joining gangs, or becoming pregnant are the teens whose parents or other significant adults have made them feel unaccepted, insignificant, incapable, and unsafe. Feeling accepted, significant, capable, and safe is basic to any positive relationship. It doesn't matter whether the relationship is between parent and child, teacher and student, coach and athlete, employer and employee, or husband and wife; if you make people feel unaccepted, insignificant, incapable, and unsafe, the results will be similar: failure, indifference, quitting, violence, hatred, cheating, and revenge. In sports, if a coach chooses to sit an athlete on the bench, doesn't

> *Things do not change, we do.*
> THOREAU

pay any attention to him, disregards his feelings, doesn't give him any hope of playing, and adds a dash of criticism, all hell will probably break loose.

To provide guidance, coaches need a practical, easy-to-understand and down-to-earth philosophy that can help them understand the basic needs, motivations, and behaviors of their players and themselves. In the following chapters, *The Power of Positive Coaching* provides a practical, workable framework for building a solid foundation of self-worth and self-esteem in young athletes. *The Power of Positive Coaching* provides a new way of looking at developing athletes as they search for identity and self-worth.

The most effective leaders are the ones who satisfy the psychological needs of their followers
DAVID OGILVY

Coaches Can Make a Difference

Coaches do have a unique opportunity to make significant contributions for change. Coaches can create within their small microcosm of sport a unique environment in which they can reach their athletes, raise their level of self-esteem, win their cooperation, and instill in them the ideal values of sport. Athletics give players a miniature world in which they can try out their skills and explore themselves. How they respond and what they learn will later contribute to their adult performance. Modern sports education is one of the greatest vehicles for reaching human potential.

Athletes deserve the best; and over time, what goes around, comes around. If athletes are respected and accepted, they will learn to respect and accept; if they are abused and rejected, they will learn to abuse and reject. Young athletes will imitate. They reflect how the coach thinks, how the coach communicates, what the coach values, how the coach solves problems, what the coach does with feelings, how the coach cares, and how the coach is in the world. Whether coaches know it or not, they are teaching and modeling self-esteem—or a lack of it—to their players all the time.

TIME OUT: SELF-ASSESSMENT

Are You a Nurturing Coach?

This assessment is primarily for individuals who are presently coaching. If you do not have any coaching experience please use this guide to evaluate one of your former coaches or answer the questions the way you think you will behave when you do become a coach. **Treat the results as a guide only. There is a margin of uncertainty in all surveys of this kind.**

Instructions: Mark one answer for each question. Four points are awarded for a "yes" answer, two points are awarded for a "maybe" or neutral answer, and no points are awarded for a "no" answer.

DO YOU:	YES	MAYBE	NO

1. Like being with young people?
2. Listen to players' concerns both on and off the field?
3. Maintain your composure during stressful interactions with people?
4. Win graciously without being arrogant or obnoxious?
5. Display faith and confidence in your players' abilities and judgments?
6. Discipline all players fairly and equally regardless of their "star" status?
7. Control your temper under pressure situations?
8. Accept athletes for who they are rather than what you want them to be?
9. Act as a positive role model for the team?
10. Accept criticism from your players?
11. Admit to your players that you are wrong?
12. Lose graciously without blaming others (especially players) or making excuses for the loss?
13. Eliminate your swearing or use of other foul language?
14. Accept and treat all athletes (regardless of abilities, color, or gender) equally and fairly?
15. Win fairly and within the rules?
16. Talk honestly with parents of players?
17. Coach an athlete who may dislike you?
18. When angry, clearly express your inner feelings in a respectful manner?
19. When necessary, become involved in the personal problems of your athletes?
20. Let the athletes be in charge of activities such as leading warm-ups, designing practices, or working out on their own?
21. Allow yourself the time to take classes

If a man does not know what port he is steering for, no wind is favorable to him.
SENECA

or seminars in subjects such as adolescent psychology or sports psychology?
22. Set realistic goals for both the team and individual athletes?
23. Stop using put-downs and criticizing words when motivating or disciplining your athletes?
24. Accept compliments or encouraging words without making excuses or explanations?
25. Search for, identify, and acknowledge the strengths of all your athletes?

SCORING

Points
100	Impossible for most ordinary, truthful people.
75–99	YES, you will probably be a nurturing coach.
50-74	YES, you can learn to be a nurturing coach.
49 or less	Are you sure you are in the right profession?

QUESTIONS AND ANSWERS

A man without a purpose is like a ship without a rudder.
THOMAS CARLYLE

Question: What specific forces are changing the nature of athletic programs?

Answer: If you investigate athletic organizations around the country you will see them struggling with many issues. Three potent forces that are redefining the nature of American athletics stand out in particular. Coaches and athletic organizations that ignore these forces or underestimate their impact do so at their own risk. These are the forces at work.

1. The New Reality of the Emerging Athlete
   Regardless of the budget and budget problems, the number of coaches, the kind of equipment, or other tangibles, the team's success will be determined by the participating athletes. Coaches cannot view athletes as pieces of equipment that are discarded after use or simply bodies that fill spaces. The athlete is the center of every single strategy, goal, or vision. All teams are affected, no matter how large or small. The new reality is that how athletes think, work, and feel dictates the direction and success of the team. Success is generated through the spirit and minds of all athletes—through their competence, capacity, and commit-

ment. Competitive advantages will go to the coaches who understand this and know how to guide their athletes. It should be obvious that mismanaging athletes will create costly liabilities for the team and the athletic program.

2. Culturally Diverse Populations

   Over the years, athletics have become a mosaic blend of people: women, Asian Americans, African Americans, Hispanic Americans, European Americans, the disabled, and others. Diversity has challenged the traditions of sports and should lead to openness and acceptance; but for many coaches and athletic programs, diversity has created only conflict and misunderstanding. Our social system has moved toward a society that demands that all people have the right to be treated as equals. As was stated earlier in this chapter, "each athlete, despite his or her individual differences and abilities, has an equal claim to dignity and respect. Neither coach nor player is superior or inferior. No individual ability or trait such as sex, age, color, wisdom, money, or position guarantees superiority or the right to dominate." If coaches and athletes are to be successful in their relationships, they must confront their own prejudices and strive to bring everyone together into a harmonious effort based on respect and acceptance.

   > *There are two ways of meeting difficulties: you alter the difficulties, or you alter yourself to meet them.*
   > PHYLLIS BOTTOME

3. Evolution of Change

   Rapidly advancing technological and societal changes, Title IX, economic restrictions, and changing rules have created a situation that requires more research, understanding, acceptance, and accommodation by coaches and athletic programs. Many coaches are struggling with the changes but, in the process, are becoming overstressed, frustrated and cynical. Coaches who can see the positive side of change and work from that positive position will escape much of the anguish that is often associated with change.

   These three pressures, plus the fact that coaches are getting pressure from higher administration as well as the media and community to win, are changing the nature of athletic programs. In addition, many coaches feel that today's athletes lack the sense of commitment and work ethic of the "good old days." Unfortunately, to cope and survive, many coaches feel that they need to use force and power to control their situations more efficiently. They become controlling and self-centered. In the end, such an approach will only create more problems. This book is about doing it differently.

Question: What skills are required for effective coaching in today's society?

Answer: It is assumed here that a coach is one who (a) manages the activities of the individual players and team and (b) assumes the responsibility for achieving chosen objectives through these efforts. Within this definition, Katz [1974] believes that effective coaching requires three basic skills: professional, human, and conceptual. These skills are interrelated and never independent of each other. Each of the three skills is briefly discussed below.

1. Professional skill is the most familiar because it is the most concrete. It is the one in which coaches are trained. It implies a knowledge and understanding of, and proficiency in, a specific sport. It also involves organization, methods, processes, procedures, and techniques. Professional skill involves specialized knowledge, analytical ability, and application of the tools and techniques of a specific sport.

2. Human skill requires a coach to work effectively as a team leader and to build cooperative effort within the team he or she leads. Professional skill requires working with the technical ins and outs of the sport; human skill is concerned primarily with the ins and outs of each team member. Human skill is principally the ability to work with people. It is essential to effective coaching at every level.

   Coaches with highly developed human skill are aware of their own attitudes, assumptions, and beliefs about each team member. Coaches should also be able to accept viewpoints and beliefs that may not agree with their own. The coach should be a skilled communicator and listener who is both empathetic and understanding about the thoughts, behaviors, and feelings of others. Good coaches have insight into the athlete's heart. They are aware of and sensitive to the hopes and aspirations of each team member.

   Ideally, a coach should strive to create an atmosphere of support and security in which players feel free to express themselves without fear of retaliation, abuse, or ridicule. The coach should encourage players to participate in the planning and execution of those things that directly affect them. The coach should be sensitive to the needs and motivations of players so that he or she can judge the possible reactions to various courses of action that are undertaken. More important, the coach can then act in a way that takes the players' needs into account.

3. Conceptual skill involves the ability to see the team as a whole. It recognizes how the various parts and functions of the team depend on each other and how changes in one

Unless the job means more than the pay it will never pay more.

H. Bertram Lewis

part affect all the others. Conceptual skill also recognizes the relationship of the team to the school, other athletic teams, and the community as a whole. Any decision that the coach makes should benefit the overall welfare of the total organization. The success of a coach's decision, consequently, depends on his or her conceptual skill and those who put the decision into action.

TIME OUT: SELF-ASSESSMENT

Is Your Present Coaching Job Right for You?

This quiz is for anyone who has already been coaching for a number of years. It is not a measure of your intelligence or aptitude for coaching. It is simply a quiz to help you determine whether your present coaching position is right for you. **Treat the results as a guide only. There is a margin of uncertainty in all questionnaires of this kind.**

Democracy has the only approach to human relationships that can make for a free flow of life forces.
FRANCIS
KINGDOM

Instructions: Circle the appropriate response.

1. It is Monday morning, and you have to go back to your coaching job. Are you
   A. Excited about getting back and working on some new strategies or drills?
   B. Wishing you had an excuse for not going today?
   C. Not particularly happy about returning, but you realize that once you are into the routine of practice, everything will be fine?

2. Would you say that your present coaching position
   A. Limits the use of your coaching abilities?
   B. Requires skills and/or knowledge that are beyond your present abilities?
   C. Continues to bring out the best in you?

3. Which statement best applies to you and your coaching position?
   A. I like my job, and I am happy where I am.
   B. I wish I were doing something else.
   C. I like coaching, I just wish I were coaching somewhere else.

4. I find my present coaching position
   A. Boring.
   B. Okay. It can be boring at times but it does have its moments of excitement.
   C. Very exciting and far from boring.

5. If your athletic program were cut and your team were elimi-
nated, what would you miss the most?
   A. The relationship that you have with the players.
   B. Coaching the athletes to become better skilled.
   C. The paycheck.

6. Do you
   A. Like working with young people?
   B. Have a general dislike for young people?
   C. Feel you are indifferent to young people?

7. I usually share my athletic stories and concerns
   A. With anyone who will listen.
   B. Only with special people such as family and friends.
   C. I don't usually talk about my coaching experiences.

8. Why did you choose your present coaching position?
   A. I really wanted it, applied for it, and got it.
   B. I wanted something else, but I took it because it became
   available.
   C. I did it because the team needed a coach and no one
   else would do it.

9. Do you think that your athletes
   A. Dislike you?
   B. Think you are okay and appreciate your efforts?
   C. Really like and enjoy being with you?

10. Your athletic director has just announced that the athletic
budget has been significantly reduced and all coaches will
have to take a 20% pay cut. You will
    A. Quit.
    B. Reluctantly quit because you will have to find something
    else to meet your living expenses.
    C. Keep on coaching.

Scoring and Analysis
Find your score by adding up the sum of your circled responses.

1. A. 5	B. 1	C. 3
2. A. 1	B. 3	C. 5
3. A. 5	B. 1	C. 3
4. A. 1	B. 3	C. 5
5. A. 3	B. 5	C. 1
6. A. 5	B. 1	C. 3
7. A. 5	B. 3	C. 1
8. A. 5	B. 3	C. 1
9. A. 1	B. 3	C. 5
10. A. 1	B. 3	C. 5

Your score will range from 10 to 50.

Score Analysis

10-23   You are dissatisfied, and you dislike the present place that you are in. Coaching may not be the best profession for you, or perhaps you need to find a more enjoyable position elsewhere. Think about what you want, and see if there is another way in which you can use your abilities.

24-37   You are generally satisfied with what you are doing but not particularly driven to achieve your potential even though you may be successful at your job. You probably have other things in your personal life that are equal to or more important than coaching and have justified your need to find a balance between them.

38-50   Your high score reflects that you are happy and actively involved in your present coaching position. You find coaching exciting and challenging. Coaching is a very important part of your life and personal identity.

Major Points Discussed in Chapter 1

1. The vast majority of coaches place the emotional and physical well-being of their athletes above winning.
2. Coaches need more training in nurturing the emotional and social development of their athletes.
3. Many coaches who want to encourage the positive emotional benefits of sport participation are seeking help in learning how to achieve this goal.
4. Society and, consequently, sports have gone through significant social changes throughout the years.
5. Historically, coaches held a position of supreme dominance and authority. However, that is not the situation today. Most athletes expect and demand to be treated with dignity and respect.
6. No individual ability or trait such as sex, age, color, wisdom, money, or position guarantees superiority or the right to dominate any individual.
7. Every athlete is entitled to respect and dignity.
8. Today's athletes are similar to the athletes of the past in that they have the same basic human needs to be fulfilled.
9. Coaches are in a unique position to make significant contributions for positive change. Coaches can live by the philosophy "Athletes first, winning second" and still have winning records and championships.

10. Coaches must be aware of the following forces that changing the nature of athletic programs.
    a. The new reality of the emerging athlete.
    b. Culturally diverse students
    c. Evolution of change.
11. Coaches need the following basic skills to be successfu their coaching efforts.
    a. Professional skills.
    b. Human skills.
    c. Conceptual skills.

2

What Kind of Coach Are You?

Our policy flows from the belief that men and women want to do a good job, a creative job, and that if they are provided with the proper environment, they will do so.

William Hewlett

A Journey with an "Empowered" Team

Imagine going to practice and encountering an exciting, inspiring, and intoxicating atmosphere. Athletes are brimming over with enthusiasm, commitment, and pride. They are eager to work hard, listen to the coach's words, and are willing to share their ideas. Some of the athletes are mentoring others, others are sharing and cooperating as they discuss how to overcome weaknesses in their offenses and defenses. They laugh easily and playfully kid with the coach and among themselves. They enjoy being there. They like and respect the coach.

As the practice progresses, the athletes meet among themselves, sometimes going to the coach with creative ideas and special requests. They approach each drill and assignment with purpose and intensity. Each athlete continuously works on different ways to improve his or her skill levels.

People are more easily led than driven.
DAVID FINK

When an athlete speaks, others listen. When an athlete takes charge of a drill, others are quick to respond and help because they know that on another occasion, they may be the leader and need support. Each athlete has trust in the coach because the coach listens and is flexible enough to accommodate each of them whenever possible. As the coach listens to the athletes' words, the coach hears voices that are supportive, sincere, and personal. No one fears or hides from the coach, nor is there secretive mumbling behind the coach's back. There is an atmosphere of support, trust, respect, and no antagonism because a philosophy of teamwork and partnership makes up the team structure.

The most penetrating aspect of the empowered team is that each person—whether it be the coach, the athlete, the manager, or anyone associated with the team—is treated with dignity and respect. When the team shows that it truly cares about each individual athlete, each athlete will reciprocate this faith with loyalty and hard work. Empowered athletic teams have a common vision surrounded by shared goals, shared respect and shared values.

This empowered team may seem like a distant dream. For many teams, it is. But some of the thousands of athletic teams from youth sports to college athletics in this country are slowly transforming themselves into empowered teams based on trust, respect, and dignity.

Many coaches sell themselves short, performing well below their full potential. Instead of striving for optimal performance, they accept stress and mediocrity as the norm. As a result, they lead stressful lives and build unhealthy teams.

This book is about doing it better. It's about designing and building empowered athletes and teams through positive relationships based on mutual dignity, respect, and trust. Whether a person is the coach of a high school team or a parent coaching a park district summer soccer team, this book is written for them. No athletic team is exempt. The concept of an empowered team is relevant to all coaches, athletic teams, and organizations.

Coaching Styles

To expect to rule others by assuming a loud tone is like thinking oneself tall by putting on high heels.
JOHN
PETIT-SENN

Who a coach is and what the coach does in the athletic arena have a tremendous influence on the athletes that the coach teaches. The words that a coach speaks and how the coach says them, the body language, the coach's facial expressions from pursing the lips or drawing the brows together to smiling—all have an impact on the atmosphere that the coach creates for each athlete and the team as a whole. This is referred to as the coaching style.

It is important that coaches know their style of coaching. Each and every day, coaches communicate messages that tell each athlete how the coach feels, not only about the athletes, but also about himself or herself. It may be scary for coaches to see who they really are, but it is also reassuring to know who they are not. The good news is that no matter what inadequacies some coaches might possess, once they become aware of the kind of coach they are, they can take steps to become even better. By its very nature, coaching is a series of learn-by-doing experiences. This means that coaches can change their coaching style.

Hart [1990] and other authors of traditional management books have described the three basic leadership styles as autocratic, permissive or laissez-faire, and democratic. Most coaches lean toward one of the three styles. Each is described below.

The Autocratic Coach

The autocratic coach controls and directs and is like a dictator who makes all the decisions. The autocratic coach gives the athlete the message "I am the boss and you will do as I say." These coaches believe that they have not only the knowledge and experience, but also the power to assume the role of supreme ruler. They tell everyone what to do. They expect athletes to listen and comply. They tend to be pushy and punitive. Everyone has had experiences with individuals like this, experiences that have provoked both anger and frustration. In the long run, healthy individuals cannot sustain positive relationships with individuals who treat them as inferior and incapable.

Dictatorial coaches mistakenly believe that when they constantly direct and correct, they are helping their athletes to flourish and grow. They believe that their words are the only truth and solution to any problem. Athletes respond to these messages in some of the following ways:

Every person is either growing or degenerating
UNKNOWN

"The coach never listens to me."
"The coach treats me like a two-year-old."
"He just pushes me around."
"Why can't she be nice once in a while."
"Why is she always picking on me?"
"Is he ever pushy!"
"Why doesn't she just shut up?"
"I hate him."
"I'm never going to tell her anything again."
"I'm just going to ignore him."
"I'm going to quit."
"I'm going to get even."
"My feelings don't really matter."
"The coach doesn't even know who I am."

If a coach hears similar statements from his or her athletes, they are probably telling the coach something that goes beyond their spoken words. The underlying message is that the coach is dictatorial, controlling, and/or demanding. The athletes are telling the coach that they feel discounted and that what they think really doesn't matter. A coach who chooses to motivate athletes through fear instead of respect will have a team that never reaches its full potential.

How Players Respond to the Autocratic Coach

A demanding, controlling coach elicits many behavioral symptoms from the players. If athletes are displaying any of the following behaviors, the coach should ask himself or herself what might be happening to cause the feelings that they represent:

Talking back
Anger
Stubbornness
Uncooperativeness
Lying
Disrespectful attitude
Defensive attitude
Keeping a distance from you (both physically and emotionally)

Controlling and directive coaches justify their approach with the belief that they are providing the athletes with the structure and discipline that are necessary to succeed in life. Most psychologists would suggest that structure and discipline are most effectively developed in an atmosphere of love, acceptance, and warmth. Many dictators are successful in sports, but they are often unsuccessful in human relationships. Many people in positions of authority say that they would rather be respected than liked. Wouldn't it be better if they could have both?

Just think about how many teams achieve mediocre success with athletes who are treated disrespectfully. Then imagine what might happen if those teams had athletes who were fully engaged, energized, appreciated, and empowered.

Indifference is probably the severest criticism that can be leveled at anything.
UNKNOWN

The Permissive Coach

Permissive coaches are ineffectual coaches. They are usually inadequately trained or just too lazy to meet their coaching obligations. Unfortunately, many permissive coaches are coaches who have already retired on the job. These coaches can also be competent coaches who are unavailable or preoccupied with other issues that they think are more important. Often, the "bench" athlete is the victim of this type of uncaring coach. The message to the athletes is "I cannot give you what you need; I am overwhelmed." or "You are not terribly important to me."

Permissive coaches make few decisions and provide little teaching. The athletes of permissive coaches respond in these ways:

"I don't respect her."

"I can't count on her."

"I feel sorry for him."

"Boy, is he a joke!"

"She's just our babysitter."

"He's just putting in his time."

"I'm not important."

"She is never around for me."

"He doesn't even know my name."

"He only cares about the starters, he doesn't care about me."

The insensitive coach who is unintentionally aloof, cold, impersonal, and uninterested in an athlete usually finds it very difficult to get that athlete to put out any extra effort.

How Players Respond to the Permissive Coach

If athletes are displaying any of the following behaviors, the coach should ask himself or herself what might be happening to cause the feelings that they represent:

Lack of respect

Manipulative tactics

Frequent angry outbursts

Withdrawal

Anxiety

Frustration

Fortunate indeed is the man who takes exactly the right measure of himself.
PETER LATHAM

Permissive coaches are usually afraid. They are afraid of not being liked by their athletes and have a difficult time saying "no." They feel relatively helpless, and their coaching responsibilities are overwhelming to them. They feel inadequate, and coaching enhances their inadequacy. They are very immature and do not know how to assume responsibility.

The Empowering Coach

Democratic or empowering coaches like and respect themselves and their players. To empower is to give ability to or to make effective or powerful. Democratic coaches empower their athletes because they give them the opportunities to express their individuality and at the same time validate or affirm their athletes by (1) providing a safe and confirming atmosphere, (2) giving them the feeling that they are accepted and cared for regardless of the situation, (3) listening to them and taking them seriously, and (4) being honest and open. The message that empowering coaches convey is "I like you. You are a good person."

Real success is not an outward show but an inward feeling.

HAROLD
WHITMAN

Athletes respond to messages from the empowering coach in some of the following ways:

"He likes having me around."

"She trusts me."

"She gives me responsibility."

"He takes me seriously."

"She listened to me."

"He was willing to change his mind."

"He takes an interest in me.

"She thanked me."

"She thinks that I contribute."

An empowering coach has to be quick because he or she is going to have to get out of the way of athletes who are rapidly growing and prospering in this environment.

How Players Respond to the Empowering Coach

As a result of the consistent words and actions of the empowering coach, athletes respond in some of the following ways:

Confidence

Resourcefulness

Helpfulness

Enthusiasm

Happiness

Cooperativeness

Responsibility

Empathy

Empowering coaches want the best for their athletes. Of course, they want them to reach their athletic potentials, but they also want them to be good, successful, happy, and capable people in the process.

Let goodness go with the doing.

MARCUS
AURELIUS

Some ways of empowering athletes include:

- allowing the athlete to develop the capacity to set their own goals and the desire to reach them,
- accepting each athlete as a unique individual,
- giving them responsibility,
- accepting their opinions,
- making each athlete feel capable of succeeding,
- being a good listener,
- establishing reasonable limits for behavior,
- allowing the athletes to share in the decision-making process,
- providing a safe environment,

- organizing and planning practices,
- taking time with each athlete, and
- establishing fair discipline policies.

Empowerment means letting the athletes flourish and grow, giving them more responsibility, accepting their ideas, and providing an atmosphere that promotes self-confidence. Empowerment is a competitive necessity. It is what leads to winning teams.

TIME OUT: SELF-ASSESSMENT

What Kind of Coach Are You?

This exercise lists certain phrases that we all say some of the time. The situations and the words you use may be slightly different from what is listed below, but the message is still the same. Check off only those phrases that you think you say often.

If you are not currently coaching, you can still check off items on the list. If you find that you are using a lot of the phrases in your everyday life, you will probably be using them when you become a coach. You may also want to think about a former or current coach and check off the phrases that apply to him or her.

If you are a coach, if your athletes are cooperative, and if you are willing to hear the answers, have your athletes rate you with this list. Compare their list with yours. You may be surprised.

1. I told you to do it now.
2. I don't know. That's not my area of expertise.
3. I'm really proud of you.
4. Because I said so.
5. What do you think I should do?
6. I like the way you did that.
7. I can't believe you did that again.
8. Remind me again and I'll try to help you tomorrow.
9. Thanks for helping me out.
10. Get over here, now!
11. I can't communicate with him. Maybe you can speak to him.
12. You've put a lot of work into getting better.
13. I make the rules around here.
14. I can't deal with this anymore.
15. You have really stayed in great shape.

Little happens in a relationship until the individuals learn to trust each other.
DAVID JOHNSON

16. Stop it this minute!
17. Don't bother me right now.
18. You must be disappointed. You worked
    so hard to make the first team.
19. Why don't you do it this way?
20. I'm busy. Just go and practice on any-
    thing you need to work on.
21. That's a great idea. Let's do it.

Scoring and Analysis

Items 1, 4, 7, 10, 13, 16, 19 are all statements of the autocratic or controlling coach.

Items 2, 5, 8, 11, 14, 17, 20 are all statements of the permissive coach.

Items 3, 6, 9, 12, 15, 18, 21 are all statements of the democratic or empowering coach.

Count your check marks for each of the three categories. If you checked more than four statements in any category, you have some tendencies to fall into that style of coaching. It is important that you understand the effects of the messages you are sending to your athletes. How are they feeling when they hear your words?

Congratulations if you scored high in the empowering coach category. You are doing a good job in helping your athletes reach their potentials.

If you are not an empowering coach and would like to learn more about how to become one, read the remainder of this book. If you are an empowering coach and would like to learn additional strategies, continue reading the remaining chapters.

Leadership is serving a relationship that has the effect of facilitating human development
WILLIAM A. WARD

Many coaches mishandle their power and misperceive their role as a leader. Few coaches are taught the art of leadership. Consequently, they tend to model the way they were coached. Unfortunately, many coaches imitate the ultrastrict behaviors and refuse to give the athletes any freedom or responsibility in the mistaken belief that control is what gets things done and handing it over to anyone else will hinder success. Controlling coaches usually work extremely hard and are admired for their intensity, after all, they plan, direct, control, and coordinate. In fact, controlling or directive coaches will usually find themselves physically and emotionally involved in every activity of the job because they believe that without them, the job won't be done right. These coaches are afraid that if they lose control, they will lose everything.

Coaches As Leaders

Coaches are leaders of young athletes, and they must plan, organize, direct, and coordinate the efforts of their teams; set goals; maintain the team; handle conflict; and much more. Leadership goes beyond just teaching athletic skills. Good coaches incorporate leadership techniques into their teaching. The coach is more than an instructor; he or she is a leader. Candace Goode Vick [1985] charted and summarized the differences between the two:

Which are you: An instructor or a leader?

INSTRUCTOR	LEADER
1. An instructor's job is to teach a skill, a technique, an activity, a game, or a subject.	1. A leader's job is to influence the growth of the followers to better citizenship.
2. An instructor's main aim is to improve the skill of the individual.	2. A leader's main aim is to improve character and life.
3. An instructor is primarily activity-centered.	3. A leader is person-centered as well as activity-centered.
4. Instructors are mainly concerned with how well a person can perform now in the activity or game.	4. A leader is mainly concerned with how well people will perform in adulthood, what ideals, what values, what goals they will reach for.
5. Instructors watch what is happening to the ball and its effect on the scoreboard.	5. A leader is concerned with what is happening to the followers.
6. Instructors want results now.	6. A leader aims for results in the future.
7. An instructor stresses and uses position, rank, and authority to get compliance.	7. A leader uses influence to create the desire to follow the advice being given.
8. An instructor considers the game, the activity, or the program an end in itself.	8. A leader uses activities as tools to teach attitudes and ideals.
9. An instructor is content to work with those who come to the activity.	9. A leader is concerned about those who don't come and does something about it.

Every human being is intended to have a character of his own; to be what no other is, and to do what no other can do.
CHANNING

QUESTIONS AND ANSWERS

Question: How would you define "empowering" leadership as it relates to the "empowered" team concept discussed early in the chapter?

Answer: Empowering leadership is a process. It is not something that you automatically possess. The foundation of empowering leadership is based on the development of two important ingredients: respect and trust. The development of these two components requires patience. They cannot be acquired overnight but must be proven over time. Athletes will listen to your words and then observe how you act on those words. If your actions do not back up your words, respect and trust will not develop.

Respect is enormously important in coaching because it means that the coaches and athletes are highly regarded, honored, or esteemed. Although respect is usually ceremoniously acknowledged in conversation and at special gatherings, it is often largely ignored in the daily workings of the athletic arena. The lip service that is given to respect comes in many forms:

As is our confidence, so is our capacity.
WILLIAM HAZLITT

- Developing rules or a code of ethics for all athletes while making special exceptions for more skilled athletes.
- Asking for opinions of athletes and never acting on them.
- Touting opportunities for women while not promoting women's teams or athletes on the same basis as men's.
- Voicing a loud commitment to sportsmanship and fair play while pressuring athletes to commit illegal or questionable acts on the athletic field. Voicing a commitment to academics while pressuring teachers to keep athletes eligible by changing grades.

Both athletes and coaches suffer when the human element in athletics is disrespected and devalued. When relationships are dishonest, team policies are unfair, and communications are secretive or degrading, athletes will develop low morale and high turnover, and the coach will have difficulty attracting high-quality athletes. Absenteeism, tardiness, early departures, passivity, indifference, and belligerence are some of the other symptoms of disrespect. Building respect is created by understanding its components and acting on them.

Trust is a firm belief or confidence in the honesty, integrity, reliability, and fairness of the coach and/or the athlete. It is something that requires time to mature and can be lost in a few seconds of thoughtlessness. Once lost, it is difficult to recover, and in some cases it may be lost forever. Distrust will break down morale, loyalty, and performance and leads to cynicism, retaliation, destructive rumors, and other forms of anger.

Trust is a two-way street; it involves both the ability to trust others and the quality of being trustworthy ourselves. If trust does not flow in both directions, it will eventually break down. Trust is composed of the following qualities:

- Honesty or the believability of your words. Inconsistencies will destroy trust. Once athletes stop listening, you will never be taken seriously.
- Your commitments are backed by your actions. If athletes cannot depend on you to fulfill your commitments, they will become indifferent to your words.
- Concern for the athletes' emotional and physical welfare. As a coach, you do not abuse feelings. Each athlete is important. You protect the athletes from humiliation or unnecessary criticism, allowing them to perform with comfort and security.

Question: Are there any practical things a coach can do to promote the "empowered" team concept?

Answer: Empowered teams cannot afford to house unruly athletes, insecure coaches, or a team structure that stifles involvement and innovation. To prevent this, coaches must encourage two basic principles: participation and psychological ownership.

Participation goes beyond performance. True participation means that athletes who are on the team have a right and responsibility to contribute. It means that athletes share responsibilities and work together with teammates and the coach to accomplish mutual team goals. It means that all athletes have a right and responsibility to contribute to and share in the successes and failures of athletic competition. Participation validates an athlete's existence on the team because what he or she does has meaning and has impact both on the team and on others.

Psychological ownership or possession arises when the athlete recognizes that his or her efforts do make a difference and that his or her contributions are an integral part of the total team process. Possession translates into pride and loyalty because one's participation becomes relevant and focused and consequently leads to commitment. Without emotional connection there is indifference because nothing really matters.

Question: As high school athletes, my teammates and I feared our dominating coach. However, our team had great success. How do you explain this success?

Answer: Some coaches mistakenly believe that fear of the coach is a powerful motivation for success. Fear may motivate some athletes, but it is emotionally devastating to others. Tiedemann [1976] states that this strategy is likely to be effective when a team is winning regularly. However, he further states that when a team is losing consistently, fear of the coach creates a highly negative atmosphere and increases the likelihood of rebellion among the players on the team. *The Power of Positive Coaching* believes that empowering coaches can have both winning records and positive relationships based on dignity and respect.

Major Points Discussed in Chapter 2

1. Empowered teams encourage an atmosphere of support, trust, and respect. They have an underlying philosophy of teamwork and partnership.
2. There are three basic coaching styles.
   a. The autocrat, who controls and directs and makes all of the decisions.
   b. The permissive coach, who makes few decisions and provides little teaching.
   c. The empowering coach, who gives the athletes opportunities to express their individuality and at the same time validates them by:
      - providing a safe and confirming atmosphere,
      - accepting and caring for them regardless of the moment,
      - listening to them and taking them seriously,
      - being honest and open.
3. Coaches must instruct, but they must also be leaders.
4. Empowering leadership is a process that is based on respect and trust.
5. Empowering coaches encourage the two basic principles of participation and psychological ownership.

The Inner Athlete: Understanding Basic Needs

Building Strong and Independent Athletes from the Inside Out

The best way to motivate a subordinate is to show him that you are conscious of his needs, his ambitions, his fears, and himself as an individual. The insensitive manager who is perhaps unintentionally aloof, cold, impersonal, and uninterested in his staff usually finds it very difficult to get his people to put out extra effort.

Dr. Mortimer R. Feinberg

Just as skilled architects design buildings to be inspiring, to stand strong, and to resist the elements over the years, effective coaches who teach and care for young people work to build in them the strength and skills to live healthy, happy, and productive lives both on and off the athletic field. Like architects, effective coaches know that to build strong and independent structures, one must work from the inside out.

Construction of the Inner Framework: The Foundation of Positive Coaching

The inner framework that coaches help to build within young athletes evolves through the quality of the relationship between coach and athlete. Young athletes look to significant adults in their lives as well as their peers for a reflection of who they are and how they are. They observe the coach's responses and reactions; they hear the coach's words. They sense the coach's feelings and notice whether they are taken seriously and listened to and whether they are respected and enjoyed. The conclusions they draw from these reflections often become their truth or the inner framework that tells them who they are and what they deserve in athletics.

Enough evidence has been accumulated to help coaches in this construction process. If athletes have healthy self-esteem (belief in oneself, self-respect, and self-liking), they are well on their way to becoming successful in the athletic arena. Research reported by the California Task Force to Promote Self-Esteem and Personal and Social Responsibility [1990] supports the theory that a sense of self-worth is critical to learning and growing. Athletes with healthy self-esteem believe that they are competent and worthwhile. They develop positive attitudes about what they can accomplish and are equipped to handle frustration and problems in athletics. In addition, athletes who have a sense of self-worth are more willing to take on new challenges. Their positive beliefs also help them to become more compassionate, responsible human beings.

The maintenance and enhancement of the perceived self are the motives behind all behavior.

A.W. COMBS

How athletes view themselves and their feelings of self-worth will affect their health, relationships, competence, goals that are set and achieved, performance, and happiness. This self-image or inner picture will influence how athletes treat themselves and others and how they accept and respect the coach. It will affect their performance and will influence their capabilities, how much they are liked, how they are accepted by others, and how they show their acceptance in return. The coach plays a crucial role in developing and supporting a positive self-image in each and every athlete. A coach can be a major contributor to the self-image and self-esteem that each individual athlete has of himself or herself.

Athletes with healthy self-esteem are not egotistical. They have an inner happiness based on feelings of self-worth and respect. They are happy with themselves and happy with who they are. They don't waste their time or energy trying to impress others. They know they are valued, and they value themselves.

Having athletes with healthy self-esteem is essential to the emotional and physical success of any team. An empowering coach must help his or her athletes to believe in themselves by nurturing the inner picture that develops in each one of them.

The coach who has the best chance of promoting a positive self-image and supporting a foundation of healthy self-esteem in the athletes is the coach who has a positive self-image, models it, and wants to instill it. A coach must coach the athletes with dignity, acceptance, and respect. He or she must give the athletes the supporting structure of appropriate rules, fair discipline, and reasonable expectations. He or she cannot assault the athletes with ridicule, humiliation and contradictions.

Mirror, Mirror on the Wall: Perceptions of Self

How athletes feel about themselves has a direct effect on how they live all aspects of their lives, including athletics. Their feelings of self-worth form the core of their personalities and determine the use they make of their minds and bodies. The importance of self-esteem in an athlete's life cannot be overlooked. An empowering coach who cares must guide athletes to believe in themselves. Even though an athlete may not believe in himself or herself in other aspects of life, a coach can empower the athlete in the athletic arena. By doing so, the athlete will have added a positive piece to the foundation of his or her own self-image.

Everyone, whether they realize it or not, has a self-image. Everyone perceives themselves in some way—as smart, fast, motivated, lazy, incompetent, shrewd, or misunderstood. Everyone has adjectives that describe themselves. It is the "I" behind the eyes. It is the "I" who thinks, hears, talks, and feels. It is the "I" that perceives and interprets all that comes at us.

Of all the judgments and beliefs that athletes have, none are more important than the ones that they have about themselves. Their beliefs about themselves are the most telling factors in determining their success and happiness in athletics and in life. Their self-images are based partly on the kind of reinforcements they receive from their coaches every day. Every outward expression of the coach's face and body, whether positive or negative, reflects the secret truths that the coach holds within his or her heart.

Self-confidence, in itself, is of no value. It is useful only when put to work.
Anonymous

All athletes need to see themselves as significant and worthy. They need to believe that their existence on the team makes a difference and that what they do with their time, energy, and talent is meaningful to themselves and others. They need to know that they are worthy of the coach's attention and that they are cared for and accepted. All athletes want to feel valued. If they don't feel valued, their effectiveness and commitment are diminished. Coaches must continue to work on, maintain, and improve the self-images of all athletes because self-image is the motive behind behaviors on as well as off the athletic field.

TIME OUT: IN THE COACH'S CORNER

"Why Doesn't the Coach Play Everyone?"

A letter to the editor from a local newspaper:

Dear Editor,

During last Friday night's high school championship game, our team was clearly overmatched and the winner of the game was essentially determined by half-time when we were behind by 21 points. The score continued to widen but the coach continued to play the starters. He never went to the bench and my son and a number of others never entered the game. This is not the first time this has happened. My son has played some during the season, but I know many "benchies" (they nicknamed themselves) who have never been given any opportunity. I am puzzled by the coach's philosophy.

What we see depends mainly on what we look for.
JOHN LUBBOCK

I realize that the coach does not think my son is the most talented player on the team, but he practices just as hard as anyone else. In fact, during the middle of the season he sustained an ankle injury during practice but endured the pain, taped it and continued to practice with the same enthusiasm and effort. He never missed a practice all year.

Shouldn't all athletes at this level be given some opportunity to play? If they are good enough to make the team, they must have some ability. Why shouldn't coaches be responsible for creating situations in which all players can contribute in game situations? Or has high school sports become so competitive and winning games so important that high school sports has lost sight of it's true purpose?

Coach, do you just keep these "benchies" on the team so that your starters have bodies to beat on during practices? Just the fact that they nicknamed themselves "benchies" should tell you something about what you are doing to their self-esteem and confidence. C'mon coach, these kids deserve better!

Signed,

A disgruntled high school football fan and parent

Response

If you were the coach, how would you respond to this letter? How you respond will help you define your coaching philosophy.

The Power of Positive Coaching supports the disgruntled football fan. Each player is making a tremendous sacrifice in time and energy. They have all committed themselves to an activity that requires long hours of practice, evening and/or weekend games, traveling to distant locations, balancing their study requirements, occasionally giving up social events, and enduring physical and emotional challenges.

One might argue that sports should be comparable to life in that all things are not equal or fair or that only the best prevail. This argument is only partially true. In high-level collegiate or professional sports this philosophy might apply. However, high school or youth sports should be a training ground for development in life. Here is where kids should be given the opportunity to learn and mature, to test their skills, and to make mistakes. It should be in this arena, during their early lives, that they should be given opportunities and challenges. Let kids learn from these athletic experiences so that they will be better prepared to cope in the "real world." Without the opportunity to truly test their skills, kids have less hope of ever achieving success.

Kids do recognize that not everyone can be a star athlete and that people have different levels of talents. Many athletes know that they will not have as much playing time as others, but the thought of having no chance of playing is crippling to anyone.

Love begins when a person feels another person's need to be as important as his own.
UNKNOWN

Responsible, empowering coaches know that they cannot assume what a high school athlete was yesterday is all that he can be today. Empowering coaches should always be striving to find ways for all their athletes, regardless of skill level, to test their skills in the athletic arena and, consequently, to develop into the athletes that they are capable of becoming.

Building Healthy Self-Esteem by Nurturing the Athlete's Basic Emotional Needs

Plants require good soil, an adequate water supply, and lots of sunshine to grow and flourish. Young athletes also need optimal growing conditions. If one neglects their needs—soil, water, and sunshine—the plants may wilt and die. Young athletes, too, have basic needs on both a physical and emotional level. These human needs must be met for appropriate growth to occur both on and off the athletic field.

It is important to recognize that wants and needs are separate matters. *Wants* can be frivolous and greedy and often are never satisfied. In many cases, if one want is met, there will be at least two more to replace it. *Needs* are the deep roots of one's existence. They are meaningful, worthy, and not as changeable as wants.

Athletes *want* fame; they *need* recognition. Athletes *want* prestige; they *need* respect. Athletes *want* freedom and permissiveness; they *need* discipline. Athletes *want* ease and comfort; they *need* achievement and work. Athletes *want* sympathy; they *need* empathy. Athletes *want* approval; they *need* acceptance.

A modified version of Conklin's [1979] rule is "to the extent that a coach gives athletes what they need, they will give the coach what he or she needs." This is the key to leading, motivating, guiding, and influencing young athletes. Unfortunately, many coaches have this simple rule backwards.

Some coaches believe that an athlete should get praise and recognition after putting forth some extra effort. Some coaches will start having confidence in their players only when the players start performing adequately in games. However, the coach must recognize and encourage to bring forth the extra effort. The coach also must express confidence in the players first; then they will start coming through with better performances.

That is the way the rule works. First coaches give the athletes what they need; then the athletes will give the coaches what they need. This requires patience and knowing what it is that athletes need, how to give them what they need, and what it is you, the coach, need and what you are willing to give in order to get it.

This rule is not about manipulating and moving athletes around for one's own satisfaction and ego or about developing strategies for gaining power and dominance. It is not about finding emotional buttons to push to get one's own way. This rule is about giving and succeeding.

The Importance of Understanding Basic Emotional Needs

Children need love, especially when they do not deserve it.
HAROLD S. HULBERT

Although people come into this world dependent on others for their survival, everyone has the innate desire to grow and become independent. Young people need others, others need them, and the need to be self-sufficient is basic to all people. These needs are like the soil, water, and sunshine. Understanding basic human needs and nurturing the athlete's growth and development are the foundation on which coaching should be built.

A coach who is going to empower an athlete must know and respond to the athlete's basic needs. As a father or mother, of course, the coach would have little difficulty identifying the needs of his or her own child. However, a coach in the team setting may find it far more difficult to respond to the basic needs of each individual athlete. Each player is usually seen as only one small part of a much larger whole. It is easy for an athlete's basic needs to be overlooked in a group. An empowering coach must always remember that human needs do not exist in a social vacuum. Human emotional needs develop and find expression through relationships such as that between the coach and the athlete.

Youngs [1991] and other sources have listed the following basic emotional needs as fundamental:

1. **The need to be accepted and to belong.** The need to be accepted and to belong is an important, human need and is the foundation of the others. All human beings need to feel a sense

of belonging. Without a sufficient amount of acceptance and belonging, people will perish just as surely as if you deprive them of food and water. Athletes need to know that their coach cares about them and is on their side. The concept of acceptance in this book is based on respect, affirmation, caring, empathy, fairness, sensitivity, and warmth. Acceptance, as it is defined in this book, is recognizing and appreciating the athlete's intrinsic worth. It is unconditional, not contingent on anything particular about the individual. The athlete does not have to accomplish anything to receive this acceptance. Each athlete has inherent value, and so acceptance is not something to be earned. Athletes who are accepted unconditionally will absorb the message that they are wanted, worthwhile individuals even when they are not the best players or make mistakes.

The concept of belonging means that people must feel connected with other people to feel secure. This sense of security enables them to reach out and identify with others in a positive way. The need for acceptance and belonging is discussed in greater detail in Chapter 4.

2. The need to feel significant. Athletes need to feel that they are important, that their participation on the team has meaning and purpose, that they make a difference, that their existence matters, and that they are needed. Athletes need to feel that their contributions are appreciated and necessary. Athletes will give up or lose their motivation to compete or progress when they believe that they are not important to the team and its members. This need is discussed in greater detail in Chapter 5.

The deepest urge in human nature is the desire to be important.
JOHN DEWEY

3. The need to feel capable or competent. Athletes need to feel that they can take on responsibility and that they are skilled and can do things well. Coaches and athletes who feel capable know that they can learn to do things. They recognize that there is often as much to learn from failure as from success. They are challenged by tasks even though they face difficult odds. They have inner strength and reasoning power that keep life and athletics in proper perspective. This need is discussed in greater detail in Chapters 6 and 7.

4. The need to feel safe. Athletes need to feel that they are safe and in control of themselves while performing in the athletic arena, that they have mastery over their well-being. Without a feeling of physical and emotional safety or security, an athlete will find it difficult to move beyond fear and anxiety. Strong fear and anxiety will hinder performance and promote possible injury. Intense fear or anxiety can affect thinking, remembering, behavior, and physical performance. How long an athlete will stay with a team is directly related to how safe he or she perceives the athletic environment to be. This need is discussed in Chapter 8.

Seek not every quality in one individual.
CONFUCIUS

Athletes who believe that they are capable, significant, accepted, and safe develop a positive attitude about coping with the problems and frustrations that frequently occur in athletics as well as life. Positive beliefs reinforce the "I can do it" or "Just do it" attitude. On the other hand, athletes who believe that they are not capable, significant, accepted, or safe seldom find fulfillment and meaning in their athletic participation. They will find it difficult to help their teammates do the same.

Meet their needs of feeling capable, significant, accepted, and safe and the team will thrive. Ignore or abuse these needs and the team will be dysfunctional. Symptoms such as demanding undue attention, seeking revenge, quitting, rebelling, always seeking approval, fear, and self-doubt are signs of dysfunctional teams. Missing practices, chronic injuries, passive efforts, and jealousy among athletes are also common symptoms found on the athletic field.

Understanding the nature of young athletes by understanding their basic emotional needs provides a foundation on which coaches can base their efforts to help athletes feel good about who they are and what they can do both on and off the athletic field. When coaches understand an athlete's emotional needs and use them to encourage and to empower, they will have made a significant step towards an empowered team.

A coach cannot be expected to meet every basic need all of the time, but the caring and empowering coach will express awareness of and concern for these needs. All plants need sun, water, and good soil, but different plants need different amounts of each. Give a cactus too much water and it will weaken; withhold sunlight from a rose and it will wilt. The same principle applies to the athletes. They all have basic needs, but each athlete is unique.

Empowering coaches know that most problems can be resolved by working on and improving human relationships, because once they meet the athletes' needs, they will usually meet their own. Empowering coaches will find ways to be sensitive and to make allowances for an athlete's basic needs. Being aware of and attending to those needs is an investment that will bring immediate and future behavioral dividends.

TIME OUT: SELF-ASSESSMENT

You Need to Take Care of Yourself
Whether you are a coach or a student, you probably get wrapped up in your job or studies and sometimes lose sight of your own needs. Don't let that happen to you. You need to attend

to your own needs and work toward fulfilling them. Whether you are a coach or a student, meeting your own needs will make it easier for you to help others meet theirs.

Directions: Below is a checklist of some of your lifestyle habits. Check off the ones that you are attending to on a regular basis.

PHYSICAL NEEDS

_____ Do you maintain a healthy/balanced diet?
_____ Do you get enough sleep every night?
_____ Do you get an annual physical examination?
_____ Do you see a dentist twice a year?
_____ Do you exercise regularly?
_____ Do you maintain a reasonable weight?

SOCIAL NEEDS

_____ Do you feel comfortable and confident meeting new people?
_____ Do you establish social relationships with people of both genders with equal ease and enjoyment?
_____ Do you participate in a wide variety of group activities such as religious, recreational, and occupational?
_____ Are you open and accessible to others in the development of intimate relationships

SPIRITUAL NEEDS

_____ Do you get in touch with nature at least once a week?
_____ Do you get spiritual (religious or other) nourishment at least once a week?
_____ Do you take time out to do the things that you truly love in life?
_____ Do you take time to be by yourself for a little solitude?

EMOTIONAL NEEDS

_____ Do you laugh at lot?
_____ Can you forgive yourself when you make a mistake?
_____ Do you get hugged and touched at least once a day?
_____ Do you nurture your friendships?
_____ Do you have at least one person with whom you can share your true feelings?
_____ Can you ask for help when you really need it?
_____ Do you have a constructive way to vent your negative emotions?
_____ Do you like yourself?

To be what we are, and to become what we are capable of becoming, is the only end of life.

SPINOZA

STRESS MANAGEMENT

_____ Do you seek out change and accept its presence with a sense of confidence and anticipation?

_____ Do you turn to friends for counsel and assistance during periods of disruption in your life?

_____ Do you seek professional counseling if stress becomes too difficult to handle?

_____ Do you reevaluate your experiences with stressful events in anticipation of similar future events?

Look over the statements you checked. Are you happy with your total? If not, slow down and think about what you might be able to do to bring your life back into balance. Don't wait, do it now!

QUESTIONS AND ANSWERS

The easiest thing of all is to deceive one's self; for what a man wishes he generally believes to be true.
DEMOSTHENES

Question: I agree that raising the self-esteem of my players is important. Can you recommend some creative ways in which a coach can find playing time for reserve players?

Answer: The following excerpt was taken from William Warren's [1983] book *Coaching and Motivation: A Practical Guide to Maximum Athletic Performance.* (Englewood Cliffs, NJ: Prentice Hall, Inc. Reprinted with permission.)

> ***Dean Smith's Strategy: Making Every Minute Count***
> *University of North Carolina Basketball Coach Dean Smith uses a "Blue" team composed of third stringers who otherwise might receive little or no playing time. These players, spelling the regulars and front line subs for 2–3 minutes at a time, play with an intensity that is truly amazing to watch. Possessing a nickname denied the first two teams, "Blue" team members take considerable pride in their ability to come in cold and not only to keep the Tarheels in games, but in many cases to catch up or extend the team's lead. Coach Smith is as likely to put his "Blue" team in pressure situations as when the team is far ahead or hopelessly behind. "Blue" team players know and respect this, and they routinely give some of the finest efforts in all of college basketball to justify Coach Smith's faith in them.*

When coaches believe in the "athletes first, winning second" philosophy, they will find it easier to be more creative.

Question: *Can you change someone's perception of himself or herself?*

Answer: Yes! A coach must realize that an athlete is not constant. She is constantly changing her behavior. An athlete is not who she was yesterday. Nothing significant may have happened to her—no injuries, no losses, no arguments, no soul-searching event—but she will be different. In that 24-hour period, she became a day older and experienced and learned some new things, however negligible, that have become part of her. As a result, her perception of today's events is different, however slightly and undetectably, from what it was yesterday. So, yes, perceptions can be changed because they are constantly changing. It has been said that perception is more powerful than fact. What players perceive to be true carries more weight than what is actually true. Therefore it is to the coach's advantage to create positive perceptions because they will generate more opportunities and better results.

> *Small opportunities are the beginning of great enterprise.*
> DEMOSTHENES

Question: Are there different levels of change?

Answer: Browner [1964] reported two levels at which people change. *Simple*-level change is superficial change that comes about simply from attaining new information or learning new skills. For example, athletes improve in endurance, athletic skills, and strength through training. Consequently, new behaviors are produced. Change in the deeper sense, however, is at a more *basic* level, such as change in a player's perceptions of self, a different attitude toward fair play and cooperation, or a feeling of responsibility toward others. Growth at the basic level brings about changes in outward behavior because each athlete is now inwardly different. The growing athlete changes because he or she has to change in response to new insights and understandings that he or she gains from the coach and athletics. However, if a coach wants player growth at a more basic level, it usually requires a change in the coach himself or herself.

Question: Are the goals of young people the same as the goals of sports education?

Answer: Young people are in the process of growing and developing and trying to determine who they are and what role will they play in life. Many young people will use athletics as a means to that end. Payne and Hahn [1989], in their book *Understanding Your Health*, listed four of the most important developmental tasks that are critical for young people to accomplish. These are (1) forming an initial self-identity, (2) establishing a sense of relative independence, (3) assuming increasing levels of responsibility, and (4) developing the social skills needed for social interaction. If these skills sound familiar, they are. They are some of the same goals that coaches have for their athletes: responsibility, self-reliance, self-discipline, and social interaction. These developmental tasks are also complementary with the four basic emotional needs discussed earlier. Without fulfilling the basic emotional needs, a coach cannot help athletes to achieve their developmental tasks.

Young athletes, of course, may not be able to verbalize these tasks or even be aware that they are in the process of becoming the person they hope to be. But the athlete's behavior and actions clearly reflect them. Coaches must understand these tasks and recognize their own role in this process and, whenever possible, provide the skills and strategies to help their players achieve these tasks.

By meeting the athletes' basic emotional needs through the activities discussed in later chapters, a coach can provide the basic tools athletes need to achieve the four developmental tasks. The goals of any athletic program should include avenues to help athletes achieve the four tasks. Athletes who perceive themselves as being unacceptable, insignificant, incapable, or unsafe will have great difficulty achieving them:

A man achieves according to what he believes.
UNKNOWN

1. **Forming an initial self-identity.** Many young people use athletics as a means of attaining some self-identity. For most of childhood and adolescence, most children are seen by adults as someone's son or daughter. Very few people recognize children as unique people. Young people usually wish to present their uniqueness and competencies. Young people are constructing perceptions of themselves both internally and externally and are formulating behavioral patterns that will project this identity to others. One's identity will be based on the judgments, both good and bad, that one makes on the athletic field as well as in life. Using good judgment requires an openness to new information, the ability to see new alternatives, and the courage to make decisions. Most important, it requires the willingness to evaluate the choices. How people adjust to their frustrations and stresses on the athletic field will influence who that person is. Youngsters who lack these skills will find themselves in a continual series of crises because they cannot apply effective solutions to their problems.

Each athlete is a unique individual functioning within the total team structure. Each athlete is special in his or her own way, and that uniqueness contributes to the total personality of the team. Each athlete must be given the freedom to search for his or her own identity within the guidelines of acceptable team participation. Athletes cannot be placed into a coach's preconceived mold. Participation in athletics is just one small piece of a larger puzzle that can help young people answer the question "Who am I?"

2. **Establishing a sense of relative independence.** In childhood, the primary responsibility for socialization lies within the family. However, as youngsters begin to move through adolescence, they want some degree of separation from that dependent relationship. They seek out their peers and move to outside activities that begin to disengage them from the family. Within this process, individuals must develop self-discipline, which requires self-evaluation, self-understanding, recognition of one's own feelings, goals, and the willingness to accept responsibility for one's own actions. Athletics is just one of many activities that can be a safe, secure path toward independence. The young people will need to draw on physical, emotional, social, intellectual, and spiritual strengths that they have attained from both the family and the coach to undertake the athletic experiences that will bring independence.

Love is the basic need of human nature, for without it, life is disrupted emotionally, mentally, spiritually, and physically.
Dr. Karl Menninger

3. **Assuming increasing levels of responsibility.** All young people are expected to assume increasing levels of responsibility. That is a significant part of adulthood. In athletics the opportunity to assume responsibility can come from a variety of sources. Responsibility is involved in establishing new friendships, helping others to achieve, cooperation in teamwork, being on time for practice, fulfilling training assignments and schedules, and a variety of other tasks. The ability to assume responsibility requires recognizing limits and identifying what needs to be done. Weakness in this area will cause athletes to blame others or the system and to see themselves as victims.

4. **Developing the social skills needed for social interaction.** The fourth developmental task is that of developing appropriate and dependable social skills. Participation on an athletic team requires the ability to function and communicate with different kinds of people. Athletes will probably need to refine a variety of social skills, including communication, which requires a person to express him- or herself clearly and to be able to listen to others. These interpersonal skills

are necessary for making friends, joining groups, developing intimacy, and managing conflict. Weakness in this area shows up as dishonesty, inability to share feelings, and difficulty in giving and receiving love or help.

TIME OUT: SELF-ASSESSMENT

How Is Your Self-Image?
This scale is designed to assist you in understanding your self-image. Positive attitudes toward oneself are important components of maturity and emotional well-being.

Life is a mirror and will reflect back to the thinker what he thinks into it.
ERNEST HOLMES

SA = Strongly Agree   A = Agree
D = Disagree   SD = Strongly Disagree

Directions: After reading each statement carefully. Circle the letter in the columns on the right that corresponds to your response to each statement. **Treat the results as a guide only. There is a margin of uncertainty in all questionnaries of this kind.**

SELF-IMAGE ASPECT	SA	A	D	SD
1. I feel that I'm a person of worth, at least on an equal plane with others.	A	B	C	D
2. I feel that I have a number of good qualities.	A	B	C	D
3. All in all, I am inclined to feel that I am a failure.	A	B	C	D
4. I am able to do things as well as most other people.	A	B	C	D
5. I feel I do not have as much to be proud of as others.	A	B	C	D
6. I take a positive attitude toward myself.	A	B	C	D
7. On the whole, I am satisfied with myself.	A	B	C	D
8. I wish I could have more respect for myself.	A	B	C	D
9. I certainly feel useless at times.	A	B	C	D
10. At times I think I am no good at all.	A	B	C	D

How to Determine Your Score:
Use the following table to determine the number of points to assign to each of your answers. To determine your total score, add up all the numbers that match the letter (A, B, C, or D) you circled for each of the ten statements.

STATEMENT	A	B	C	D
1.	4	3	2	1
2.	4	3	2	1
3.	1	2	3	4
4.	4	3	2	1
5.	1	2	3	4
6.	4	3	2	1
7.	4	3	2	1
8.	1	2	3	4
9.	1	2	3	4
10.	1	2	3	4

Total: _____ This is your self-esteem score.

Interpretation of Your Score

Classify your score in the appropriate score range.

SCORE RANGE	CURRENT LEVEL OF SELF-ESTEEM
Less than 20	Low self-esteem
20–29	Below-average self-esteem
30–34	Above-average self-esteem
35–39	High self-esteem
40	Highest self-esteem

The higher your score, the more positive your self-esteem. High self-esteem means that individuals respect themselves and consider themselves worthy but don't necessarily consider themselves better than others. They don't feel themselves to be the ultimate in perfection; on the contrary, they recognize their limitations and expect to grow and improve.

Self-esteem is the most important variable in human development and maturation. It is the master key that can open the door to the actualization of an individual's human potential.

Source: Reprinted from *Society and the Adolescent Self-Image* © 1989 by Morris Rosenberg, Wesleyan University Press, by permission of University Press of New England.

Major Points Discussed in Chapter 3

In summary, a primary goal of coaching is to help young athletes mature in both athletics and life by providing them with a well-stocked toolbox: self-identity, independence, responsible behavior, and functional social skills. Athletics, along with an empowering coach, can assist young athletes in mastering the developmental tasks that will make participation in athletics and life more satisfying and productive.

1. To build strong, independent athletes, coaches must work from the inside (emotional makeup) out.
2. A strong inner framework evolves through the quality of the relationship between coach and athlete.
3. Research has shown that a sense of self-worth is critical to learning and growing.
4. Athletes with healthy self-esteem have an inner happiness based on feelings of self-worth and respect.
5. The best chance a coach has of promoting a positive self-image and supporting a foundation of healthy self-esteem is to have a positive self-image, model it, and want to instill it.
6. The beliefs that athletes have about themselves are the most telling factor in determining their success and happiness in athletics and life.
7. The four basic needs that require fulfillment in any relationship are:
   a. the need to feel accepted,
   b. the need to feel significant,
   c. the need to feel capable, and
   d. the need to feel physically and emotionally safe.
8. A coach cannot be expected to meet every basic need all the time, but the caring and empowering coach will express awareness of these needs and concern for meeting them.
9. Coaches can help change their athletes' perceptions of themselves.
10. The everyday goals of young people are complementary with the goals of sports education. They are:
    a. forming an initial self-identity,
    b. establishing a sense of relative independence,
    c. assuming increasing levels of responsibility, and
    d. developing the social skills needed for social interaction.

CHAPTER

4

Emotional Affiliation: Acceptance and Belonging

*At the heart of personality is the need to feel a sense of be-
ing lovable without having to qualify for that acceptance.*

Maurice Wagner

Acceptance—the sense of belonging, of being connected to
those you care for—is an essential element in building self esteem. One of the most compelling motivations that any athlete
has is the need to feel that he or she belongs. Nothing contributes to one's self-esteem more than being accepted by another.
For many athletes, being accepted by their coach and teammates is just as important as being accepted by their parents.
Since athletes choose to participate in athletics, it is important
that they feel accepted by those whom they consider to be important to them: the coach and their teammates. There is nothing more sad and frustrating than being surrounded by people
yet feel only loneliness on the inside. Anybody and everybody
needs to feel like somebody.

Athletes need to feel that there is some meaning to their existence on the team. They are no different from other adolescents. The research on school dropouts indicates that being
unaffiliated—not belonging—is one of the leading causes of
dropping out of school. In athletics, coaches are in a unique
position because athletes come to them to try out for, and hope-
fully become part of, the athletic team. Once an athlete becomes a member, however, he or she doesn't necessarily feel
part of the team. Belonging means a variety of things to different athletes. It can mean new friendships, cooperation with
others, peer acceptance, feeling valued by the coach and/or
teammates, and excelling in the sport. Just as adolescents will
drop out of school because they don't feel that they belong, so
will athletes drop out of the athletic program if the need to belong is not being fulfilled in that arena.

When athletes lack the sense of feeling likable and accepted, many will seek to be esteemed and respected through athletics but will find little or no peace in the process. Sports may raise one's level of self-esteem, but this does not reflect acceptance. Acceptance is unconditional, not contingent on one's accomplishments or personality. It is inherent, not earned.

Isolation is the sum of wretchedness to man.
THOMAS
CARLYLE

Many coaches are initially surprised to find out just how important they are to their athletes. When athletes are asked to list the most meaningful people in their lives, coaches and significant teachers rank just behind parents. Being in this position, coaches have a significant impact on both the physical and emotional growth and development of their athletes.

Messages of Acceptance

Coaches can build a sense of acceptance and belonging by their actions as well as their words. Coaches should show an interest in all their athletes, from the star player to the least talented member of the team. By having a player on the team, a coach has made a commitment to him or her. It is not always possible to "connect" during practice sessions and games. What is most important to athletes is that the coach is interested in them as people and not just because of their athletic ability. Take some time outside of practice to interact and find out what's going on in their lives. "How's it going?" and "Can I be of any help?" are simple openers that will make it clear to the athletes that they count in the life of the coach.

According to Clarke [1978], the following messages of acceptance can be expressed verbally or by the coach's actions:

"You have a right to be here."
"I'm glad you are who you are."
"It's okay for you to have needs."
"You don't have to do tricks to get attention and approval."
"You can stand up for the things you believe even if there is some risk involved."
"You can own the consequences of your actions; others don't have to rescue you."
"It's okay to make mistakes as long as you accept responsibility for making amends."
"You can express your own thoughts and feelings without fear of rejection."
"It's okay to disagree."
"You can trust your own judgment."

By accepting athletes for who they are and building on their strengths and successes rather than their weaknesses and failures, coaches can help athletes to cope with their problems; develop self-confidence, responsibility, and self-reliance, and learn to accept themselves.

Accepting the Athletes for Who They Are

The concepts of intrinsic worth and unconditional acceptance are at the center of Positive Coaching. Athletes need to know that the coach accepts and cares about them, that the coach has their best interests at heart, that the coach wants them as part of the team, and that the coach appreciates them for their contributions. Athletes need to feel that the coach is working with them to become all that they are capable of becoming both on and off the athletic field.

An ancient Chinese proverb says, *"A child's life is like a piece of paper on which every passerby leaves a mark."* Coaches have an opportunity to leave a mark of caring and acceptance.

Demonstrating That You Care for and Accept Each Individual Athlete

We are all so much together, but we are all dying of loneliness.

ALBERT SCHWEITZER

Most coaches probably care for and like the athletes that they coach. However, because of their personal shortcomings and faulty communication styles, some coaches do not make their athletes feel cared for or accepted.

The more caring and acceptance a coach can give to the athletes, the more the coach will help the athletes to care. The more they have, the more they will be able to give away. The less they have, the less they can give away. Athletes who feel cared for and accepted will not need to use or abuse others to find their place in the athletic arena. If the coach can learn to give caring and acceptance away, they will always come back with added interest. Conversely, if the coach gives anger and hate away, they too will always find their way back to the coach.

Sometimes, coaches who really care about their athletes don't know how to convey care and acceptance. What does communicate caring and acceptance?

1. Take the athletes seriously. The things that happen in the lives of the players both on and off the field are of tremendous importance to them. The coach should value what they share. By listening and taking an interest in what they do, the coach lets them know that they are being taken seriously, that the coach cares for them, and that they can always come to the coach.

2. Listen carefully. This is one of the most basic and important life skills. It tells the athletes that they are valuable and worthy of the coach's time and attention. See Chapter 9 for detailed discussion on the art and science of listening.

3. Tell the athletes that you care for them. If a coach really cares about someone, he or she should say it directly. Don't drop hints or beat around the bush. Don't be coy or embarrassed. Say, "I'm glad you're a part of this team," or "I really enjoy being with you." These are significant statements to the athletes. These kinds of statements help players to feel connected to the coach and give them an idea of how the coach feels about them.

4. Touch respectfully. Because touching can be a sensitive issue, many coaches have adopted self-imposed rules that forbid physical contact between themselves and the athletes, even though they know that appropriate touching can carry a message of care and respect. It is obvious that nobody wants any of their personal rights violated. Touching however, can be done without having sexual or abusive connotations. Hand shaking, for example is an acceptable greeting among most Americans. Some cultures, however view touching as a very personal matter and coaches must be aware of this fact. The question that most coaches ask is "What is appropriate touching"?

Part of the answer is based on why a person is touching someone. If a coach is disciplining an athlete, the coach's touch is going to be rejected. However, if the coach is encouraging the athlete, an appropriate touch is usually welcomed. A safe zone of touch is from the shoulder to the hand. A "pat" on the shoulder, a handshake, and a "high" five are some of the ways that a coach can show caring and acceptance.

5. Smile. Sometimes, just a sincere smile with eye contact is all that is needed to make a connection that says, "I care about you and support you."

6. Use simple hand gestures. Acknowledging players with a "thumbs up, an okay sign, a hang-loose sign, or a simple wave to say hello or good-bye signals recognition, acceptance, and caring.

7. Be sensitive to ethnic and racial terminology. Terminology changes over time, as ethnic and cultural groups continue to explore who they are through their history and their relationship to the dominant culture. In the 1990s the following terms have gained general acceptance:

African American: In the 1960s the term *negroes* was replaced with *Blacks* and *Afro-Americans*. In the 1990s the term *African American* has gained general acceptance. The Census report still uses the term *Black Americans*.

Asian American: Most Americans of Asian ancestry do not want to be referred to as "orientals." In California, *Asian Ameri-*

can and *Pacific Islanders* are the terms that are currently preferred. However, as the cultures of the athletes are differentiated, most of them would prefer to be identified by their origin such as Japanese American, Chinese American or Thai American.

Hispanic American: This is the generally accepted term. However, most Americans of Mexican ancestry prefer *Chicano* or *Latino* or *Mexican American* to *Hispanic American.*

Native American: Native American is the accepted term. There are two groups of Native Americans: *American Indians* and *Native Alaskans.*

European American: The term white or caucasian has given way to the term *European American* although the Census reports still use the term *white.*

To find out what terms are used and accepted within a community, coaches need to simply ask their athletes.

8. Be sensitive to the pronunciation of names. Individuals take pride in their names and every coach should learn to pronounce each name correctly. Continual mispronunciation or the use of nicknames to avoid pronouncing an ethnic name is disrepectful.

9. Provide sincere encounters. Every athlete needs occasional sincere encounters with the coach. A sincere encounter is simply focused attention. It is a vital contact that is direct, special, and unique for each individual player. Players are highly sensitive to the degree of focused attention they receive. When it is lacking, they know. If the coach uses this time to do mental note taking, athletes will know. Wandering thoughts such as, "I need to remember to call in the order for shoes" and "I forgot to schedule the next coaches meeting" during sincere encounters will only put distance in the relationship. Athletes are sensitive to the coach's inner presence. Without it, time together is wasted and sometimes harmful. A coach's lack of inner presence can be easily interpreted as a negative message because the coach's behavior is indifferent and the player may feel that the coach is not interested in him or her.

> *A human being can go without food longer than he can go without human dignity.*
> HARRY GOLDEN

However, learning to focus attention doesn't come automatically. Just as it takes time to train athletes to focus on the moment for competition, sincere encounters also requires concentration and practice. Most coaches have spent so many years hurrying and concentrating on things to do that it is hard to switch to focusing on the moment during a sincere encounter.

Just as in competition, a coach needs to let go of every thought and concentrate on the here-and-now. There must be no planning ahead or reminiscing. A coach must be totally with the athlete, even if only for a few moments. A coach needs to let go of everything except the sincere encounter.

Obviously, the more encounters, the better. Realistically, coaches are busy, and sincere encounters do take time. When teams are large, the thought of sincere encounters can be overwhelming. If this is the situation, a coach should take full advantage of any assistant coaches and assign them to players. However, a coach doesn't have to give exclusive attention all the time. It is when the coach never has time that players will feel unfulfilled. If athletes occasionally feel a coach's heartfelt presence, they will accept times when his or her attention is elsewhere.

Coaches need to think about ways in which they can make an athlete feel connected with them. Busy coaches need to find creative ways to let the players know that they count. A simple note sent in the mail or delivered by a teacher can have a lifelong impact. It doesn't take much. It's often the little things that win the biggest points. When players feel the quality of the coach's presence, they will conclude that they matter. Most athletes who look back on their careers will always remember the coach who took the time to get to know them.

> Prejudice is a mist, which in our journey through the world often dims the brightest and obscures the best of all the good and glorious objects that meet us on the way.
> SHAFTESBURY

TIME OUT: IN THE COACH'S CORNER

A Simple Gesture

History was made in the baseball world in 1947. It was in that year that Jackie Robinson became the first black baseball player to play in the major leagues. The Brooklyn Dodgers' owner, Branch Rickey, told Robinson, "It'll be tough. You are going to take abuse, be ridiculed, and take more verbal punishment than you ever thought possible. But I'm willing to back you all the way if you have the determination to make it work."

In short order, Robinson experienced Rickey's prediction. He was abused verbally and physically as players intentionally ran him over. The crowd was fluent with their racial slurs and digging comments. Opponents ridiculed Robinson as well as the Dodger team.

Around midseason, Robinson was having a particularly bad day. He had fumbled grounders, overthrown first base, and had an equally disastrous day at the plate. The crowd was celebrative in their boos. Then something special happened. In front of this critical crowd, Pee Wee Reese walked over from his shortstop position, put his arm around Jackie Robinson, and indicated his acceptance of the major league's first black baseball player.

Robinson later reflected, "That gesture saved my career. Pee Wee made me feel as if I belonged."

Consider the number of newcomers who happen in our lives every week. They too are waiting for the displayed acceptance from the crowd. But more important, they need to feel as if they belong in our world and are considered an important contributor. We have a significant impact on the lives of others by simply letting them know we accept them.

Source: Reprinted with permission from *The Speaker's Sourcebook: Quotes and Stories.* © 1988 by Glenn Van Ekeren. Englewood Cliffs, NJ: Prentice-Hall, Inc.

Personal Biases Affect Acceptance

Unfortunately, some coaches find it difficult to completely accept the athletes for who they are. Many coaches carry biases into their profession. Their biases are their sets of beliefs, values, and assumptions that they hold because of their past experiences and their philosophy of life. They will like some athletes better than others. Some athletes, because of their background, sex, appearance, abilities, size, nationality, behavior, or whatever will be more appealing than others to a given coach.

In addition, a coach may inwardly feel that an athlete isn't talented enough, outgoing enough, fast enough, or smart enough. The athlete never completely measures up to what the coach wants. While many coaches rarely display overt rejection, they may, unconsciously and unwittingly, express their lack of acceptance in more subtle ways, such as displaying disappointment, anger, or irritation or by becoming overly critical, protective, and demanding.

It is essential that a coach be fair in his or her treatment of different athletes. A coach must ask himself or herself, "What preconceived notions do I have about young people in relation to their ethnic, gender, or personal differences? Do I generalize about certain groups of people and create stereotypes? Am I creating an atmosphere that values diversity and encourages cooperation among players from various racial and ethnic backgrounds? Am I acting on any prejudicial assumptions about people of color or ethnic minorities that are contradicting the human values that I am trying to teach? Am I supporting any certain preconceived characteristics that are giving mainstream athletes a better chance to learn over athletes who have different ethnic characteristics?" These are just some of the questions that coaches need to sort through to separate facts from opinions.

The uncommitted life isn't worth living.
Marshall Fishwick

All athletes need to be accepted for who they are without having to qualify or change for that acceptance. So a coach must look carefully at and accept each athlete as he or she is. A coach may not always have to accept what the athlete does. However, a coach must focus on the player's behavior rather than his or her personality. If a coach has trouble changing his or her own personal biases or habits, then a coach must understand how difficult it is to change others.

QUESTIONS AND ANSWERS

Question: Can a player be motivated without feeling accepted or a part of the team?

Answer: Yes, athletes are motivated by a variety of factors. There is no one single factor. However, Tutko and Richards [1971] stated that if players are to be effectively and significantly motivated, they must:

1. feel unique or special in some way,
2. be handled on a personal basis, and
3. clearly understand and agree with team goals.

The first two conditions are closely related to the need for acceptance. In fact, a closer examination of these conditions reflects the necessity of meeting all four of the basic needs (acceptance, significance, capability, and safety) discussed in Chapter 3.

One of the toughest things in dealing with diversity is getting people to understand what's going on inside their own minds when they make decisions about people.
KIM BREESE

Question: I am a very busy coach. Do you have some suggestions for "connecting" with my athletes?

Answer: I know a coach who takes time to remember each player on his or her birthday with a card. I also know a 50-year-old man who still cherishes a 35-year-old hand written note from his high school coach. It simply said, "I'm really happy that you are a part of this team. Your contributions and hard work are really appreciated."

You can also plan to connect with your athletes by making it a priority. Set aside a small amount of time on a regular basis and meet with one or two different athletes each time. Simply write this meeting into your daily or weekly schedule and do not allow other things to interfere with that scheduled time. This practice will be well worth the investment of your time.

TIME OUT: SELF-ASSESSMENT

Are You Prejudiced?

Each of us, because of our personal experiences, carries biases and prejudices into our profession. Some of your values, beliefs, and assumptions are so ingrained that you are usually unaware of them. Consequently, you will generalize about certain groups of people and create stereotypes. If you trick yourself into believing that your subjective opinions are true facts, you lose a tremendous opportunity to see young athletes as they really are. It is important that you examine yourself honestly and carefully to help you take stock of your inner feelings.

The purpose of this quiz is to help you determine your familiarity with and acceptance of people who are unlike yourself. **Treat the results as a guide. There is always a margin of uncertainty in questionnaires of this kind.**

Look at people; recognize them, accept them as they are, without wanting to change them.
HELEN BEGINTON

Score your questions:

1. Never   2. Seldom   3. Sometimes   4. Often   5. Always

1. _____ Do you have negative feelings about Americans who don't speak English or use broken or heavily accented English?
2. _____ Do you have negative feelings about gay colleagues or athletes?
3. _____ Do you feel uncomfortable where you are different, for example, where you are surrounded by others who are of a different color and/or speak a different language?
4. _____ Do you dislike males who have "feminine" traits or females who have "masculine" qualities?
5. _____ Do you tell ethnic jokes?
6. _____ Do you discount opinions of athletes who are different from you? (For example, someone who has brown skin, has a heavy accent, or is of a particular nationality)?
7. _____ Do you dislike to hear different cultural language or slang?
8. _____ Do you dislike the African-American style of rapping in terms of voice volume, facial gestures, hand movement, and posturing?
9. _____ Do you avoid trying to learn or to speak the language of some of your athletes from different cultures?
10. _____ Do you dislike the idea of interracial dating or marriage?
11. _____ Do you converse with close friends (not acquaintances) and speak negatively about some minority group or groups?
12. _____ Do you resent the special opportunities given to minorities?
13. _____ Do you take the time to study the different cultures that your athletes represent?
14. _____ Do you find assertive female athletes to be pushy or abrasive?
15. _____ Do you feel it is ever appropriate to imitate certain ethnic groups by overexaggerating certain stereotypical ethnic speech patterns or mannerisms.

The privilege of a lifetime is being who you are.
JOSEPH CAMPBELL

Add your scores for all 15 statements. The total represents your score.

SCORE	WHAT YOUR ANSWERS MEAN
60–75	You probably have a number of cultural biases and tend to have a fear of or are intolerant of people of different cultures. You need to work on overcoming your prejudices by separating opinion or emotional reaction from the hard truth. Seek a professional who can help you in this process.
35–59	You appear to have some biases, but you are somewhat aware of your biases and try to treat people equally whenever possible. Keep plugging away. Continue to expand your knowledge and diversity.
Below 35	You have few ethnic or cultural biases and tend to judge most people individually, rather then by placing them into generalized groups. Congratulations!

Whether it's on the athletic field or in the workplace, the same rules apply: the teams that win are the teams that complement one another and whenever you find a situation where people who are of a different sex or a different color can't play together on a team, that team doesn't win.

JOHN SIMS

Major Points Discussed in Chapter 4

1. One of the most compelling motivations that any athlete has is the need to feel accepted.
2. A coach's acceptance of an athlete should be unconditional, not contingent on anything particular about the individual who is accepted.
3. The concepts of intrinsic worth and unconditional acceptance are at the center of Positive Coaching.
4. Coaches can show that they care about their athletes by:
   a. taking them seriously,
   b. listening carefully to them,
   c. letting them know that the coach cares about them,
   d. touching them respectfully and appropriately,
   e. smiling at them,
   f. using simple hand gestures of approval, and
   g. providing sincere encounters with each athlete.
5. Some coaches find it difficult to completely accept the athletes for who they are. Their personal biases affect their acceptance of the athletes.
6. It is essential that coaches be fair in their treatment of different athletes and not let their biases or prejudices interfere.

Emotional Significance: Give Athletes a Sense of Purpose

I saw the angel in the marble and I just chiseled until I set him free.

Michelangelo

Athletes who feel purposeful have an inner knowledge that their participation has meaning and direction. Feeling a sense of purpose is one of the deepest human needs. Athletes with a sense of purpose have specific goals for what they want to do and be. Having purpose makes them feel like somebody. They become motivated, optimistic, and energized in the process.

It is the coach's responsibility to help each athlete discover personal meaning by helping the athlete determine his or her purpose and providing the support necessary to accomplish it. This means helping each athlete set and achieve worthwhile goals. When athletes are involved in decisions, they'll feel accountable for what happens.

The coach acts as a guide by helping all athletes determine the direction in which they should be heading. When they have a goal, athletes know where to focus their time and energy which increases the likelihood of success. Best of all, success in one area leads to success in another area—and that is the whole idea. Athletes who have no goal have nothing to aim for, and over time they will hit that "nothing" with great success.

Setting Goals

There are five easy steps to help athletes set goals:

1. Determine whose goal it is. If athletes do not really want something, chances are they won't make the commitment needed to achieve it. A smart coach helps all players see each goal as their own. If a player "owns" the goal, he or she will be more motivated toward achieving it. When the coach is helping athletes set goals, take a few minutes to talk about what they are going to get out of accomplishing it—the benefits. The more reasons they think of for achieving the goal, the stronger will be their desire. A stronger desire will result in greater effort.

Efforts and courage are not enough without purpose and direction.

J. F. KENNEDY

2. Make sure the goal is attainable. The athlete has to believe that the goal is achievable. It doesn't have to be easy, but the athlete should have a fair chance of meeting it. In contrast, if the goal is too easy, what's the challenge?

3. Divide the goal into small, achievable steps. Goals seem a lot easier to reach when they are broken down into manageable tasks. Long-term goals need to be broken down into a series of smaller short-term goals. Each small accomplishment should be recognized as the athlete moves toward the greater whole.

4. Set realistic deadlines. Setting deadlines forces the coach and the athlete to plan and organize. A deadline also acts as a point of reference to determine the success in achieving the short- and long-term goals. It forces an evaluation to determine where the athlete is at that point in time.

5. Put the goal in writing. Asking the athlete to put the goal in writing helps him or her to clarify it as well as organize and plan it. It helps to internalize the goal. The goal should also be posted where the athlete can see it. Crossing off each short-term goal as it is accomplished has wondrous effects.

TIME OUT: IN THE COACH'S CORNER

Leaders Help Others to Reach Goals

Paul "Bear" Bryant, the football coach who won 323 major college football games, more than any other coach in history,* used a technique from which all leaders could benefit. At the beginning of each football season at Alabama, Bryant had every member of his squad write out his personal goals. Only after reading and studying those goals did Bryant design a game plan and objectives for his football team.

Why did this work so well? This simple technique had a threefold message. Bryant was conveying to his team (1) I care about you and what you want; (2) you should be thinking ahead; and (3) we are building a team in which each of you can pursue your personal goals, and I'm going to include those goals in our total team plan in as many ways as possible.

Knowing this, Bryant's squad gave their coach all they could give, and in so doing they strove for their own personal goals as well as producing strong, winning records year after year.

Source: Reprinted with permission from *The Speaker's Sourcebook: Quotes and Stories.* © 1988 by Glenn Van Ekeren. Englewood Cliffs, NJ: Prentice-Hall, Inc.

*Other coaches may have surpassed Bryant's record since 1988, when this article was written.

Successful Teams Have High Expectations

Schools that establish high expectations for all kids—and give them the support necessary to achieve them—have incredibly high rates of academic success. Rutter [1984] concluded that successful schools shared certain characteristics: an academic emphasis with high standards, teachers' clear expectations and regulations, and a high level of student participation. Equally important, Rutter found that the number of problem behaviors experienced by students decreased over time in the successful schools and increased in the unsuccessful schools.

The best kept secret in America today is that people would rather work hard for something they believe in than enjoy a pampered idleness.
JOHN N. GARNER

Successful athletic teams share the same characteristics of successful classrooms: clear expectations and a high level of participation. Consequently, it is essential not only that coaches help all athletes to establish high expectations for themselves, but also give them the support and encouragement to meet these expectations.

Athletic Participation and Involvement

The need to feel needed is often more powerful than the need to live. People have committed suicide when they felt that their lives had no meaning or significance. Wehlage [1989] has confirmed that teenagers who feel alienated from family, school, or the community are more likely to abuse drugs, get pregnant, or father a child, fail in school, commit vandalism, develop depression, or commit suicide. Wehlage stated, "The challenge clearly for these social institutions—and especially for the schools—is to engage youth by providing them opportunities to participate in meaningful, valued activities and roles—those involving problem-solving, decision-making, planning, goal setting, and helping others."

Bernard [1991] states, "Once again, the operating dynamic reflects the fundamental human need to bond—to participate, to belong, to have some power or control over one's life. . . . When schools ignore these basic human needs, they become ineffective and alienating places."

This is also true in athletics. All athletes need to feel that they are an important member of the team. Athletes must believe that their participation makes a difference, that their existence and contributions to the team matter. Athletes who feel alienated will be indifferent, aimless, and unmotivated.

Seymour Sarason [1990] says it well: "When one has no stake in the way things are, when one's needs or opinions are provided no forum, when one sees oneself as the object of unilateral actions, it takes no particular wisdom to suggest that one would rather be elsewhere." It would seem logical that when athletes have no stake in the outcome of any athletic contest, when their needs or opinions are discounted, when they see themselves only as bodies rather than as individuals on the field, when they feel that their presence on the team doesn't really matter, it takes no particular wisdom to suggest that they would rather be elsewhere.

Every athlete is waiting for the coach to give him or her some responsibility, something that he or she can feel good about. When it happens, it's almost miraculous. Things begin to happen in ways that nobody, not even the coach or the players, could ever have guessed.

> *Lack of something to feel important about is almost the greatest tragedy a man may have.*
> ARTHUR MORGAN

Providing Opportunities for Contribution

Every athlete as a team member must be given the opportunity to be meaningfully involved and valued. Kurth-Schai [1988] reported, "youth participation in socially useful tasks is associated with heightened self-esteem, enhanced moral development, increased political activism, and the ability to create and maintain complex social relationships." When athletes are needed as contributors, they will bond, grow in dignity and self-respect, and get involved.

Here is a partial list of activities in which athletes can become *involved*:

1. Organizing and planning practices
2. Leading warm-ups
3. Making team travel plans
4. Managing team finances
5. Caring for athletic equipment
6. Helping to coach less skilled teammates
7. Maintaining the athletic field or court
8. Buying equipment

9. Maintaining scorebooks
10. Writing articles for school newspaper
11. Being the audio-visual manager
12. Being the team's public relations director
13. Creating posters and announcements
14. Raising funds
15. Preparing the team's banquet program
16. Being a computer consultant
17. Being the team statistician
18. Being the alumni director for the team
19. Team scheduling

Involvement leads to accountability, accountability leads to ownership, and ownership will lead the athletes to involvement. Involvement is a cyclic process.

TIME OUT: IN THE COACH'S CORNER

"Why Aren't My Players Motivated in Practice?"

Coach Foster was frustrated by the attitude of many of her players. They didn't seem motivated in practices. Each evening she took much of her work home. She diligently planned each practice. Drill by drill and strategy by strategy, each had a specific purpose. Before each practice, she lectured her athletes and gave an overview of the practice and its purpose. She carefully explained the reason behind each specific drill and strategy. She thought that if the athletes knew the purpose, they would be more responsive to her practice demands. She thought, "How could my players not respect and appreciate me for all the work I'm doing? No other coach in the league does as much as I do." But she also thought, "Why aren't they responding? How can they be so unmotivated?"

She was worried, even though her team was in first place. It was imperative that they didn't become too complacent and lazy during the second half of the season. It was this kind of attitude and behavior that she thought could cost her team the conference title.

During practices, she was frustrated and pleaded with her players to get motivated. Phrases like, "Come on gals, you're being lazy" and "What you do in practice will carry over into the games" were repeated continually throughout practice. Choice words reflecting anger and frustration were also beginning to surface. Yet the energy level never really rose. Coach Foster's tolerance was reaching its limits.

Ability is of little account without opportunity.
NAPOLEON BONAPARTE

Multiple Choice

If you were Coach Foster, which of the following would you do?

A. Continue designing drills and strategies and explain their purposes, and hope that the players will become motivated once they truly understand and appreciate your efforts.
B. Show your anger and frustration by yelling more.
C. Use some form of punishment to motivate the players.
D. Allow the players to have input into the practice sessions.

Response D is correct. Athletes' motivation during practice can be enhanced if athletes have input into the practices. Allowing input provides a number of advantages:

1. It forces the athletes to think critically about the team's practice needs.
2. With input, the athletes will take greater ownership of the practice sessions. The greater the ownership, the greater the motivation to participate.
3. It assures the coach that the players know the basics behind the plays because they are implementing them in practice.
4. The players grow and mature. They become more responsible, self-reliant, and self-disciplined through this process.
5. Working together builds teamwork between the players and the coach.

Response A doesn't work. Coach Foster has always planned and explained the practices, and the players were not responding. Why continue this strategy if it is not working?

Response B may work for a short time, but in the long run, screaming and yelling will only distance the coach from the players, and soon the yelling will increase as the players begin to ignore the coach.

Response C may also work for a short time, but in the long run, like screaming and yelling, punishment will distance the coach from the players. See Chapter 11 for the devastating effects of punishment.

The very essence of all power to influence lies in getting the other person to participate. The mind that can do that has a powerful leverage on his human world.
HARRY A. OVERSTREET

QUESTIONS AND ANSWERS

Question: I would like to allow my athletes to be meaningfully involved, but to suggest that they be involved with some of the activities you listed (such as planning practices, making team travel plans, fund raising, and team scheduling) is a bit scary. It seems like they are taking over my job. How much should I really let them do?

Answer: This is a tough question because each coach, team, and situation is different.

The coach: Each coach has her own value system, and many coaches feel compelled to assume the responsibility for all decision making. Each coach must examine the importance that she places on organizational efficiency, personal growth of players, and team winning. Coaches also differ greatly in the amount of trust they have in their athletes' abilities as well as the coach's feelings of security when she allows players to make decisions.

The players on the team: Each team is different, being made up of people with different personalities and different wants and abilities. Some want more responsibility; others need more independence. Some will have the necessary knowledge and experience to deal with a problem; others may not be interested in the problem.

Situations: Situations will vary in complexity. Such factors as the pressure of time, the nature of the problem, and group effectiveness will play a role in how much input players might have in planning.

> *If you want to get the best out of a man you must look for the best that is in him.*
> BERNARD HALDANE

These three factors will influence a coach's action in a decision-making situation. So there is no one absolute answer. Most coaches should start slowly allowing players to make decisions in nonthreatening situations. For example, little harm is done if a player makes mistakes while leading warm-ups. On more important issues such as helping to arrange practices or make travel plans, the coach can work closely with athletes to help guide them through the process. Small steps are taken in the beginning, and as the players learn to walk on their own, the coach can gradually relinquish input to empower her athletes in the decision-making process. In addition, when athletes begin to take ownership of the situation, they are more motivated to participate.

The successful coach is one who can accurately perceive when it is necessary for him or her to direct and make decisions but can provide the freedom of decisions to the players when it is called for.

Question: How much should I participate with the players once I delegate responsibility to them?

Answer: This depends on whether your presence will inhibit or facilitate the planning process. There may be some instances when you should leave the group to allow players to solve the problem by themselves. At other times, you can contribute beneficial ideas. However, if you are delegating responsibility, you need to clearly indicate that you are merely a contributing member of the group rather than the leader.

Question: What if I don't like the decision that the players have made?

Answer: A coach is always held responsible for whatever decision the group makes. Therefore you must be ready to accept whatever risk is involved when you delegate decision-making power to your athletes. However, you cannot give your players more freedom than you yourself have been given by your superiors. Therefore limitations must be set. To reverse a decision will only create distrust and disrespect and will send the message that the athletes are incapable. If a wrong decision is made, it becomes a wonderful opportunity for learning.

If it were considered desirable to destroy a human being, the only thing necessary would be to give work a character of uselessness.
FYODOR
DOSTOYEVSKY

TIME OUT: IN THE COACH'S CORNER

Discovering the Potential of Each Athlete
This exercise is a treasure hunt designed to help you (1) discover the potentials in each of your players and (2) make sense of what you uncover. Be honest.

If you are not a coach, choose an athlete or friend and discover his or her potential.

1. Observe and talk with an athlete during the week, and write a description of him or her. Pretend that you are writing it to someone who has never met the athlete. Describe each athlete physically, emotionally, intellectually, socially, and athletically. How does the athlete act in school and in practice? Does the athlete get along with others? What is it about him or her that you have difficulty accepting? Is the athlete even-tempered? Does he or she have a lot of friends? Does the athlete interact socially with others? Does he or she have a sense of humor? How does the athlete dissipate nervous energy? What do you like best about the athlete? What does he or she do outside of school and athletics? What are his or her athletic talents? What does the athlete do that annoys you? Does the athlete practice effectively? Is he or she performing up to his or her present capabilities? What keeps the athlete from improving? What is the athlete doing that is making him or her perform better? Is the athlete a responsible person? What are his or her limits? What are his or her bad habits?

Keep your description as detailed as possible. Keep adding to it during the week. You will find yourself thinking about the athlete and looking at him or her more carefully. You will discover qualities and behaviors that you never noticed before. Add to your description by checking with other people such as parents, teachers, and friends. You will probably be surprised and delighted by the added insights.

2. Now analyze your description by constructing a list of the positive qualities that you want to nurture and the negative qualities that you want to change. This partial list is written about Sue, captain of the high school basketball team.

POSITIVE QUALITIES	NEGATIVE QUALITIES
"Clutch" player	Easily frustrated by other players
Great Sense of Humor	Too much of a perfectionist
Good grades	Loses temper too easily
Knows the game of basketball	Not very outgoing with others
Determined	Stubborn
	Bossy

Examine the Positives
Look for positive qualities that already exist. Reflect on those positive qualities and appreciate the athlete for having them. Continue to reinforce those behaviors with recognition and encouragement. The athlete will learn to value these qualities and see himself or herself as capable and special in these areas. If the list is long, choose a few qualities to begin with and gradually add others to your reinforcement strategy. In time, you will get used to finding the special qualities in each athlete.

Purpose is what gives life a meaning.
C. H. PARKHURST

Examine the Negatives
Both positive or negative behaviors are based on fulfillment of one or more of the basic emotional needs. When an athlete starts a fight with a teammate, shows off in an obnoxious way, complains about rules, or deliberately misses practice, he needs something. If you can determine what need is being expressed, you can help that athlete meet the need in a more appropriate manner.

For every item on the negative list, ask yourself these three questions:

1. What need does this behavior really reflect?
2. How can I help meet this need in a more positive way?
3. Can I find a positive quality in this behavior?

Re-evaluating Some of the Negatives

Carefully reexamine the negative list and identify some of the items that are really your problem and not the athlete's. Are some of the things you listed a matter of your own personal preferences? No amount of nagging or reminding will change a shy, quiet athlete into a verbal, outgoing team leader. Forget about hairstyles and dress; you will only create tension or conflict and, in the long run, spoil the relationship.

Major Points Discussed in Chapter 5

1. Coaches must help each athlete set and achieve worthwhile goals.
2. The process of setting goals includes the following:
   a. Determine who's goal it is.
   b. Make sure the goal is attainable.
   c. Divide the goal into small achievable steps.
   d. Set realistic deadlines.
   e. Put the goal in writing.
3. Successful athletic teams have clear and high expectations and a high level of participation.
4. All athletes need to feel that their participation makes a difference and that their existence and contributions to the team really matter.
5. Coaches need to find ways in which all athletes can contribute within the team structure.
6. The three factors of the coach, the players, and the situation will determine how much responsibility the coach can give to the athletes.

6

The Capable Athlete: Structure for Success, Not Failure

All of us do not have equal talents, but all of us should have an equal opportunity to develop our talents.

John F. Kennedy

Build Positive Images within Your Athletes

Athletes, children, students, and even adults develop perceptions of themselves based on how they think others see them. Athletes will find in the eyes and attitudes of adults who coach them mirrors in which they discover and perceive themselves. How athletes perceive themselves through their coaches will be a major factor in how they comprehend themselves within the playing arena.

The athlete's self-image becomes internalized as the athlete tests himself or herself in the athletic arena. The athlete adopts attitudes of worthiness or worthlessness as he or she ventures through the athletic world with an eye on the coach's reactions. It is easier for athletes to develop positive attitudes about themselves if they are with coaches who see them as competent, responsible, and worthwhile.

Individuals see themselves as they think others see them. The words and attitudes that coaches choose and the way they use them significantly contribute to an athlete's destiny. Words and attitudes have the power to lift up or put down. So if coaches fill players with visions of incompetence, failure, and worthlessness, the players will probably perform poorly. When athletes hear coaches call them "clumsy" or "lazy" they may not only think of themselves as clumsy or lazy but behave in that manner as well. Coaches can assist in forming a positive view by focusing on the athlete's capabilities. If a coach encourages and affirms an athlete's capabilities, the athlete will respond with greater confidence and maturity.

The Power of Words

If we maximize communication, we can minimize coercion.

EDGAR DALE

Coaches' language and attitudes can have both positive and negative effects. On one hand, words can create barriers that block trust, confidence, performance, and communication. It is important to remember that the barriers coaches help to erect within their athletes are almost always internal ones. The absence of achievement is most often due to a genuine belief that one could never achieve at a high level. As significant adults in the lives of children, coaches often reflect attitudes or use words that undermine the athlete's self-confidence. Attitudes and words can make players feel inadequate and not capable and can destroy the positive beliefs that the athletes may have in themselves. It is a language of disrespect for others. It can be nasty, condescending, and harmful.

The job of motivating players to have greater aspirations in life and athletics is essentially the task of working on their self-image. Any time a coach finds an athlete reflecting indifference, negativity, and pessimism about his or her own abilities, the coach has much work to do.

However, the language and attitudes of coaches can also have the opposite effect. Words can consistently affirm and validate young people by instilling a belief in their capabilities and potential. Words can be respectful and caring, encouraging and not charged with negative emotions. Words can provide positive feedback. The only authentic barrier to an athlete's own greatness is his or her fear of his or her own greatness. Eliminating those fears is the avenue the coach needs to take in working on the athlete's self-image.

The coach's most fundamental task is to provide a learning environment that fosters the athletes' perceptions of themselves as capable, significant and accepted. Everyone knows that having a positive self-image is important, yet concerned and caring coaches often interact with athletes in such a way as to promote a lowered self-image. Many destructive words keep repeating themselves simply because the coach doesn't know of better ways to deal with problems.

The greatest discovery of my generation is that human beings can alter their lives by altering their attitudes of mind.

W. JAMES

TIME OUT: IN THE COACH'S CORNER

The John Lucas Philosophy

When John Lucas became head coach of the San Antonio Spurs,* he brought with him a philosophy that was unheard of in the National Basketball Association. As a recovering drug addict and director of a drug rehabilitation center in Houston, Lucas allows his players to take responsibility for their actions on the court. His basic philosophy stems from the "12-step program" that helps people take control of their own lives. It is not unusual for his players to diagram plays and dictate strategies during time-outs or to be in charge of different drills during practices.

In the *Los Angeles Times* [1993], Lucas was quoted as saying, "I'm getting out of their way. I'm letting them have their team. They do some things they probably thought they would never do as a player. With this team, I have such smart players. I've got to keep challenging them. . . . I felt a sense of purpose that I had to refocus our team about building confidence for themselves, believing in themselves and doing what they say they are going to do."

Coaches and athletes who feel capable and responsible know that they can learn and accomplish things. They have the inner strength and reasoning power to take on challenging tasks even though they face difficult odds. John Lucas fostered an attitude and environment in which his players could grow and prosper. He treated his athletes as they ought to be and, consequently, helped them become what they are capable of.

Wisdom is knowing when to speak your mind and when to mind your speech.
EVANGEL

*Lucas left the San Antonio Spurs at the end of the 1994 season.

Barriers that Condemn Athletes to Failure

Coaches sometimes set up their athletes for failure. They may do it unintentionally, but they do it just the same. H. Stephen Glenn [1989] developed a list of behaviors or barriers that he believed undermine self-confidence and trust and, consequently, lead to failure. Discussed below are variations and modifications of Glenn's barriers. These behaviors act as obstacles to success.

1. Having unrealistic athletic expectations of the athletes. Players want to live up to the coach's expectations—unless those expectations are unrealistic or impossible. Unrealistic expectations lead to disappointment, dissatisfaction, discouragement, and finally despair. Of course, coaches should set high standards, but in the process they should avoid pointing out the athlete's failure to achieve these standards. Having high expectations means that a coach believes in the athletes' capabilities but the coach needs to give the athletes time and space to grow to meet those expectations—not all at once, but in small increments. If coaches have unrealistic expectations and focus only on them, they will seldom view the athlete as successful. If coaches communicate their judgment of failure, athletes will feel frustrated, unaccepted, and incapable.

Coaches must be patient and encourage and celebrate each successful step and focus on that moment rather then comparing it to the athlete's potential. Coaches should allow each athlete to enjoy his or her journey to personal success.

A true critic ought to focus rather upon excellencies than imperfections.
JOSEPH ADDISON

2. Evaluating the athletes' social behavior according to adult standards or evaluating the athletes on the basis of expectations that have not yet been achieved. In addition to athletic performance expectations, coaches must have realistic expectations of the athletes' emotional and social behaviors. Coaches often forget what it is like to be a young athlete. They mistakenly expect, demand, and require the players, to think, act, understand, see, and do things as they do. Coaches need to respect their players and recognize that young athletes are still young people in the process of becoming adults. Young athletes are still searching for their identity, discovering themselves, and sorting out their feelings. It is a very important time in their lives. Young people are going to make mistakes, act out, do things that are considered foolish or immature, speak out, and be influenced by their peers. Coaches must recognize that young people are only doing their "job." It is their job to individualize and become independent and capable. Coaches must recognize and respect this process and provide any necessary support. Adults' unrealistic expectations produce impotence, frustration, hostility, and aggression in young people.

What coaches must realize is that the athlete is not bad; only the behavior or performance is bad. An athlete is not "dumb" if he or she fails an exam. The performance on the test was bad, but things can be done to improve the results of future tests. Focus on test improvements, not on the athlete. Athletes will sense the distinction. Young players are neither good nor bad; however, what a coach thinks makes it so. Players will become aware of the coach's faith in them. It will give them added encouragement to overcome difficulties, which will seem less formidable to them now that they have been minimized.

It is much easier to be critical than to be correct.
DISRAELI

3. Criticizing or "dumping on" players when they are already down. Criticism is closely related to the behavior of expecting. When an athlete fails to live up to the coach's expectations or standards, he or she will often be criticized for that failure. Criticism contributes to lowered self-images. The more criticism athletes receive, the more likely they will be to avoid doing the things that engender that criticism. Such statements as "You will never be good at playing defense" or "That's the third time you've missed a key shot—I guess you'll never be a clutch player" are the tools that athletes use to sculpture a poor self-image. Coaches often believe that they are providing help to their athletes when they constantly correct and criticize them, assuming that the athletes will grow from these negative remarks. There are other ways to encourage and motivate an athlete to a more effective performance. Criticism is the least effective and perhaps the most damaging of all the available techniques.

The language of criticism includes such statements as "Why don't you ever . . . ?" "How many times do I have to tell you?" and "When will you ever grow up?" Coaches must realize that a young athlete's view of the world is different from an adult's view of the world. Coaches are faulting the athlete for not seeing what the coaches see. Criticizing responses are based on disrespect and will ultimately lead athletes to failure. Ridicule, put-downs, blaming, fault finding, comparing, and labeling are also common. Messages that judge or criticize will make players feel inadequate and unworthy. These messages will begin to chip away at the players confidence, potentials, and abilities. Players will often respond to these messages with defensiveness. anger, and withdrawal because they need to protect their self-images.

The more coaches rely on external criticism, the greater the chance that the athlete will internalize these words. Before long, the athlete will create a self-image based on self-criticism. Nobody enjoys being criticized. Coaches should not build on weakness—only on strength. Unfortunately, some coaches, spend too much of their time watching to see what their players are doing wrong and criticizing them for it instead of finding what is right and building on those strengths. As Dreikurs [1964] stated, "anyone who stops to think will realize that we really do follow our noses. If our nose points to mistakes, we arrive just there. If we center our children's attention upon what they do well, express our confidence in their ability, and give them encouragement, the mistakes and faults may die from a lack of feeding."

Coaches seem to live in a sort of fear that their athletes will learn bad habits and do things the wrong way. They watch their athletes constantly and try to prevent mistakes. They constantly correct and criticize. Such an approach shows a lack of faith in the athletes. It is discouraging and sometimes humiliating. With a constant emphasis on the negative, the athlete loses the energy to progress toward achievement.

When athletes are constantly corrected and criticized, they may get the feeling that they are always wrong and become very fearful of making mistakes. This fear may cause many athletes to lose their ability to function and may even cause them to give up in despair.

Criticizing others is a dangerous thing, not so much because you may make mistakes about them, but because you may be revealing the truth about yourself.
JUDGE HAROLD MEDINA

Recognition and encouragement are powerful tools. Encourage and recognize athletes for attempting a task, even if they were unsuccessful, and acknowledge them for taking the risks. Using these tools creates an environment in which athletes know that they are being supported in their efforts.

4. Talking too much and not allowing the athletes to discover useful explanations for themselves. Coaches who play the "know-it-all" role try to show their players that they have traveled life's roads for a long time and have accumulated most of the answers. Consequently, they lecture, advise, and make appeals to the athletes' reason. They try to show how superior they themselves are. Though teaching and lecturing are legitimate functions of the coach-player relationship, players regard them as illegitimate at times. Coaches must try to become aware of when "logic and facts" begin to evoke defensiveness and resentment.

Encouragers know there is a big difference between advice and help.
ANONYMOUS

Lecturing is the most widely used teaching method, but it is also the least effective. It is an excellent example of one-way communication. The teacher is the only one who is active. The only indication a teacher receives of student understanding is nonverbal. The same principle applies when coaches lecture their players. The coach can't be sure that the players understand. It is also boring; it allows for no interaction. It does not allow the player to disagree or agree with expressed viewpoints, and most important, it does not require the athlete to take any responsibility for learning.

Too often, coaches step in and explain things instead of helping athletes to discover the meaning of an event for themselves. Some coaches believe that it is their job to explain everything before anything happens and more frequently after something happens. Coaches, in the role of the "know-it-all" or in the name of expediency, will step in all too quickly and explain to the players something that the players have not yet experienced. When a mistake occurs in the game, the coach takes it on himself or herself after the game to explain what happened. However, truly effective coaches work with athletes to help them develop useful explanations for themselves. If an athlete can figure it out by himself or herself, the coach can be assured that he or she really understood what happened. Further growth can then occur. The athlete will become more independent and confident in his or her decision making when new situations arise.

Coaches often become frustrated because a player keeps on making the same mistake over and over. Each time the mistake is made, the coach explains what happened, why it happened, and what can be done to fix it. By stepping in too quickly, coaches prevent athletes from thinking through the occurrence and learning from it.

Reflection on one's experience is a far more effective teacher than coaches could ever be. A coach can help athletes to internalize the learning by helping them to reflect on the experiences that occurred. It is a process of understanding what happened, why it happened, and how one can learn from it. Instead of quickly explaining and lecturing, H. Stephen Glenn [1989] suggests that one may ask thoughtful questions such as "What do you think happened?" "What do you think caused that to happen?" and "How could you do it differently the next time?"

This process conveys the message that the athlete is capable of developing good judgment, mastering situations, and gaining understanding. As a result of this process, a mistake, if budgeted right, can be investment spending for the future. By explaining and lecturing all the time, coaches slow the development of the athlete's judgmental skills as well as his or her sense of feeling capable and competent. Of course, the coach must provide an evaluation when it's clear that the athlete doesn't know what is correct or incorrect. If the behavior or performance is correct, the coach should recognize and acknowledge the athletes for it and tell them what he or she liked about it.

Until I can risk appearing imperfect in your eyes without fear that it will cost me something, I can't really learn from you.
RUDOLPH DREIKURS

Asking the players the "What," Why," and "How" is also an excellent tool for postgame evaluations. Whether the game was won or lost, this process will help the players to analyze and internalize the successes and the mistakes of the competition. If players have input, they will be more likely to take ownership of the situation and, consequently, be more committed to the learning process, in particular, to the skills and strategies they need to work on.

5. Excessive directing. For the sake of efficiency, expediency, and time, coaches find it easiest to direct, order, or command athletes to do things. When coaches step in too quickly and direct, they produce hostility and resistance and, most important block communication. These messages tell a player that his or her feelings or needs are not important; he or she must comply with what the coach wants. (Examples: "I don't care if you're thirsty; wait until you're excused." or "Stop complaining. You're the biggest baby on the team.") Being directed makes people feel impotent and frustrated. Ordering or directing also implies that the other person's judgment or knowledge is inferior to yours.

Criticism is the art of appraising others at one's own values.
GEORGE JEAN NATHAN

Unfortunately, some coaches add to their directing threats of punishment for refusing to comply. (Example: "Stop complaining or I'll give you something to really complain about.") These messages evoke fear and hostility and make the athlete feel

fearful and submissive. Some players will respond to threats by
doing something they have just been warned not to do, just to
see whether the consequences promised by the coach will ma-
terialize.

In general, the more directive coaches are, the more rebellious and resistant athletes become. In addition, when coaches
are constantly directing, athletes will respond by doing nothing
at all or less than what was expected. A very authoritative high
school coach once said that he directed his players to "load the
equipment on the bus" because they had to leave quickly for an
away game. Most of the players tried to get on the bus and did
nothing to help. The coach then proceeded to scream at the
players and hovered over them as they were forced to load
things on the bus. As a matter of defense, the coerced athletes
reverted to passive-aggressive behavior by leaving a few items
behind to irritate the coach.

If, instead of being directed, players are invited or encouraged to assist or contribute, they are generally more willing to
cooperate. After learning a different behavioral model, that
same coach was faced with a similar situation, but this time he
said, "I would appreciate anything you could do to help me get
the equipment on the bus." Most of the players cooperated and
loaded the equipment on the bus. Some even asked if there was
anything else they could do. By inviting their contribution, the
coach encouraged their participation and promoted extra effort.

6. Assuming the worst. Making assumptions prevents
growth and development. To make assumptions about athletes
doesn't allow them the opportunity to learn, change, and grow.
When we assume we say, "What you were before is all I allow
you to be now." A coach said that she had a freshman player
who forgot her athletic shoes for an away volleyball tournament. For the next four years the coach reminded her before
each game "Don't forget your shoes." She assumed that no
growth had taken place in the four years. Many coaches make
assumptions about players because of a single incident and ste-
reotype that person for the remainder of his or her athletic career. There is an abundance of stories about players who
changed to a new coach and blossomed because the new coach
did not hold negative assumptions and the person was given a
chance to develop.

Athletes have multiple self-images that are constantly shifting between highly positive and fearfully negative. On one day
they may feel quite capable as a tennis player; on the next day
they may feel like a beginner. Athletes cannot be stuck into specific slots or reduced to computerized data. Besides being
unique, athletes are ever-changing entities. Just when you

*It's always wise
to raise ques-
tions about the
most obvious
and simple as-
sumptions.*
C. WEST
CHURCHMAN

think you have them figured out, they surprise you by being better then what you imagined or even the opposite of what you imagined. Young athletes are not fixed pieces of computer software, they are dynamic, ever-changing, and unique.

7. Maintaining standards that are too low. Instead of allowing athletes to develop and test their strengths and abilities in a variety of ways, a coach may confront them with his or her own prejudices, preconceptions and beliefs. The coach lacks faith in the athletes' abilities and sets his or her own standards by which the athletes must perform.

Too often, coaches train athletes at the level at which they think the athletes are, rather than the level at which they could or might be. If coaches treat athletes as the coaches think they are, the athletes may stay that way. If it is the coach's job to help athletes grow and change, then the coach must allow them to grow and change. It seems more logical for a coach to encourage players to find out what is possible than to make assumptions that may keep them from reaching their potential. A coach should examine what is possible today and build higher levels of confidence in the players' abilities as growing and changing athletes.

Presume not that I am the thing I was.
SHAKESPEARE

In summary, of all the judgments and beliefs that athletes have, none is more important than the ones they have about themselves. The barriers that athletes erect are almost always internal psychological ones. The absence of achievement is most often due to a genuine belief that one could never achieve at a high level. Consequently, the job of motivating athletes to have greater aspirations in athletics is essentially the task of working on their self-perceptions. Wherever a coach finds negativity, pessimism, or indifference, he or she has an assignment for self-perception improvement to work on.

TIME OUT: IN THE COACH'S CORNER

"Coach, I Quit!"
Listening to someone without judging his or her actions is difficult. However, learning to focus on the individual's behaviors rather than the individual's personality is one of the most important skills a coach should learn and practice. Two scenes representing the same situation are described below. Scene 1 represents an attack on both the person and the behavior. Scene 2 is a respectful approach in which the coach validates the individual's feelings and focuses on changing the individual's behavior.

Scene 1

Bob, visibly upset, approaches the football coach and says in a hesitant voice, "Coach, I'm quitting the team."

"Bob, I don't understand. What's the matter?" Coach Smith replies in a puzzled but concerned voice.

Bob responds in a straightforward but rehearsed manner, "Coach, I've been to every single practice and you're not letting me play in any of the games. I don't think it's fair."

Startled for a moment, Coach Smith puts down the clipboard that he has been looking at and gathers his thoughts. He responds in a somewhat condescending manner, "Bob, I think you are being very selfish. You can't be thinking only about yourself. There are others who are in the same situation that you're in. But they aren't complaining. Football is a team sport. You are part of the team. Your efforts during practice are necessary for total team success."

Treat people as they ought to be, and you help them become what they are capable of being.
GOETHE

Coach Smith thinks that he is offering sound logic. He does not realize that he is fueling Bob's frustration by calling him selfish and trying to make him feel guilty about his attitude.

Bob responds, with anger and frustration, "But it's not fair, you're not giving me a chance. I'm just wasting my time."

Coach Smith now feeling a bit defensive, says, "Bob, life isn't always fair, nor is football. I wish I could play everybody, but I can't. I can only play those who I think are talented enough, and right now you are not good enough. With more practice and improvement, you might just get to play."

"All I want is a chance!"

Coach Smith, cuts Bob off and continues to preach. "You may get that chance someday. But for now you have to be patient, and things will work out. I remember having another player who went through the same thing you're going through. But with perseverance, he made the starting team and eventually earned a college scholarship."

Bob is thinking, "Who cares what happened to him? Why is he telling me some stupid story that has nothing to do with me?"

The scenario continues with the same circular dialogue until Bob angrily quits the team and leaves the office. As Bob is leaving, Coach Smith shouts, "Clear out your locker and turn in your equipment before practice."

How could the coach have done it differently?

Scene 2

Bob, visibly upset, approaches the football coach and says in a hesitant voice, "Coach, I'm quitting the team."

"Bob, I don't understand. What's the matter?" Coach Smith replies in a puzzled but concerned voice.

Bob responds in a straightforward but rehearsed manner, "Coach, I've been to every single practice and you're not letting me play in any of the games. I don't think it's fair."

Startled for a moment, Coach Smith puts down the clipboard that he has been looking at and gathers his thoughts. He responds, "It sounds like you are feeling frustrated about not getting any playing time."

"That's right, coach. I don't think you're being fair. I'm just as good as some of the other guys that you let play."

Realizing how important it is for Bob's feelings to be validated, Coach Smith tries to put himself into Bob's shoes. He carefully responds, "Let me make sure I understand. You feel frustrated because I haven't given you a chance to prove yourself."

"Absolutely."

"And if you play, you'll feel like you are contributing?"

"Yes! I feel like a nobody. I know I can play and help the team."

At this point, the conversation can go in one of two possible directions. If Bob is correct and the coach realizes that he hasn't given him a chance, he might respond, "Bob, you might be right. Maybe I haven't given you a fair look. Let me think about this, and I'll see how I can work you into the next game."

However, if Coach Smith doesn't think Bob is ready to play at this time, he needs to clearly explain (without name-calling, preaching, or criticizing) what specific skills Bob needs to improve before he can be given a chance to play. Bob may not agree with the coach's assessment of his skills, but he has been treated with respect. Coach Smith has made no evaluation of Bob's behavior or attitude.

At this point, Bob feels that he was not only heard, but also understood. He must now make his own decision whether to quit the team or to work on the specific skills suggested by the coach.

If you expect perfection from people, your whole life is a series of disappointments, grumblings and complaints.
BRUCE BARTON

QUESTIONS AND ANSWERS

Question: Why do some coaches resort to verbally attacking their players with put-downs or name-calling?

Answer: A put-down is a humiliating remark or degrading gesture directed at some aspect of one's behavior or action. How athletes deal with put-downs makes a statement about their self-concepts and self-esteem. The sad part is that if they accept the negative remark, their self-perception is going to suffer and affect their ability to succeed. In reality, disparaging remarks don't really reflect the players' inferiority or inadequacy; they reflect the low self-esteem and poor self-image of the coach who makes the remark. Coaches who make disparaging remarks are reflecting their own unhappiness. They are trying to feel better by feeling superior to the athlete.

Question: How can I structure a team for success rather than failure?

Some people in weighing the faults of others, keep their thumbs on the scale.

UNKNOWN

Answer: Here are some ways to help athletes succeed.

1. Adjust the degree of challenge or difficulty of a skill according to the athlete's present ability.

2. Make certain that athletes are both physically and mentally prepared before moving on to new skills.

3. Structure the physical and emotional environment so that it is organized and supportive.

4. Give athletes plenty of time to practice before they move on to new skills.

5. Help athletes establish specific and achievable goals for improvement.

6. Schedule specific time blocks that allow the athletes to take their time or work at their own pace.

7. When athletes reach physical or mental blocks to improving, go the extra mile and provide the needed help.

8. Prepare athletes for game situations that may catch them off guard by having them practice various situations that they may unexpectedly encounter.

9. Let athletes know that it is okay to fail and that failure can be a wonderful opportunity for learning.

10. Maintain daily practice routines.

TIME OUT: SELF-ASSESSMENT

Stroking Yourself

Who is your biggest critic? You probably are. When you make a mistake or do something stupid, do you start an internal monologue of criticism? If you do, you need to turn the internal criticism into internal stroking. You already know that you can tear yourself down; you also have the ability to build yourself back up.

Internal stroking helps to develop a loving and positive attitude toward yourself. It means that you strive to see the best in yourself and to like yourself. If you don't like yourself, others probably won't like you either.

Part 1

Draw a line down the middle of a piece of paper. On the left side, write down all of the negative thoughts that you had about yourself today. Focus on statements such as:

"How could I be so stupid?"

"I look like a slob."

"How could I have forgotten? What a dummy!"

"Why did I say that? I can be so critical!"

Listening to some people means being exposed to a monologue.
UNKNOWN

Part 2

After recording your negative thoughts, take a deep breath and relax. Put your pencil away and close your eyes for a moment.

After a moment or two, slowly open your eyes, pick up your pencil, and on the right side of the paper, write positive replies to the criticisms you recorded on the left side. Create a dialogue between the two sides.

"How could I be so stupid?"

"I'm not stupid. I just made an honest mistake. I apologized and did what I had to do to correct it. No one is perfect. I can handle this and I can forgive myself."

"I look like a slob."

"No I don't. I just got a little stressed today. I think I'll wear that new shirt tomorrow. People will take notice."

"How could I have forgotten? What a dummy!"

"I'm no dummy. Things were just too hectic this morning. Next time I'll plan ahead a little better and put what I need to bring in my briefcase the night before."

"Why did I say that? I can be so critical!"

"I mean well and don't intentionally try to hurt people's feelings. The next time I'm going to take a deep breath and focus on the positive things."

I am an enemy of long explanations; they deceive either the maker or the hearer, and usually both.
GOETHE

Overcoming your critic is not easy. Don't get discouraged. It takes time. After all, your critical voice has probably been with you for years. But the more loving strokes you give yourself, the greater chance you will have of overcoming your critic.

Major Points Discussed in Chapter 6

1. Athletes will develop perceptions of themselves that are based on how they think others see them.
2. The coach's words can consistently affirm and validate the athletes by instilling a belief in their capabilities and potential.

3. Barriers that condemn athletes to failure includes:
   a. having unrealistic athletic expectations of the athlete,
   b. evaluating the athletes' social behavior according to adult standards or evaluating the athletes on the basis of expectations that have not yet been achieved,
   c. criticizing or "dumping on" players when they are already down,
   d. talking too much and not allowing the athletes to discover useful explanations for themselves,
   e. excessive directing,
   f. assuming the worst, and
   g. maintaining standards that are too low.
4. Coaches need to structure athletes for success rather than failure.

7

The Capable Athlete: Encourage Success, Not Failure

Small opportunities are often the beginnings of great enterprises.

Demosthenes

Encouragement

Encouragement is a process of giving positive recognition, support, and confidence to the athletes. Encouragement reassures the athletes. It neutralizes any doubts that they may have about themselves. It focuses on both the physical and emotional resources and provides positive recognition of the athlete's strengths as well as setting a foundation from which he or she can grow. Coaches must recognize the differences between advice and help. Coaches will be more successful if they encourage athletes rather than nagging them. Here are some strategies to help coaches encourage their athletes.

1. **Search for, identify, and acknowledge the athlete's strengths.** Most coaches are experts at scouting for potential athletic talent. But coaching goes beyond this one dimension. Coaches must also identify a variety of other skills. Athletic strengths are important, but so are other skills such as sportsmanship, social interaction, a work ethic, leadership, being responsible, and being cooperative. Once these other skills have been identified, tell the athlete that they are appreciated for having them. Don't be afraid to thank the athletes for being cooperative or kind. Look for the positive things and reinforce the players for having those traits.

2. **Display faith and confidence in the player's abilities and judgments.** Coaches must be aware of and acknowledge the strengths and positive attributes that an athlete possesses, especially at times when the athlete needs emotional support. It's easy to feel justified in getting angry at an athlete who performs

poorly and makes uncalled-for mistakes. However, that same situation also presents an opportunity to express faith and confidence in the player by turning the negative experience into an encouraging one. Help players to learn from their mistakes. Ask them, "What happened? Why do you think that happened? What do you think you can do the next time to help prevent those mistakes?" When the athlete has internalized the answers to those questions, let that person be free to move forward with the confidence that he or she can overcome their mistakes.

3. Give responsibility. Develop the attitude that players are responsible individuals. Expect that players will take responsibility for their own actions. For example, coaches shouldn't have to watch over the players all the time. Writing up the practice schedule with the expectation that players will fulfill their workout obligations is a simple responsibility. The giving of responsibility is a gift to athletes because it tells them that the coach respects, trusts, and values them. It tells them that they can succeed and be responsible for themselves. Review Chapter 5, especially the section on providing opportunities for contribution.

True friends don't coddle your weaknesses; they encourage your strengths.
ANONYMOUS

4. Don't criticize mistakes; look for the logic behind the mistakes. Kids today grow up in a society that thrives on finding mistakes. Fault finding rivals baseball as the national pastime. Making a mistake is part of being human; it's the only thing anyone can be absolutely certain that all humans will do. However, a mistake can be an important avenue for learning. Remember, correcting the mistake is more important than the mistake itself. Review Chapter 6, especially the discussion of criticizing.

5. Recognize effort and improvement, not just final achievements. Work with the athlete to create short-term and long-term goals. Keep them realistic. Provide support and encouragement all along the way. Recognize improvements and accomplishments as they are achieved. Review Chapter 5, especially the section on setting goals.

Whether approving or criticizing, the coach's response is what helps to shape the athlete's behavior. Coaches will be far more successful if they choose to encourage rather than to criticize or praise. Many coaches praise an athlete's efforts. However, encouragement is different from praise. It is important that these two concepts be separated and not viewed as the same because each has a different result.

Praise

The Praise Craze

A controversy over the appropriate use of praise has arisen. Many educators and parenting experts have split on the merits of praise. Many believe that praise is overused, overrated, and used inappropriately. Some believe that Americans, in the name of self-esteem, have gone "praise crazy." Everyone agrees that self-esteem must arise from within, from a genuine sense of accomplishment and self-worth. But the approach has been an explosion of awards, gold stars, and certificates for such routine accomplishments as just showing up or "just being me." Many kids have become praise "junkies," expecting praise for every little thing they do.

The Ulterior Motives Behind Most Praise

Lillian Katz, president-elect of the National Association for the Education of Young Children and professor of education at the University of Illinois, was quoted in a *Newsweek* article (Surler, 1992) as saying, "Schools have established award structures—the happy helper of the week, the reader of the week. Teachers think that if they don't do this stuff, the kids won't work, but that's ridiculous. We don't need all this flattery. No other country does this."

> *Man lives more by affirmation than by bread.*
> VICTOR HUGO

Therein lies the fault of most praise. Coaches, teachers, parents, and other adults use praise to reinforce or change youngsters in some specific way. They have ulterior motives for their praise. Praise reinforces the "proper" behaviors that the adult wants the child to continue, such as good grades, neat appearance, good manners, and acting nice. Somewhere, hidden under most adult praise is the underlying purpose of making the adult feel good—getting the behavior he or she wants, having the kids dress the way he or she wants, having a quiet classroom. It doesn't take long for anyone to see through such praise and recognize the adult's intentions. Coaches who give out praise not only to make the athlete feel good but to change the athlete so that the coach can feel good will soon be perceived by athletes as manipulative and dishonest.

Insulting Through Praise

Some coaches give backhanded compliments by mixing their praise with an insult. They give the athletes praise for what they did well but at the same time remind them of earlier failures. Some examples are:

"You certainly did better today than you did yesterday."
"You finished that race with a great kick. I was really surprised, since you loafed at practices all week"
"Congratulations, you got here on time, I didn't think you

would make it, considering you waited until the last minute to leave."

Don't use praise to punish or insult. Obviously it doesn't make the athlete feel very good.

Praise That Doesn't Match the Athlete's Perception

Another problem arises when the coach's praise doesn't match an athlete's own perception of success. When praise doesn't match the athlete's self-evaluation of performance or behavior, the player loses respect for the coach's integrity and honesty. More important, when praise doesn't match an athlete's self-evaluation, it denies the athlete's feelings. It tells the athlete that the coach doesn't really understand him or her. Praise in this instance becomes a barrier to further communication.

He who praises everybody praises nobody.
UNKNOWN

Overpraising

An athlete often knows that he or she is not "the best sprinter in the league." Overpraising the athlete because he or she won today puts pressure on the athlete to be great every day. When the athlete eventually comes in third or fourth, will that make the athlete feel like he or she is lousy or inadequate?

Many coaches have come to realize that overpraising can become detrimental because as soon as they draw attention to what the athlete did well, he or she will do the opposite. This phenomenon is due to overpraising. The tension of being over-praised is too much of a burden to carry. Allow the athlete to be himself or herself and not "the best sprinter in the state."

An Alternative to Praise

This does not mean that coaches should never say anything nice to their athletes. Athletes do need encouragement and feedback. However, using the language of typical praise is not as effective as was once thought. Thomas Gordon [1989] recommends an alternative to praise that he calls "Positive I-Messages." The purpose of the Positive I-Message is to send a clear message that expresses to another person how his or her behavior made you feel. Positive I-Messages are self-disclosing, self-revealing messages that clearly share what is going on in you, not evaluations of the other person. "Positive I-Messages" encourage positive action and behavior.

These messages consist of three parts: (1) your reaction to or feelings about the behavior or performance, (2) a description of the behavior or performance, and (3) why it makes you feel that way.

1. Your reaction to or feelings about the behavior or performance. The first part of this message expresses or shares how you feel inside about the behavior or performance. You are sharing something about yourself, and it tells the athlete what is important to you. It tells them about your needs and moods and how to please you or when to avoid you. This is important because it is not a statement or evaluation about the athlete. *"I was really pleased when. . . ."* and *"I was so relieved when . . ."* are disclosures of your personal feelings rather than evaluations of the athlete such as "You must be a genius in chemistry" or "You are the best field goal kicker on the team." Thomas Gordon believes that this distinction is crucial because evaluations are the very parts of praise that cause so many problems.

2. A description of the behavior or performance. After your feeling has been expressed, the next part of the message is to describe what it is that made you feel that way. "I was really pleased when *Mrs. Jones told me that you were doing well in English class.*" or "I was so relieved when *you kicked that field goal.*"

3. Why the behavior makes you feel that way. The final part of the message is to convey the effect your athlete's behavior or performance has made on you. "I was really pleased when Mrs. Jones told me that you were doing well in English class, *because it makes me proud to coach athletes who also work hard in their academics.*" or "I was so relieved when you kicked that field goal because *I felt our defense would hold and we would win.*"

Sharing reactions such as these with the athletes makes the coach more understandable rather than someone who unpredictably goes from hot to cold without reason. This form of praise enables athletes to learn something about the coach and themselves. For instance, you appreciate that the players clean up the mess after practice—you like a clean locker room. You are glad that your athletes are able to diligently practice while you talk with the assistant coaches—you need quiet while you discuss strategy.

Here are some examples that compare typical praise with encouraging Positive I-Messages:

Situation: Your basketball team has just won a game, and your center did an excellent job of controlling a much larger offensive opponent under the boards.

"You really played great, and the way you contained their big man was terrific. You were awesome!" (Praise)

People have a way of becoming what you encourage them to be—not what you nag them to be.

SCUDDER N. PARKER

"I was really happy with your defense under the boards because I felt we could win if their inside game was kept under control." (Positive I-Message)

Situation: Some of your players helped out without being asked and cleaned up all the mess that remained after a victory party in the school cafeteria.

"Thanks a bunch for cleaning up the mess. You are really nice and thoughtful." (Praise)

"I was so grateful when you cleaned up. It makes me feel really good when I see players being responsible for their actions. Thank you." (Positive I-Message)

The preceding examples and situations are summarized as follows:

"I Feel" (Share your feelings and emotions)	"About" (Clarify the behavior)	"Because" (Benefits to the coach)
1. pleased	1. that you are doing well in English class	1. I'm proud to coach athletes who work hard in their academics.
2. relieved	2. you kicked that field goal	2. I felt our defense would hold and that we would win.
3. happy	3. with your defense under the boards	3. I felt we could win if their inside game was kept under control.
4. grateful	4. for cleaning up	4. It makes me feel really good when I see players being responsible for their actions. Thank you.

TIME OUT: IN THE COACH'S CORNER

Practicing Positive I-Messages

Rewards and punishment are the lowest form of education.
CHUANG-TZU

Read the following examples, and finish the exercise by converting the you-message into a positive I-message. Of course, these messages must be believable to the athletes. Therefore they should be spontaneous and genuine and free of any ulterior motives. It may be difficult at first. The more you work at identifying your feelings, the easier it gets.

You-Message	I-Message
1. "You're terrific for getting to practice on time."	"I am so relieved when everyone gets to practice on time. It sure makes it easier for me to get things organized"
2. "You sure were smart when you didn't let that other player push you into a fight."	
3. "Hey, great shot! You are the best shooter on this team."	
4. "You sure used good judgment on that backhand shot when you went cross-court instead of down the line. You're one smart player!"	
5. "You girls were so good while I was talking with the principal."	
6. "You guys were so thoughtful to clean up the mess after the party."	
7. "You are really being a great student by always doing your homework."	
8. "You were brilliant. Your play calling was outstanding!"	

QUESTIONS AND ANSWERS

Question: Can you provide some strategies for encouraging my athletes?

Answer: There are a number of strategies you can use to encourage athletes. Here are a few:

1. Give responsibility. Keep the attitude that your players are responsible for their own actions.
2. Ask your players for opinions and suggestions on as many issues as possible.
3. Encourage participation in the decision-making process. Let your players get involved in making decisions about such things as game strategies, play-calling, organizing practices, rules, player discipline, social events, and other issues that affect themselves and the team directly.

4. Accept mistakes. Use mistakes as an opportunity for learning rather than as an opportunity for punishment.
5. Show appreciation for contributions both on and off the field.

Question: Are Positive I-Messages the same as encouragement?

Answer: Yes. Encouragement is a process of giving positive recognition, support, and confidence to the athlete. Recognition and appreciation are specific, and they focus on how we feel about what the athlete accomplished. Encouragement clarifies how the player's actions affected the coach. This process allows the player to clarify the benefits that resulted from his or her performance or behavior. This gives the player a foundation on which to build self-esteem and make decisions.

Major Points Discussed in Chapter 7

1. Five strategies for encouraging athletes for success are the following:
   a. Search for, identify, and acknowledge the athlete's strengths.
   b. Display faith and confidence in the player's abilities and judgments.
   c. Give responsibility.
   d. Don't criticize mistakes; look for the logic behind them.
   e. Recognize effort and improvement, not just final achievements.
2. Many people believe that praise is overused and used inappropriately.
3. Use Positive I-Messages instead of praise.
4. Positive-I Messages are messages that clarify how the players' actions affected the coach.
5. The Positive I-Message consists of three parts:
   a. the coach's reaction to feelings or about the behavior or performance,
   b. a description of the behavior or performance, and
   c. why the behavior makes the coach feel that way.

8

The Need to Feel Safe

Fear is an instructor of great sagacity, and the herald of all revolutions.

Ralph Waldo Emerson

The Importance of Physical and Emotional Safety

Physical and emotional safety means that athletes feel that they are in control of their own selves within the athletic environment—they have mastery over their being. Without a feeling of physical and emotional safety, athletes will find it difficult to move beyond strong fear and anxiety and be willing to enthusiastically explore new challenges. Strong fear and anxiety limit athletes—sometimes in small ways, sometimes in ways so large that they become imprisoned by them.

This chapter is not about the fear and anxiety that are related to the improvement of competitive performance. Therefore, it is not about whether or not mild anxiety and fear may improve performance or whether or not too much will cause the athlete's performance to become awkward or deteriorate.

This chapter is about the fear and anxiety that are related to daily situations when the athlete's physical safety and emotional well-being are threatened. It is about feeling fear and anxiety and having no control over the situation. This chapter is about understanding the need for both physical safety and emotional security within the team environment.

Athletes who choose to participate in athletics are generally aware that there is a certain amount of physical danger and risk in sports. However, athletes must also see the athletic arena as a place (1) where all precautions have been taken to ensure their physical safety and (2) where their emotional well-being is not being violated. It is important for any coach to make safety (both physical and emotional) the highest priority. Without a feeling of safety, athletes will become victims of fear and anxiety. Would most people stay on the job if they were afraid for their own physical or emotional safety? Probably not.

How long athletes will stay on a team is directly related to how safe and orderly they perceive the athletic environment to be. This perception of safety is also related to how well they will perform on a daily basis and how much they will respect and trust their coach and teammates. Unfortunately, not all coaches provide a safe environment for their athletes.

The mere appre-hension of a coming evil has put many into a situation of the utmost danger.
LUCAN

How long adults stay on a job is determined largely by whether or not they consider the environment to be safe and orderly. This perception is also related to their level of performance and productivity, how much trust they have in their fellow workers, and how much they support their boss. Employees who do not feel safe while at work suffer more depression and mood swings and have the highest absenteeism and quitting rates. Therefore it would be prudent to apply the same results to the athletic arena.

Physical Safety

Threats to one's physical safety include fear of injury due to feelings of being unprepared, undertrained, unprotected, overwhelmed, or overmatched. The athlete may also fear participating in an unprotected athletic environment where there are safety hazards and unsafe equipment. In addition, the threat of excessive violence will threaten the athlete's perception of physical and emotional security.

Each individual sport has unique physical safety problems. However, common principles can be applied to all sports. Elkow, as cited in *Sports Safety* (Yost, 1971), reported that the primary considerations of any athletic program are to:

1. prevent accidents,
2. eliminate hazards,
3. develop individual and group safety consciousness,
4. develop wholesome attitudes, habits, and practices pertaining to safety, and
5. develop attitudes of personal responsibility for safety.

It is important to remember that all the latest equipment, controls, and procedures will not keep athletes safe until these are properly used. Most accidents involve human error, so safety is primarily a people problem. In order to achieve these five considerations, Elkow reported that "a coach must have a thorough understanding of the sport: equipment and facilities, the leadership provided, fitness requirements of the participants, nature of the skills necessary for success, and the demands placed on personnel involved in the activity by themselves and their community."

In addition to making the environment safe, a coach must make sure each athlete is mentally ready to participate and accept challenge. Listed below are some ways to increase safety and help athletes to overcome fear and injury. Some of these same factors were listed in the question and answer section of Chapter 6 but, because of their importance, are repeated here.

1. Adjust the degree of challenge or difficulty of a skill according to the athlete's present ability.
2. Make certain that athletes are both physically and mentally prepared before moving on to new skills.
3. Structure the physical and emotional environment so that it is organized and supportive.
4. Give athletes plenty of time to practice before they move on to new skills.
5. Schedule specific time blocks that allow the athletes to take their time or work at their own pace.
6. Let athletes know that it is okay to fail and that failure can be a wonderful opportunity for learning.
7. Maintain daily practice routines.

Fewer accidents occur when the athletes believe that the coach is committed to their safety. And until the athlete is comfortable within the environment, he or she will never be fully aware of his or her full potential.

It is never safe to look into the future with eyes of fear.
E. H. HARRIMAN

Emotional Safety

Human interrelationships are integral to any athletic team. An athlete's emotional development can be positively or negatively affected by this experience. When a coach uses harsh words, threats, sarcasm, and undesirable discipline techniques and places too much stress on performance and competition, many athletes become uneasy and nervous.

Emotional safety also means that athletes can trust the coach to be there for them and that the coach is willing to respect their points of view. They know that the coach won't always agree with them but is on their side and is willing to work with them rather than against them. They can count on the coach because they know that they are valued and the coach will not hold their actions against them personally. An important part of emotional safety is feeling respected.

The emotional setting is just as important as the physical one, and the coach is responsible for establishing a safe emotional atmosphere within the athletic arena. The overall atmosphere should be one of acceptance, one in which the coach knows the athletes well and is sensitive to their individual needs. Athletes should feel free to express their feelings honestly without fear of ridicule or rebuke. They should also feel free to fail occasionally without punishment. A coach can promote well-being by being kind but fair, promoting coach-athlete relationships, setting reasonable goals for each athlete, encouraging positive behavior, challenging athletes within their capabilities, and tolerating occasional frustration.

Coaches may find the following categories useful in determining whether or not they provoke emotional "fear" in their athletes.

1. Warning and threatening tells the athlete that the coach has little respect for his needs or concerns. "You're going to stay here all night until you get it right" and "If you don't get your act together you're off the team" are examples of making the student feel fearful and submissive.

2. Being criticized makes players feel stupid, unworthy, and inadequate. Demeaning words will chip away at the athlete's self-confidence and self-image. Critical remarks usually provoke defensiveness and anger on the part of the player. Coaches who use criticism usually find that their players have little respect for them.

3. Name-calling and ridiculing have effects similar to those of criticism. Coaches who send these messages in an attempt to influence players are usually disappointed.

4. Sarcasm tells players that the coach is not interested in them and doesn't really have any positive feelings toward them. Sarcasm usually hurts and is viewed as a put-down.

The Effects of Emotional Assaults

When players are emotionally assaulted, they feel both hurt and anger. If the athletes cannot express those feelings, they will suppress them, and resentment will build. It is unhealthy to be consumed inwardly by resentment. Athletes usually pay a price when they "swallow" feelings, and the relationship between them and the coach will be impaired.

The progression from unexpressed anger to resentment to hostility

If emotional assaults continue and the athlete repeatedly represses the anger and resentment, internal pain builds up, causing an intense rage or hostility. The athlete becomes a "time bomb," easily able to explode at even the most minor irritations or annoyances. The hostile athlete will eventually withdraw from the entire situation by quitting or express rage in the form of insulting behavior or words at teammates or others in inappropriate situations. What the teammates don't know is that the hostile athlete is responding not to the present situation, but to the accumulation of unresolved pain and anger.

The Toll on the Body

Marks [1978] reported that "strong fear and anxiety cause unpleasant feelings of terror; paleness of the skin; sweating; hair standing on end; dilation of the pupils; rapid pounding of the heart; rise in blood pressure; tension in the muscles and increased blood flow through them; trembling; a readiness to be startled; dryness and tightness of the throat and mouth; constriction of the chest and rapid breathing; a sinking feeling in the stomach; nausea; desperation; contraction of the bladder and rectum leading to urges to pass urine and feces; irritability and a tendency to lash out; a strong desire to cry, run, or hide; difficulty in breathing; tingling in the hands and feet; feelings of being unreal or far away; paralyzing weakness of the limbs; and a sensation of faintness and falling."

Athletes can live under fear for only so long. The body and mind can endure only so much. Eventually, over time, athletes who feel personally victimized by continued physical or emotional assaults are likely to develop anxiety, depression, and helplessness and will live in fear, not knowing when the abuse will happen next. They will lose faith in the coach and develop a persistent preoccupation with the problem. Some think that there is no escape except to quit. Others become preoccupied with revenge.

When athletes view the environment as hostile, they are likely to dislike the team, the coach, and their teammates. Fear promotes anxiety, stress, and depression. It reduces the ability to perform and creates an atmosphere of distrust.

TIME OUT: SELF-ASSESSMENT

Recognizing Symptoms of Anxiety

It is important that coaches be aware of the physical and emotional reactions to fear and anxiety. You can get a measure of your anxiety by checking how much you are bothered by the following symptoms:

Fear builds walls that shut out the light.
UNKNOWN

Symptom	Not at all	Moderately	Severely
1. Feeling hot	_____	_____	_____
2. Feeling dizzy or light-headed	_____	_____	_____
3. Feeling unsteady	_____	_____	_____
4. Having trembling hands	_____	_____	_____
5. Having a flushed face	_____	_____	_____
6. Fearing the worst happening	_____	_____	_____
7. Being terrified	_____	_____	_____
8. Feeling nervous	_____	_____	_____
9. Feeling a loss of control	_____	_____	_____
10. Being able to relax	_____	_____	_____

The highway of fear is the shortest route to defeat.
W. BROWNNELL

Source: From *Coping with Life Challenges* by C. L. Kleinke. Copyright © 1991 Brooks/Cole Publishing Company, a division of International Thomson Publishing Inc., Pacific Grove, CA 93950. By permission of the publisher.

These items come from the Beck Anxiety Inventory (Beck, Epstein, Brown, & Steer, 1988) as cited by Kleinke [1991]. Items 1 through 5 measure somatic symptoms; items 6 through 10 measure subjective anxiety. This inventory was developed as an index of anxiety independent of feelings of depression. There is no score to this inventory. It is a tool to help you recognize any symptoms of fear or anxiety that you or someone else may be having. Once the symptoms have been identified, it is important to deal with the problem. If you do not have the problem-solving skills or communicative tools to deal with the problem, seek help from a counselor or psychologist.

QUESTIONS AND ANSWERS

Question: Is it possible to be too overprotective?

Answer: Since there are so many hazards and so many different degrees of risk in athletics, coaches must seek a practical changing balance between protection and athletic participation. If athletes are overprotected, their personal responsibility and adjustment may be retarded. On the other hand, if athletes are underprotected, in the absence of proper safety practices they may be seriously injured or even killed. This is a fine line, and a coach must always teach on the side of safety before moving to the next level.

Question: What is the most common liability problem that coaches face?

Answer: Both coach and school board can be held responsible in case of "negligence" and be held financially liable for accidental injury to an athlete. Coaches should, of course, familiarize themselves with the school and athletic laws in their own state regarding negligence and liability to civil suit.

The law of negligence is based partly on the theory that everyone has the right to live safely and must be protected from the negligence of others. In the school or athletic situation the coach has a duty to the athlete. In many cases the failure to act to prevent an accident to an athlete would be considered negligence on the part of the coach.

The law of negligence implies, as far as the duty of the coach to the athlete is concerned, that there be foreseeability. The coach acting as a reasonably careful and prudent person should anticipate danger or an accident.

A coach's negligence is generally predicated on (1) failure to foresee risks, (2) failure to take reasonable action to avert risk, (3) failure to give adequate warning or instruction in "difficult feats," and (4) failure to provide proper emergency care to the injured athlete or increasing the severity of the injury through improper methods of first aid.

If a man harbors any sort of fear, it percolates through all of his thinking, damages his personality, makes him landlord to a ghost.
LLOYD DOUGLAS

Major Points Discussed in Chapter 8

1. Without a feeling of physical and emotional safety, athletes find it difficult to move beyond strong fear and anxiety.
2. Threats to physical safety include fear of injury due to feelings of being unprepared, unprotected, overwhelmed, or overmatched.
3. Emotional safety is when athletes feel safe from intimidation, emotionally painful put-downs, threats, and criticism from the coach and their teammates.
4. Strong fear and anxiety can hinder performance on both physical and emotional levels.
5. How long athletes will stay with a team is directly related to how safe and orderly they perceive the athletic environment to be.

Any fool can criticize, condemn, and complain and most fools do.
DALE CARNEGIE

Effective Communication

9

Effective Communication: Listening to and Acknowledging the Athlete's Thoughts and Feelings

He who listens, understands.

African proverb

Effective communication is one of the most important skills in coaching. Success will depend not only on how well a coach listens, but also on how well a coach communicates his or her thoughts and feelings to the players, parents of the players, other coaches, officials, and all other individuals who are actively concerned with the athletic team.

Communication skills are just as basic as driving a car. A person needs to know how to start and stop. In between starting and stopping, one needs to know when to accelerate, when to put on the brakes, and how to keep the vehicle on course.

Listening Reflects Acceptance and Significance

Of all the things that can make an athlete feel accepted, significant, and worthwhile, none is more vital than being listened to. Yet listening is a skill that is usually overlooked because many coaches would rather talk than listen. Coaches who are good listeners become very popular with the athletes. More important, they even learn something. Listening is a very powerful sign of respect. Listening is, perhaps, the most important vehicle for meeting an athlete's need for emotional acceptance, significance, and security. Being listened to makes an athlete feel worthwhile. For the athlete, being listened to means being understood and feeling that his or her thoughts and feelings really do count.

Many coaches are inclined to preach, advise, patronize, or evaluate their athletes rather than listen to and understand them. Coaches may mistakenly believe that what they have to say to their player is more important than what the players have to say. Many coaches tend to tell their athletes what and how they should feel and think. Sometimes when athletes express how they feel, coaches may even tell them to deny those feelings and then proceed to tell them how they should feel. For example, an athlete expresses disappointment in losing an event, but the coach says, "You shouldn't feel that way. You did your best."

Unfortunately, many coaches believe that they are communicating with their players when in reality they are talking too much and hoping to hear their own words coming from the players' mouths.

Psychologists and counselors work on the principle that merely talking about one's inner emotions in relation to life's frustrations can be healing therapy. Letting clients talk is an important part of the foundation for most treatment. Careful study of good salespeople shows the importance of good listening. The best salespeople are those who have empathy and listen the most. They know that if you want to get somebody to do something or to buy something, you "can't talk them into it."

Empathy, Not Sympathy

Empathy is a process that involves being sensitive to another individual's changing feelings and connecting emotionally to that other person. Empathy involves a process of "living for a time in the other person's life," entering his or her private perceptual world, and seeing events through his or her eyes. Empathy involves avoiding judgments about what the other person is feeling and instead trying to understand those feelings fully from the person's perspective.

A coach will witness countless cues to an athlete's emotional experience. These cues are found in what the athlete says and how he or she says it, as well as his or her actions and expressions. Empathy involves correctly perceiving what the athlete is expressing through nonverbal cues and responding in a manner that conveys understanding.

Empathy involves letting the athlete know that he or she is understood. It is more than just saying, "I understand how you feel." Rather, empathy requires the accurate perception of the athlete's emotional experience and then the communication back to the athlete precisely what is understood.

Empathy is not sympathy. Sympathy is the concern that a coach may feel or show for an athlete. Empathy is an attempt to feel with the athlete, to understand the feelings from the athlete's point of view. Empathy is focusing on the athlete's problem and not on the coach.

It is quite apparent that most people like to talk, to express themselves, to be heard. When allowed to do that with an attentive listener, they respond positively and favorably. They become more receptive to the things that the listener suggests.

Athletes need to be understood. This is especially true when they are upset. They need the acceptance of others. The coach's acceptance does not mean that he or she must agree with the player's feelings and opinions. It simply requires that the coach listen and understand.

For example, a player comes to the coach and says that she hates playing and is going to quit the team. The coach does not want her to quit, and she probably doesn't really want to quit, but something is obviously upsetting her. It would be difficult to convince her about the benefits of remaining on the team because she would probably feel that the coach doesn't understand her anger. Though the coach may already know the solution to the problem, jumping in too soon will usually result in rejection of the solution. When individuals are upset, they are not ready to hear instant solutions. They need to be heard and understood, and they need to have their feelings validated.

Acknowledge the athlete's feelings first. A coach might say, "Sounds like something is really upsetting you." Acknowledging the athlete's feelings gives her a chance to talk and sort out her feelings. If this process continues, she will gradually calm down and will be ready to look for ways to solve her problems. When a coach understands a player's thoughts and feelings, he or she establishes a foundation for problem solving.

If a player expresses sadness, anger, or disappointment and wants to be left alone after losing a contest, the coach must acknowledge those feelings and wishes. If a coach believes that it is important to follow up on those feelings, the coach should allow those feelings to dissipate and discuss the issue at a less emotional time. Acknowledging a player's thoughts and feelings is not the same as approving of them, nor does it imply that the athlete is going to have his or her own way. It is simply a way of saying to the athlete that he or she is understood and that the coach can empathize with his or her thoughts and feelings.

Listening for Feelings

Recognizing feelings is often difficult. Without a vocabulary for feelings, it is hard to explore and understand the needs of others. The following is a list of some words that describe internal feeling states:

I have often regretted my speech, never my silence.
PULILIUS SYRUS

It takes two to speak the truth—one to speak and another to hear.
H.D. THOREAU

angry	anxious	apathetic
bitter	bored	broken-hearted
calm	cautious	cheerful
comfortable	confident	confused
contented	daring	delighted
distressed	distraught	displeased
eager	ecstatic	elated
enchanted	excited	frustrated
foolish	glad	happy
hesitant	hopeful	hurt
humiliated	incensed	irritated
joyful	jubilant	nervous
proud	relieved	resentful
sad	selfish	silly
sorry	uneasy	uncomfortable
unhappy	weary	

It is better to ask some of the questions than to know all the answers.
J. THURBER

The following attitudes are necessary for reflective listening:

1. The coach must be willing to hear what the athlete has to say and be willing to take the time to listen.
2. The coach must be willing to be helpful to the player.
3. The coach must be willing to accept the the player's feelings.
4. The coach must see the player as a person who is capable and competent enough to understand his or her own problems.

Practice the Art of Listening

Most people are not taught to listen. However, listening skills are not difficult to learn. They are just difficult to use. The foundation of attentive listening skills is that the coach must want to listen. The coach must have a strong desire to hear what the other person has to say. Once a coach learns to use listening skills and teaches them to the players, the coach will transform relationships, help solve problems, and raise self-esteem.

1. Stop. Do not fidget, turn your back, or conduct some other business and try to listen at the same time. Show your athletes that you are interested in them. Be interested and look interested. Be sure your facial and eye expressions as well as your posture (body language) and tone of voice all communicate appropriate feelings and meanings. When a player shares something with you, let your face express your interest. Make eye contact, face the speaker, and lean slightly forward.

Well timed silence hath more eloquence than speech.
M.T. TUPPER

2. Look. Be aware of the tone of voice, the pauses, movement, posture, speed and inflection of voice, tears, and all the other things that relay important information to you. Sometimes the actions reflect a totally different meaning than the actual words. Be aware of nonverbal cues or behaviors. Try to hear the feelings and meanings behind the words.

3. Listen. Most of the time, when someone is talking, the listener is only partly listening because the listener is usually thinking about what he or she is going to say and waiting for the opportune time to cut in on the other person so that he or she can speak. Conversations that occur at this level, are minimally effective. Try to focus on your players' words and feelings instead of thinking about what you are going to be saying next. Don't make impulsive judgments about your players and their feelings. Try to focus on your players' words and feelings instead of thinking about what you are going to say next. Try to put yourself in their shoes and try to understand what is happening. Also, let the players own those feelings. Do not tell them that you know and understand how they feel. Even though you may think you are helping by telling them that you know how they feel, your "reassuring" words are usually a turn-off.

4. Caution. Let them finish; don't interrupt the train of thought and feelings. Even though you may have a different opinion, keep it to yourself until your player requests it. If the players know they are really being listened to, they are more likely to choose their words carefully because they are more accountable for what comes out of their mouths. While you are a listener, let the speaker do the talking. It is occasionally okay to briefly interject an occasional "uh-huh" or nod of the head. Any subtle gesture that reflects that you are listening is okay. The main point is that you do not interrupt the flow of words and feelings.

Reflective Listening

Reflective listening is a way to show players that their message has not only been heard but been understood as well. This skill becomes a way in which the coach can become the mirror by which the players can hear and "see" their feelings more clearly. While there is no one correct way to carry out this skill, a few guidelines are the following:

Everyone has a right to his own opinion. It is generally no use to anyone else.

DUBLIN OPINION

1. Reflect the content of the communication by paraphrasing what is being said instead of evaluating it. Simply repeat exactly what is said. If a player says, "Nobody on the team likes me!", you would say, "You think no one on the team likes you?" Keep your voice calm, maintain eye contact, and be patient when you say this.

2. Show that you empathize by reflecting the players' feelings. When you reflect feeling, you listen with your eyes and hear the tone of voice that captures the nature and intensity of the emotion behind the words. In fact, your player may be saying a great deal more with his or her body language and tone of voice than the words alone convey.

3. Ask open-ended questions to encourage the players to share or continue to share their feelings. Asking them to elaborate on their thoughts and feelings shows that you are interested in what they have to say. Open-ended questions neither add to nor subtract from the player's message. It shows that you understand what your player is trying to tell you. When you are listening reflectively, it is better to ask the right questions than to provide the answers. Open-ended responses encourage dialogue. The opposite of an open-ended question is a closed question. Closed questions or responses are usually directive or require only a one-word response from the listener. Closed responses do not seek understanding. Closed responses discourage dialogue.

Listed below are some examples of open-ended and closed response questions:

Open ended:	"How is the injury coming along?"
Closed response:	"Are you still having trouble with the ankle?"
Open ended:	"What options do you think are best?"
Closed response:	"Why don't you go to a doctor?"
Open ended:	"What does Jim do that irritates you?
Closed response:	"Why don't you try to get along with Jim?"

The important aspects of communicating with players are understanding and building trust and confidence. When coaches listen, they make it clear to the players that they care about their concerns, needs, fears, doubts, and hopes. Listening is accepting the player's thoughts and feelings and being okay with the fact that this other point of view might be different from the listener's.

There is no worse lie than a truth misunderstood by those who hear it.
WILLIAM JAMES

Coaches should not think that they have to lecture and teach a lesson to the players at every turn, especially when emotions are intense. A coach should listen completely to all of the athletes' thoughts and feelings and be cautious about advising too quickly. Sometimes, when no advice is requested, a coach should try not to give any at all.

When Does the Coach Get to Speak?

Reflective listening is a process that is used when something is troubling the athlete. The athlete "owns the problem." However, not every conversation involves a problem, and reflective listening is not always required. The following diagram represents the typical situations that arise in any human relationship:

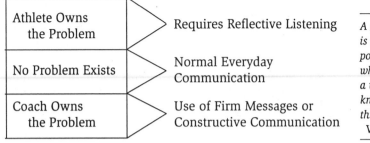

If no one has a problem, coach and athlete carry on with their everyday normal conversation. Listening is important, of course, but when no problem exists, reflective listening is not always necessary. The coach can talk as much as he or she wants, as long as the athletes are willing to listen.

If the coach "owns the problem," he or she should use firm messages or constructive communication. Firm messages are discussed in Chapter 10. Constructive communication is discussed in Chapter 11.

TIME OUT: IN THE COACH'S CORNER

"Coach, I Lost the Game!"

Listening is the most basic communication skill. But learning to listen requires both practice and patience.

Effective listening is perhaps the first tool of coaching. Two scenes are described below. Scene 1 demonstrates poor listening techniques in which the coach tries to tell the individual how he should feel. Scene 2 represents an understanding coach who validates the individual's feelings and demonstrates that he recognizes how that person feels.

Scenario

The silence and tension in Miguel's mind were almost unbearable. Even the roar of the opposing crowd could not be heard. Miguel could hear only the hollow, deep rushing sound of his own breathing as he cradled the basketball in his hands. He could feel the sweat trickle down his forehead and a coldness on his skin from the wetness of his jersey. His team was down by two points when he was fouled with just two seconds left on the clock. He had calmly sunk the first free throw to bring his team to within one point of a tie and a possible overtime game.

Miguel swallowed, bounced the ball once, then again. And just as they had done so many times in practice, his well-rehearsed body and hands lifted the ball above his head. With a fluid motion of legs, body, arms, and wrist the ball flicked from his fingers and rotated toward the basket. Miguel could only watch in disbelief as the ball spun from the rim into the hands of an opposing player.

With head down, Miguel weaved his way through the jubilant victors as they jumped up and down, pumping their fists and hugging one another as they shouted in victory.

Scene 1

Children will be mean if not heard.
GENE SPERRY

Coach Robinson catches up to Miguel and gently puts a hand on his shoulder. Miguel, feeling that he has let the whole team down, says tearfully, "Coach, I really blew it. We could have tied them and gone into overtime, but I really choked. I'm sorry."

Coach Robinson replies sympathetically, "Listen, Miguel, you did your best. Besides the game wasn't lost on that shot. There were plenty of other missed opportunities. A game isn't won or lost on one shot. Even if you did make it, we might have lost in overtime anyhow. It's okay, don't worry about it." Coach Robinson replies sympathetically.

"Yeah, but I had a chance to tie the game. I had the opportunity and I screwed up. Now it's going to be tough for us to make the play-offs."

"Don't feel bad. We will win the next one. Now, why don't you get showered up and forget about it."

Scene 2

Coach Robinson catches up to Miguel and gently puts a hand on his shoulder. Miguel, feeling that he has let the whole team down, says tearfully, "Coach, I really blew it. We could have tied them and gone into overtime, but I really choked. I'm sorry."

Realizing that Miguel's feelings need to be validated, Coach Robinson softly replies, "It sounds like you feel you lost the game for us."

"Yeah! If I make it, we go to overtime and have a chance to win. We needed the win to make the play-offs. Now I don't know if we are going to make it. I really choked. I let the whole team down." Miguel cups his hands slightly and rubs his eyes gently trying to hold back the tears.

"Are you saying that because of that one missed free-throw, we might not make the play-offs?"

After a moment of reflection, Miguel says, "No, I guess not. I just feel lousy, I missed the shot."

"I think I know how you feel. I know you're feeling lousy. I realize I can't change that feeling right now, but I want to talk with you immediately after you get cleaned up."

Coach Robinson knows that when feelings are too strong, it is better to back off and allow the person to have those feelings and to let them dissipate. Miguel needs to have some time to himself before talking about them. It is also important for Coach Robinson not to try to change Miguel's feelings by telling him to cheer up or that he shouldn't feel bad. Coach Robinson needs only to validate them at this time.

Later, Coach Robinson meets with Miguel to help him sort out his feelings. It is okay and normal for Miguel to be disappointed that he missed the basket. It is also important that he not take the blame for losing the game. Those are two separate issues.

Coach Robinson proceeds to ask Miguel questions about other missed opportunities: "Miguel were there any times when we failed to execute properly?"

"Yeah, coach. During the beginning of the second half, we didn't get back on defense quick enough, and they opened that 10 point lead on us," Miguel replies.

The word communication comes from the Latin communico, meaning share.
ANONYMOUS

"Why do you think that happened?" Coach Robinson asks.

"We were shooting from the outside, and when we missed, we all tried to crash the boards, and they left one man back for the quick outlet pass. When they got the defensive rebound, they killed us on the fast break."

"Good observation. I also noticed we were standing around a lot and not cutting through our passing lanes to make the defense work more. It looks like we have some things to work on if we are going to have any chance at making the play-offs. I'll see you at practice."

Coach Robinson recognizes that Miguel is still disappointed that he failed to make the free throw. He also knows that at a deeper level, Miguel knows that a game is not won or lost on just one shot.

QUESTIONS AND ANSWERS

Question: Can you develop empathy?

Answer: Developing empathy is a slow process that requires effort and discipline on three important dimensions:

According to Mayer and Greenberg [1964], the cognitive component of empathy requires the coach to observe the athletes behavior carefully (body language and actions) and interpret the meaning of what is being observed. Empathy depends on knowing or being aware of what the physical and emotional effects of certain events are. For example, it is important for the coach to know about the emotional realities of losing and winning. These include the effects on an athlete's thoughts, emotions, and behaviors when he or she is faced with defeat or failure.

The affective component of empathy involves being sensitive to the athlete's feelings and listening to what the athlete is saying about those feelings in words, gestures, and actions. The effective component of empathy involves the coach relating what he or she perceives to be the athlete's emotions to his or her own emotional experience.

The communicative component of empathy focuses on communicating through words or gestures to the athlete that he or she is understood, that the coach knows the facts about what the athlete is experiencing and perceives accurately what the athlete is feeling.

When athletes feel understood, they are also more likely to follow any recommendations the coach makes. When given the opportunity to express their emotional needs and concerns, athletes feel they can trust the coach to function in their best interest. In addition, athletes will be more willing to share their concerns in the future.

Of all the things you wear, your expression is the most important.
JANET LANE

Question: What do you believe is the major barrier to the communication process and what can we do about it?

Answer: Rogers and Roethlisberger [1952] believe that the major barrier is the tendency to judge, to evaluate, to approve or disapprove of the statements that our athletes make to us. For example, suppose Joe comments that he "doesn't like having to play the final game on their home court." What will you respond? Almost invariably, your reply will be either to approve or disapprove of the attitude expressed. You respond either "I don't either" or "It doesn't really matter." In other words, you evaluate the statement from your own point of view or reference. In addition, evaluations are usually elevated when feelings and emotions are more deeply involved. Stronger feelings in the initial statement usually separate any mutual elements in the communication, resulting in two feelings and two evaluations that miss each other completely. The coach could have replied, "You dislike playing our final game away from home?" or "What bothers you about playing our last game on their home court?"

Real communication, of course, occurs when we stop evaluating and empathetically listen with understanding. It means seeing the athlete's point of view and sensing how it feels to him or her.

TIME OUT: SELF-ASSESSMENT

Communication Skills Test
Directions: Respond to each of the following items by circling the number that corresponds to the description that most accurately reflects your behavior. **Treat the results as a guide only. There is a margin of uncertainty in all questionnaires of this kind.**

Rating Scale	Never 1	Seldom 2	Usually 3	Always 4

1. I like to listen to others.	1 2 3 4
2. I state one thought at a time.	1 2 3 4
3. I pretend that I'm paying attention.	1 2 3 4
4. I use sarcasm.	1 2 3 4
5. I repeat key points.	1 2 3 4
6. I respect others' right to express themselves.	1 2 3 4
7. I am easily distracted by other noises.	1 2 3 4
8. I listen to all of the other person's message.	1 2 3 4
9. I finish thoughts for the speaker.	1 2 3 4
10. I listen by nodding my head or verbally agreeing with what others are saying.	1 2 3 4
11. I keep the pitch of my voice level in tense situations.	1 2 3 4
12. I shake hands firmly.	1 2 3 4
13. I look directly at people when talking to them.	1 2 3 4
14. I walk slowly and hunch my shoulders.	1 2 3 4
15. I use my hands to augment my words.	1 2 3 4

Scoring the test: Simply add the numbers circled for items 1, 2, 5, 6, 8, 10, 11, 12, 13, and 15. Then for items 3, 4, 7, 9, and 14, reverse the order of the numbering system. For example, if you circled "4" for the third item, you would score it as "1." Add these five reverse-scored items to the total for the first ten items summed to get your total communication score.

Total Score	Your Communication Style
51 and up	Clear connection
40–50	Mixed messages
39 and below	Tongue-tied

Source: From *Psychology of Officiating* (pp. 42–43) by Robert S. Weinberg and Peggy A. Richardson, Champaign, IL: Human Kinetics Publishers. Copyright 1990 by Robert S. Weinberg and Peggy A. Richardson. Reprinted by permission.

Major Points Discussed in Chapter 9

1. Listening is a skill that is often overlooked because many coaches would rather talk than listen.
2. Listening is, perhaps, the most important vehicle for meeting an athlete's need for emotional significance and security.
3. Empathy is a process of "living" for a time in the other person's life, entering his or her private perceptual world, and seeing events through his or her eyes.
4. Empathy is not sympathy.
5. Athletes need to be not only heard but also understood.
6. The first step in the reflective listening process is the desire to want to reflectively listen.
7. Reflective listening requires the coach to:
   a. stop all other activity,
   b. look for body language and emotions to help understand the meaning behind the words,
   c. listen to words and search for the meaning rather than thinking about what you are going to say, and
   d. use caution. Do not interrupt the flow of words and feelings.
8. Reflective listening also requires that the listener
   a. reflect the content of the communication,
   b. reflect feeling, and
   c. ask open-ended questions.
9. Some of the major barriers to the communication process are the tendency to judge, evaluate, or approve or disapprove of the statements that the athlete is making.

10

Sending Firm Messages and Establishing Team Rules and Procedures

*Even though a speech be a thousand words but made
up of senseless talk, one word of sense is better, which
if a man hears, he becomes quiet.*

Dhannapada

When coaches send messages that communicate team rules and expectations or demands, they are setting the boundaries for acceptable behavior. These boundaries provide the limits within which the players can freely participate without being reprimanded. How coaches send their messages determines the parameters of behavior and answers the question of what is acceptable and what is not acceptable.

Players clarify the coach's message through their behavior. Testing is the best way to determine whether the coach really means what he or she says and whether those demands and expectations are going to be enforced or the limits can be stretched. Some players will simply go ahead and do whatever the coach said he or she didn't want them to do and then wait to see what happens. The coach's actions after the violation will determine what the player will do next.

Firm Messages

Firm messages are when "no" really means "no." Coaches are using firm messages when both their words and their actions say "stop." Their players receive a clear message that says that compliance with the rule or request is both expected and required. In addition, the players are given all the information they need to make more acceptable choices in the future. Firm messages send clear communications about rules and expectations. A coach's words must also be consistent with his or her actions.

In language, clarity is everything.
Confucius

Let players know that you want them to learn and grow and that you may have to correct them at times. This, of course, does not mean that you don't like them or that you are rejecting them; it means that there is a better way to do something. Good coaches should like their athletes, but shouldn't have an urgent need to be liked in return every minute of the day.

When giving guidance to players, coaches must give a clear message about rules and expectations. MacKenzie [1993], recommended the following guidelines for communicating clear, concise verbal messages.

1. Focus your message on the behavior, not on the player. Be sure to correct the behavior while it is happening or as soon as you become aware of it. Do not focus on the player's attitude or make a judgment about his or her worth. Tell the player (in nonjudgmental language) that what he or she did was not acceptable. If you want a player to stop interrupting you while you are talking, your message should be "Joe, stop interrupting, please," or "Joe, you need to wait until I'm finished speaking," not "Can't you see I'm busy!" or "Do you have to be such a pain in the neck?" or "Are you always so inconsiderate?"

2. Be direct and specific. Speak directly to the players, and use language that tells them precisely what you want them to do. Such statements as "I want you to be here at three o'clock this afternoon" or "It's time for you to do your free throw drill" or "You need to pick up the tennis balls right now" are direct and specific. Speak in terms that are clear rather than abstract. "I want you to quit your fooling around during team meetings" is vague. "When we have a team meeting, I want you to sit quietly in the front row and in front of me" is clear and concise.

If necessary, be prepared to tell the athletes when and how you want things to be done. If it is the team's responsibility to keep the locker room clean after practice and the players are leaving the locker room a mess, your message should be "Each of you needs to be responsible for keeping this locker room clean. That means putting all wet towels into the hamper, putting away all clothes in your lockers and picking up any used tape or other trash before you leave the locker room to go home." If your message was "You guys have to do a better job of keeping the locker room clean," who decides what "a better job" means? Without a direct and precise message, a player's performance will probably fall short of your expectations. If you want your players to do something, you must tell them in no uncertain terms. The more uncertain your terms, the more uncertain the outcome.

3. Be concise, and use your normal voice. The fewer the words, the better. Don't use 100 words when 10 will do. Don't lecture; you are sure to lose the players' attention. When expressing your carefully chosen words, keep your tone of voice calm and under control. State your matter-of-fact message in a normal voice.

Firm messages do not need to be stated emotionally. There is no need to yell or raise your voice to convince your players that you really mean what you say. Your actions or the consequences will communicate your message more forcefully than your words can.

4. Nonverbal communication is an important part of your message. Firm messages should be respectful. Therefore appropriate body language is important. Maintain eye contact, do not cross your arms and/or legs, sit or stand erect, and make sure you are close to your listener(s) but not too close. If your voice, words, and body language are out of sync, the athletes will be influenced more by the nonverbal behavior than by your words.

Nothing gives one person so much advantage over another as to remain cool and unruffled under all circumstances.
THOMAS JEFFERSON

5. State your consequences when appropriate, and follow through with actions when necessary. If you are expecting a power struggle or to be tested, you may need to specify the consequences of noncompliance at the same time you make your request. This is not a threat nor should it be punishment. It is far better to solve a problem than to apply consequences. However, when you apply a consequence, you are bridging any credibility gap that may have existed between what has been said and what action was to be taken.

For example, if you ask a player to stop throwing his football helmet when he gets upset but you expect him to throw it anyway, your message should be "Do not throw your football helmet. If you do, I'll have to put it away for the rest of practice, and you won't be able to participate in practice without it." Now your player has all the information he needs to cooperate. If he throws it again, follow through with your action and put the helmet away. Making your action consistent with what you say will establish your credibility, and your players will begin to take your words seriously and do what you request. Your words are only the first part of your message, and that may be all you will need. But your words will be ineffective if you fail to support your message with action.

A good teacher is firm and active. It is important not to confuse firmness with punishment. The two are by no means identical.
PERCIVAL M. SYMONDS

The following are examples of effective firm messages;

"Stop fighting right now!"

"Be at practice by 3:30."

"You can play by the rules of the game or leave this field and find another game to play elsewhere. What would you like to do?"

"It's 10:30, time for bed. Turn the lights out and no more talking."

"It is time for you to do your assigned workout on the weight machines."

"It is time for you to come into the gym for practice. You need to say good-bye to your friends and come inside now."

"Remove any rings, bracelets, earrings, or necklaces before getting on any piece of gymnastics apparatus."

The following are examples of effective actions after firm messages have been communicated:

Removing a player from the court for swearing.

Not distributing any towels for a few days if your players are not putting them in the hamper after practice.

Not allowing a late player onto the practice field if he or she was warned about coming late.

Not allowing a player to practice for a designated period of time when the player refuses to quit fighting with his or her teammates.

Not replacing a piece of equipment that was damaged because of carelessness.

Soft Messages

Anybody who gets away with something will come back to get away with a bit more.
HAROLD
SCHOLENBERG

Soft message are rules that are only expressed in words but not put into consistent practice. Soft messages are when "no" means "yes," "sometimes," or "maybe." The verbal message of "no" says to stop, but the action message says that it's okay to continue.

The following are examples of soft messages:

"Please try to get to practice on time, okay."

"Shoot some free-throws after practice."

"Run some laps before practice."

"That is enough from you."

"Come on, shape up."

"I don't like your attitude."

"Don't be stupid."

"It's time to do our drills, okay?"

"Come on, let's have a little cooperation."

"Would you just try to cooperate once in a while?"

"Come on, stop acting like a jerk."
"Can't you see that I'm busy?"
"Keep the noise down."
"How about picking up those balls before you leave?"
"I want you to be good when we travel to any away games."
"Let's clear the court, okay?"

The following are examples of ineffective action:

Ignoring misbehavior in the hope that it will go away.
Not enforcing the predetermined consequences of rule violations.
Trying to persuade an academic teacher to consider giving a player a "passing" grade.
Making exceptions for the star athletes.
Overlooking unacceptable behavior when you are in a good mood.
Allowing players to walk away from assigned responsibilities.

Laws should be like clothiers. They should be made to fit people they are meant to serve.
CLARENCE DARROW

Team Rules and Procedures

Players function and cooperate best within a structured environment. Players know what is expected of them because the athletic environment has been planned with their needs in mind. Rules are implemented to maintain harmonious interactions within the athletic arena as well as the appropriate use of athletic equipment and property. Rules provide a structure and a pattern to daily practice and athletic contests.

It is the coach's responsibility, sometimes with the help of the team members, to establish rules to guide the behavior of all team members. Some coaches have issues about which they feel very strongly, and they alone establish the rules for those issues. There is nothing wrong with this procedure as long as the established rules have the five characteristics of a good rule, discussed below. However, at times a coach may be very receptive to having player input about the rules. In this case the coach and players can work together to make good rules (see Chapter 16, "The Team Forum").

Setting limits on behavior means making good rules and teaching the value of the rules. Making rules and consistently enforcing those rules provide the foundation for building the inner discipline that is necessary on and off the athletic field. Without rules, there is disorder. Without rules, there is nothing to refer to when a choice about behavior arises. However, making rules requires planning and patience. Good rule making is a skill that must be learned and practiced.

The liberty of the individual must be thus limited; that he must not make a nuisance of himself to other people.
JOHN STUART MILL

What Makes a Good Rule

There are five characteristics that make a good rule.

1. The rule must be reasonable. A rule is reasonable when it takes into consideration the athletes' age and ability to perform according to the rule. If it is reasonable, it must be understood. Safety rules are the most reasonable because the reason for the rule can be explained in terms of the consequences. Other rules are not as easy to explain.

2. The rule must be clearly communicated. The rule must not be confusing or ambiguous. It should not imply what needs to be done, it must state it clearly. "All athletes must attend classes" is not a clearly communicated rule. A clearer version of this rule would be "All athletes must attend all classes every school day unless they have a written excuse from their parents or school counselor."

3. The rule must be enforceable. The rule must be one that the coach can enforce with a consequence. An example of an unenforceable rule is "Don't ever swear." The enforceable rule is "Do not swear in my presence." Ideally, we don't want kids swearing, but it would be almost impossible for the coach to enforce such a rule when the athlete swears at home or with his or her friends.

Everything educates, and some things educate more than others.
HAROLD TAYLOR

4. The rule must be consistent. The rule must be one that has general application and few circumstances in which it may or may not not apply. "Do not fight unless you are attacked and must defend yourself or you are going to the defense of one of your teammates or . . . " is not a good rule because there are too many circumstances or conditions.

Bad laws are the worst sort of tyranny.
BURKE

5. The rule must be flexible. The rule must have room for flexibility due to changes of circumstances. There are times when other priorities take precedence over a rule. For example, if your team is on an overnight trip and the curfew for being in the hotel is 9:30 P.M., and the athletes are attending a movie that ends at 9:25, some degree of flexibility would be prudent.

Making rules is not easy. For practice make rules for the following situations:

Cleaning up after practice
Curfew
Not attending class
Not completing academic class assignments
Missing practice
Using alcohol, tobacco, or other drugs
Tardiness
Fighting
Swearing

Using Procedures to Prevent Problems Before They Occur

Many of the problems that are associated with player misbehavior can be prevented through early planning and effective team management. Effective coaches use the preventive approach.

Rules, as was previously stated, are statements that specify what athletes can do or not do. *Procedures* are the ways of doing things. Procedures provide order and sequencing to make activities flow more efficiently.

Establishing team procedures beforehand can prevent a lot of potential problems and disruptions. Effective coaches must take the time to teach their athletes about procedures. Coaches should not assume that the players know how to behave. However, when coaches explain procedures, they must walk a thin line between providing helpful explanations and sounding patronizing or overly moralistic.

It is, of course, important for coaches and players to establish rules of behavior that concern attendance, tardiness, drug use, and general behavior both on and off the athletic field. However, many coaches overlook some of the most important activities that require rules to govern behavior and procedures that make everyday practices flow efficiently. These include player movement, talking, and downtime.

1. Player movement. In many sports, mass practice drills are an efficient way for large groups of athletes to learn important skills. Effective coaches devise ways to make needed movements flow smoothly. They use efficient cues such as whistles and hand signals, and they establish rules that ensure (1) safety and the prevention of potential injuries and (2) fairness, for example, taking turns, limiting the number of people in a drill, and movement from place to place.

Setting safety rules is essential in sports. These rules, in particular, must be firm, and enforced. Players may not always agree with them, but safety rules are usually the most reasonable because the reason for the rule can be explained in terms of consequences. Rules that encourage responsible behavior and inner discipline are not as easy to explain.

It is easier to suppress the first desire than to satisfy all that follow it.
BEN FRANKLIN

2. Player downtime. This refers to the time in between activities. Most athletes should be too tired during this time to get into any mischief or cause any disruptions. A simple rule to be applied during downtime is that players must respect the rights of others to finish their activity without any disruptions.

3. Player talking. Athletes who talk while you or others are talking are annoying and disruptive. Effective coaches have a clear set of rules governing player talking. Most coaches have a no-talking rule when they or others are lecturing or explaining. Such procedures as listening to others, raising hands, taking turns, and talking one at a time are also used.

Administering Consequences: Making Athletes Accountable for Their Behavior

Early planning can prevent many behavioral problems. However, every team will have a few athletes who will choose to become disruptive. They will violate rules and procedures. When rules are broken, it is the coach's responsibility to firmly and consistently apply the preestablished consequences for violating the rule. If coaches are not consistent in their enforcement and their application of consequences, the rules will soon become ineffective. See Chapter 14 for a discussion of consequences.

Without consistency there is no moral strength.
OWEN

TIME OUT: IN THE COACH'S CORNER

Keeping Within the Spirit of the Rule

Situation 1
The rule was clearly stated to the team. Anyone who missed a practice without prior permission from the coach would not be allowed to play in the next game.

Wesley was a very responsible individual. He studied hard and got excellent grades. He was never late for practice, nor did he ever miss a practice. He was liked by his teammates and the coach.

No power is strong enough to be lasting if it labors under the weight of fear.
CICERO

Wesley's mother had scheduled Wesley's important dental appointment at noon. However, Wesley didn't inform the coach about his schoolday dental appointment because he was sure it would be finished early enough for him to attend practice. After all, practice didn't begin till 3:00. In fact, Wesley intended to return for his 2 P.M. class.

The dentist had to do some minor surgery that required an anesthetic. Wesley, drowsy and incoherent from the procedure was taken home by his mother to sleep it off. Wesley had forgotten to telephone the coach.

The next day, Wesley returned to practice and told Coach Martinez what had happened.

Multiple Choice
If you were Coach Martinez, what would you do?

   A. Tell Wesley that a rule is a rule and it cannot be changed. No exceptions. Wesley should have picked up the telephone and called. Wesley will have to miss the next game.
   B. Recognize that extenuating circumstances may occur and rules should be flexible enough to accommodate them.

Response B is correct. There are times when other priorities and circumstances take precedence over the rule. Wesley did not intentionally violate the spirit of the rule. Some degree of flexibility would be appropriate on this occasion.

Situation 2

Yolanda knew the rule about attending classes. No team members would be allowed to cut any classes. The rule clearly stated that any athlete who did not have a written legitimate excuse for missing a class would be suspended from the team for one week.

However, Yolanda was confident that the coach would understand her situation and never suspend her from the team. She deliberately cut her noon English class to complete a Social Studies project that was due at the end of the day.

Yolanda's English teacher informed Coach Saunders about the unexcused absence. When the coach confronted Yolanda about the unexcused cut, Yolanda responded, "Coach, I had to miss class. I had this group Social Studies project that was due at the end of the day. I had to miss English to complete it. If we don't complete the project, I really blow my grade for the class. You understand, don't you, coach?"

Multiple Choice

If you were Coach Saunders, what would you do?

A. Exempt Yolanda from the rule because this is an extenuating circumstance, and flexibility in the rule is appropriate.
B. Suspend Yolanda for the week.

Response B is correct. Yolanda clearly knew the rule. She needed to complete the project, but her Social Studies teacher had given her plenty of time to do so. Her English period was not the time to do it. She should have managed her time better. She clearly violated the rule. Excusing her would undermine the process of developing self-discipline and responsibility.

QUESTIONS AND ANSWERS

Question: My players are always challenging certain rules. The more I explain them, the more they argue. Am I making things worse by trying to defend the rules all the time?

Answer: If players are engaging you in long explanations, debates, or arguments, they are probably testing your limits and finding out whether the rules can be renegotiated. (Do you really mean what you say?) Remain firm with your limits and argu-

The school should never lay down a rule without giving an adequate explanation as to why this rule is good for the pupil

JAMES GEISEL

ments will diminish over time. Do not get into any arguments when the consequences are being applied; this is the time when players will try to test you. If a player needs any clarification of rules, this can be done at a later time when things are calmer.

Question: How much input should players have in making the rules?

Laws are not invented; they grow out of circumstances.
AZARIUS

Answer: How much input you allow players to have in establishing rules depends on their age and readiness. Obviously, a six-year-old does not have the same capacity as a 17-year-old to make good rules. If players have input and their opinions are received, respected, and implemented whenever possible, the players are usually more willing to abide by them.

If a rule is broken, the consequences must be consistently applied. If the player believes that the consequence is unfair, it can be renegotiated at a later time, after the consequence has been allowed to run its course.

Question: If I punish my athletes after I have told them "no," won't that reinforce a clear message about what I want to convey?

Answer: The answer depends on the rules you intend to teach. If you are trying to convey a rule about stopping a specific misbehavior (such as talking back), then your athletes will probably get the message. If you use physical punishment or verbal abuse on a regular basis, however, your action message will also convey another rule: Physical punishment or verbal abuse is the way we solve problems. Is this the lesson you want to teach?

Question: If rules should be flexible and negotiable, how can I set firm limits?

If you're out to beat a dog, you're sure to find a stick.
HANAN J. AYALTI

Answer: Rules should be flexible in the sense that they can be negotiated and revised as the athletes outgrow them or as changing circumstances require. However, you cannot be flexible at the moment when the rules or firm limits are being violated. They can be open to discussion at more appropriate times.

Question: What should I do if my athletes attempt to bargain or negotiate about something that is unacceptable to me?

Answer: This is limit testing. You need to use a "cutoff" technique by responding firmly with "Those are your only choices. What would you like to do?"

Question: What should I do if an athlete refuses to respond to her "limited choices?"

Answer: If the athlete's actions reveal that she has chosen not to cooperate, then follow through with a logical consequence. The athlete will soon discover that a decision not to choose is also a choice. See the discussion about logical consequences in Chapter 14.

Major Points Discussed in Chapter 10

1. How coaches send their message determines the boundaries or parameters of behavior and answers the question of what is acceptable and what is not.
2. Firm messages are when "no" really means "no."
3. Clear and concise verbal messages require that the coach:
    a. focus the message on the behavior and not the player,
    b. be direct and specific,
    c. be concise and use a normal tone of voice,
    d. understand that nonverbal communication is an important part of the message,
    e. state the consequences when appropriate and follow through with actions when necessary.
4. Soft messages are rules that are only expressed in words but not put into consistent practice.
5. Soft messages are when "no" really means "yes," "sometimes," or "maybe."
6. The five characteristics of a good rule are that they must be:
    a. reasonable,
    b. clearly communicated,
    c. enforceable,
    d. consistent, and
    e. flexible.
7. Many of the problems that are associated with player misbehavior can be prevented through early planning and effective team management.
8. Rules are statements that specify the things that athletes can and cannot do.
9. Procedures are the ways of doing things by providing order and sequence to make things flow more efficiently.

CHAPTER

11

Coaching Without Anger: Communicating Your Needs in Words

Psychological change almost always occurs in a support-ive, warm, rewarding environment. People usually "open up" and talk about things—and try new ap-proaches to life—when they trust, admire, or want to please the therapist.

James McConnell

Communicating Your Thoughts and Feelings to the Players

The careful use of language is especially crucial in correcting an athlete's problematic behavior. Athletes who are given correc-tions without reasons tend to be less reasonable. Athletes who are not given clear statements of what is expected of them feel frustrated about doing anything right. It is difficult for an ath-lete to develop positive feelings when his or her behavior in-spires only anger and annoyance in the coach.

When players have a problem and need to discuss what is troubling them, coaches need to be good listeners. When coaches have a problem, they need to apply effective and con-structive communication skills to express their feelings about a situation that bothers them.

Wants into Words: Constructive Communication

The most important skill in asking athletes for what a coach wants is formulating a request that is respectful and construc-tive. Preparing such a statement involves getting the facts and then putting them into a clear statement of the coach's wants. This is usually all that is needed in everyday coaching. For example, simply stating that you want the team to do some stretching or to be at practice at 3:00 is all that is needed. In some cases, when things are getting out of control, a firm message usually suffices. A coach doesn't need to explain these requests.

However, sometimes it isn't enough just to say what is wanted. On occasion, athletes will do or say things that tear at the personal emotions of the coach. It is when this happens that athletes need to know the coach's understanding or perception of the situation. It may also be helpful for them to know how the situation has affected the coach emotionally. When the coach offers his or her thoughts (how the situation is perceived), feelings, and want statement, this is constructive communication.

Good communication is personal
E̲d̲g̲a̲r̲ D̲a̲l̲e̲

Constructive communication encourages closeness and mutual respect. Athletes will be more likely to respond to the coach's wants when they are aware of the coach's feelings and perspective.

For example, the coach knows that Joe is lying to him about doing his daily English assignments. The coach has been told by Joe's teammates and English teacher that Joe has not been turning in his daily assignments and that he has bragged about it during lunch hour. However, Joe has repeatedly told the coach that he has been attending class and turning in his daily assignments in English. The coach is upset that Joe is not turning in his homework, but more important, the coach is hurt that Joe is lying to him. It's rather abrupt to say to Joe, "You're a liar, I can't trust you." It is better to deliver constructive communication like this: "I feel very hurt and disappointed that you could not be honest with me. What I want is for us to try to find a way to develop a relationship that is based on honesty and trust."

When coaches leave their experience of a situation or their feelings out of a request, athletes may feel pressured to do something, but they won't know why. They are more likely to resist or argue and place barriers between themselves and the coach. It is better to give the athletes a window through which they can see and experience where the coach is coming from.

How Anger Affects Constructive Communications

Coaches have moments of rage. No matter how much a coach cares for the athletes, it's inevitable that at some point he or she will get mad at them. Unfortunately, few coaches know how to communicate anger effectively. Coaches sometimes make the mistake of saying terrible things that are later regretted.

In moments of frustration, anger, or stress, coaches have said things that they knew they shouldn't have. Unfortunately, most have engaged in personal attacks on the players. Not knowing what else to do, they have said things that have insulted and hurt others. In their anger, they have blamed, ridiculed, and referred to athletes with unkind names. As a result, they usually got the opposite of what they wanted. Instead of encouraging cooperation, they invited anger, resistance, and rebellion.

These types of comments are attacks on the athlete's self-esteem and promote defensiveness and counterattacks. If the motivation behind such verbal attacks is to inflict emotional pain, character assassination is the ultimate weapon. However, if the goal is to create mutual understanding between the two parties, it is self-defeating.

Anyone who angers you conquers you.
Sister Kenny's mother

Anger undermines constructive communication. Communication should be delayed until the coach feels that he or she is under control. Take a deep breath and say, "I am really upset and angry now. I need to move away from this situation. I will talk with you when I feel calm." Or ask for assistance from another adult or responsible player who is calm.

Angry confrontations are hurtful and punitive. Effective, constructive communications guide, protect, and help athletes to grow. An angry coach may find it helpful to think about and answer the following questions:

"Why do I feel this way?"
"What did I feel before I became angry? Was it embarrassment? Fear? Frustration?"
"Are there other problems bothering me that are making me less tolerant?"
"What is the athlete feeling at this moment?"
"Am I expecting too much from my athletes?"
"Am I being reasonable?"

Coaches who lack assertiveness need to add constructive communication to their daily speech. Long-suffering martyrs who suppress their own feelings, wants, and needs to keep everyone happy are taken advantage of and will eventually erupt in anger and resentment. The more they give, the more people want. As they learn to take an assertive stance, they will discover less anger, greater feelings of appreciation, and a better feeling about themselves.

The more skilled coaches become in using constructive communication, the more successful they will become in confronting and resolving problems with their athletes. Athletes will respond with greater trust and confidence because they know they are being treated in a fair and respectful manner.

When an Athlete's Words or Actions Affect the Coach's Emotional Well-Being

Coaches need to develop positive ways to communicate their thoughts and feelings, especially when they are hurt, frustrated, or upset. The language that coaches choose and the way they use it can ultimately affect an athlete's career. Coaches need to model self-control, responsibility, and consideration to others.

The greatest cure of anger is delay.
SENECA

Constructive communication is an effective way of dealing with undesirable behavior. It focuses on the coach's feelings about a player's behavior, not about the player. The players are okay; their behavior is not. The coach can still accept and respect them, but the coach does not like what they did. Constructive communication expresses the coach's feelings, thoughts, and wants. The first three steps of constructive communication are based on the "I-Message" model developed by Thomas Gordon [1970]. A fourth step has been added to help the athlete know specifically what the coach wants. The four steps of constructive communication are as follows.

1. Describe your feelings. Your feelings help the listener to have empathy for your experience in a situation. The best way to express your feelings is for you to take responsibility for your emotions. You say:

Handle anger by preventing it's buildup.
DALE GALLOWAY

"I feel frustrated"
"It makes me angry"
"I'm confused"
"I feel disappointed"
"I was saddened"
"I get discouraged"
"I feel anxious"

This is in contrast to destructive communication, which is accusing and places all responsibility for your feelings on the listener. Destructive communications are "You-Messages" that put down, blame, or criticize. These destructive messages provoke anger, embarrassment, and feelings of worthlessness. Athletes may take such statements as "You're lazy" or "You're worthless" as an affirmation of their lack of personal value. Other examples of destructive communication are:

"You hurt me"
"You made me angry"
"You're so inconsiderate"
"You disappointed me"

At times you may have to use the pronoun "you" when you are referring directly to a specific athlete. However, you can still use it without placing blame. "When you come late to practice" doesn't place blame; it merely states a fact. Whenever possible, talk about the situation rather than focusing on the individual.

2. Describe your thoughts about the action or event that concerned you. Your thoughts are your perceptions or understanding of a particular situation. You explain or describe your understanding of what is happening. You say:

An angry man opens his mouth and shuts his eyes.
Cato

"When people do the exact opposite of what I requested"
"When people lie to me"
"When individuals spread rumors about me"
"When people use that type of language with me"

3. Describe the tangible reason why the behavior affects you. Your explanation helps the listener to understand how his or her behavior is affecting you. You say:

"because it will adversely affect team spirit."
"because I am afraid someone will get hurt."
"because I dislike leaving the locker room messy."
"because I don't like people questioning my abilities."
"because I don't like to be lied to."

4. Describe what you want done. The most important skill is asking for what you want. Preparing a constructive request involves getting the facts (your thoughts) and processing them into a clear statement of your wants. Stay away from abstractions such as "show me some cooperation," "show respect," or "be honest." Don't ask for a change in attitude or level of interest. Instead, specify the exact behavior: "I want you to tell me the real reason why you missed practice yesterday" or "I want every one to be here Monday afternoon at exactly 3:00."

Putting It All Together: The Completed Message

The following is a model for constructive communication:

"I feel _____
about/when _____
because _____
therefore/so _____

Other words or phrases may be substituted for any of the words used in the model. In addition, the first three phrases may be stated in any order. In some instances, it may be appropriate to omit the "therefore" portion of the statement and allow the listener to determine what he or she should do.

Constructive communication clearly states what it is that you want. Constructive communication can be arranged in any order the coach desires. The statement of the problem behavior is not always necessary.

Further Thoughts about Constructive Communication

1. Nonverbal communication is an important part of your message. Remember that constructive communication is friendly, respectful, and honest. Therefore use appropriate body language. Maintain eye contact, sit or stand erect, don't cross your arms and legs, and make sure you are close enough to your listener. Speak clearly. If the coach's tone of voice and body are out of sync with what the coach is trying to say, the athlete will be more influenced by the nonverbal behavior than by the coach's words. Coaches should practice constructive communication in front of a mirror to correct problems in body language. Coaches should also listen to their own words on tape to evaluate their voice and inflection.

The best gift we can bestow on others is good example.
MORELL

2. Don't overuse constructive communication. Constructive communication should be used sparingly. If it is overused, athletes will be turned off, and it will lose its overall effectiveness. Alternative approaches such as delaying the conversation to a time when there is no conflict or making simple requests for gaining cooperation are effective.

"Is there anything that you can do to help me out?"
"It would really be helpful if you _____."

By making a request, a coach is giving the player the right to say no. If a "no" response is given, the coach must respect that decision. Doing so demonstrates respect and may very well encourage a willingness to cooperate in the future.

TIME OUT: IN THE COACH'S CORNER

The Overbearing Parents

Winston High School has just won a very close and important midseason conference game. They are well on their way to making the playoffs for the fourth. straight year. The fans and the media have been supportive, and attendance and publicity have been exceptional. The season couldn't be going much better for Coach Thompson—except for Cheryl's aggressive and

When anger rises, think of the consequences.
CONFUCIUS

overly involved parents. Their recent "know-it-all" suggestions about what the team should be doing have been wearing away at Coach Thompson's nerves.

Parental interest and involvement are always appreciated. But over time, Cheryl's parents have crossed the line between what is acceptable and what has become obnoxious interference. The coach doesn't want to hurt their feelings, nor does she want to further embarrass an already embarrassed Cheryl. However, Coach Thompson, has endured the situation long enough and is ready to tell Cheryl's parents where they can go. She also realizes that she could have prevented this situation if she had put a stop to their behavior earlier.

Coach Thompson, relaxing in her office after the game and quietly savoring the important victory, is dreading the moment when Cheryl's parents "accidentally" run into her to tell her how great Cheryl played, what the team did wrong, and what the team needs to work on for the next important game.

Cheryl's dad enthusiastically shouts, "Hi, Coach! Great game! We are going to make it to the play-offs." The supportive language continues in this direction until the manipulative conversation turns to the dreaded words that Coach Thompson has already anticipated: "You know, coach, I noticed that Keesha was making a lot of defensive mistakes. You might consider taking her out of the starting line-up or moving her to a different position. And . . . ."

> *Language is by all odds the most subtle and powerful technique we have for controlling other people.*
>
> G. A. MILLER

Coach Thompson is thinking to herself, "Oh no, here it comes again," as the words from Cheryl's mom and dad fade into space and are no longer heard. Coach Thompson's eyes are looking beyond them now, but she is not seeing anything in particular.

Multiple Choice

What would you do if you were Coach Thompson?

    A. Tell Cheryl's dad to shut up and to keep his know-it-all, meddling opinions to himself and stop coming to you with his comments.

    B. Endure the situation and ignore his comments.

    C. Use constructive communication to help Cheryl's dad understand how you feel about the situation.

Response C is the correct answer. Constructive communication is a positive way to express your thoughts and feelings. It is respectful because it focuses on the behavior, not on the individual. Cheryl's parents are okay, but their behavior is not.

After recognizing her anger and calming down, Coach Thompson might reply something like this:

"I truly appreciate all of the parent and fan support our team is receiving. I am, however, beginning to feel very frustrated with the unsolicited suggestions that I am constantly receiving. These comments suggest that I am not doing a good job. I would appreciate it if the suggestions would stop."

Response A is not appropriate because you are attacking Cheryl's dad directly. This will result in hard feelings and put a huge barrier between you and Cheryl's parents. It might also damage your relationship with Cheryl.

Response B is not appropriate because enduring the behavior is not really fair to you. You should not have to endure any unsolicited behavior. Also, your negative feelings will only increase over time.

QUESTIONS AND ANSWERS

Question: Can constructive communication be used in other ways?

Answer: Yes. Don't limit constructive communication to negative things. It is equally important that a coach communicate good feelings. Be generous with good feelings. Players need to know that they are making important contributions.

"Thank you for being so respectful during this talk, it really helped me focus on what I needed to say."

"I appreciated how hard you practiced today, I know it was a tough workout."

Question: Can I use constructive comunication to influence an athlete's behavior?

Answer: Yes. You can use constructive communication to influence an athlete's future behavior. Informing the athletes of your needs will help them plan their future behavior. Here are some examples of using constructive communication to help prevent problems in the future.

"I'd like to discuss the upcoming trip to Central City. We need to decide what special rules we will need to prevent any problems."

"This upcoming tournament is going to require a lot of my time. I will not be able to spend as much time on the practice field with you. I'll really need your cooperation during practices. I need you to follow the workout schedule on your own."

"I don't want anyone leaving the tournament without my permission, I am responsible for you and don't want to be worried if I can't find you."

By using constructive communication in this manner you invite understanding and cooperation.

Question: What if an athlete doesn't respond to constructive communication?

Answer: If an athlete doesn't modify his or her behavior, you still have a problem. You need to start mutual problem solving, which usually involves at least these four steps:

1. Identify the problem or situation from each person's point of view.
2. Brainstorm the situation by generating solutions to improve the situation.
3. Evaluate each solution to determine a course of action.
4. Make an agreement on a mutual decision that is acceptable to both of you.

A thorough discussion on the process of problem solving can be found in Chapter 15, *Conflict Resolution.*

Major Points Discussed in Chapter 11

1. Constructive communication is when the coaches put their wants or needs into words.
2. Constructive communication encourages closeness and mutual respect.
3. In moments of frustration, anger, or stress, coaches have said things that they later regretted.
4. Constructive communication includes the following four steps:
   a. The coach describes his or her feelings.
   b. The coach describes his or her thoughts about the action or event that concerns him or her.
   c. The coach describes the tangible reason why the behavior affects you.
   d. The coach describes what he or she wants.
5. Nonverbal communication (body language) is an important part of a message.
6. Don't overuse constructive communication. A coach should use it only when something really bothers him or her.

Establishing
Responsible Behavior
and Discipline

12

Athletes in Conflict: The Mistaken Goals of Behavior

Find the essence of each situation, like a logger clearing a log jam. The pro climbs a tall tree and locates the key log, blows it, and lets the stream do the rest. An amateur would start at the edge of the jam and move all the logs, eventually moving the key log. Both approaches work, but the "essence" concept saves time and effort. Almost all problems have a "key" log if we learn to find it.

Fred Smith

Whatever an athlete does, no matter how peculiar it may seem, he or she does it for a reason. And what the athlete does usually shows something about himself or herself. It is, of course, very difficult to determine what the behavior means. Sometimes, people do things that are so destructive or peculiar that a psychologist needs to be consulted. We do know, however, that people do things because they expect to make matters a little better. They expect to be a little happier because of their behavior.

Coaches may not always understand the goal of an athlete's behavior. When they begin to judge the behavior from their perspective rather than the athlete's, it becomes very confusing. Many behaviors will ultimately lead to conflict. Coaches must realize that if they are ever to understand what an athlete does, they must understand what he or she needs.

When the athlete and coach are in conflict, it is important to have the athlete involved in the resolution, but it is equally important to break a chronic cycle of dysfunctional behavior. The coach must take steps to ensure that the athlete's emotional needs are being met.

Dreikurs [1964] theorized that the true primary goal of most behavior is (1) to find a sense of belonging, (2) to feel that one has significance by having control over one's own life, (3) to feel that one has been treated fairly, or (4) to avoid stressful and frightening situations.

Athletes, like other young people, want desperately to belong. They achieve that sense of belonging through participation and their sense of usefulness to the group. A young athlete who is discouraged and, for whatever reason, feels left out or insignificant will turn his or her attention from participation in the group to a desperate attempt to find his or her place within the group. The athlete may adjust to the situation with either pleasing or disturbing behavior; one way or another, he or she will find a place.

When one or more of an athlete's basic needs are not being met the athletes may adopt certain misbehaviors to try to have those needs fulfilled. Rudolph Dreikurs hypothesized that discouraged children as well as adults may use inappropriate behaviors or "mistaken goals" to help achieve fulfillment of their needs. He proposed four mistaken goals of behavior that he hypothesized to be the root of chronic patterns of dysfunctional behavior. They are called mistaken goals because they lead to misbehavior due to mistaken beliefs about how to find belonging and significance.

If you argue and rankle and contradict, you may achieve a victory sometimes; but it will be an empty victory because you will never get your opponent's good will.
BEN FRANKLIN

The Four Mistaken Goals of Behavior

Discouraged athletes suffer from low self-esteem and have the mistaken assumption that they belong and are significant only when they are the center of *attention*. Being the center of attention gives them a sense of power and control over others. Consequently, discouraged athletes will develop great skill at attention-getting. Discouraged athletes develop a variety of ways to keep the coach and others busy with them. Obviously, athletes need the coach's attention. However, when a coach finds himself or herself chronically busy with an athlete at times when situations do not justify it and the coach feels annoyed or distressed, it is usually a sign of undue attention. Coaches must realize that as pleasant or as disturbing as the athlete may be, his or her goal is to win attention rather than to participate.

The following list gives examples of attention-seeking behaviors.

- *The Team Clown* is the athlete who is constantly clowning around, acting out, or being overly silly to get attention from both the coach and his teammates. He needs to be the center of attention or uses this behavior when he feels embarrassed or pushed into a corner. It is used as a way of "saving face."
- *The Obnoxious Athlete* usually doesn't feel good about herself and consequently does things that receive negative attention from the coach or teammates.

- *The Lazy Athlete* is similar to the obnoxious athlete in that she receives negative attention while the coach nags and other athletes do work for her.
- *The Helpless Athlete* pretends that he can't do anything without help. He only feels loved when he is being fussed over and cared for.
- *The Artificial Charmer* plays the role of the adorable and charming athlete by spouting insincere compliments to everyone. This niceness vanishes as soon as the attention is diverted toward someone else. He becomes a cold competitor in seconds.

The battle for *power* is the second mistaken goal and most frequently occurs after the coach has tried for some time to restrain the discouraged athlete's demands for attention. Discouraged athletes feel a sense of belonging and significance if they are in charge and do what they want to do. Power becomes a mechanism by which the athlete can defeat the coach or others. It is an attitude that implies that one belongs only if one is winning or, if one cannot win, one can prevent others from winning the power struggle. Discouraged athletes can feel enormous satisfaction when they refuse to comply with the coach's demands. This situation is like that when a small child calmly smirks in the face of the parents' screams and tears. The child knows that he or she has won because the parents were driven to complete exasperation and frustration.

Revenge is always the weak pleasure of a little narrow mind.
JUVENAL

The following list gives examples of controlling or power behaviors.

- *The Rebellious Athlete* controls the coach by being so out of control that the coach feels helpless. He controls some of his teammates by bullying them with his size and strength.
- *The Stubborn Athlete* who fails to get her way gains control by refusing to participate or by causing a scene.

The third mistaken goal is usually a consequence of the power struggle. The athlete in his or her discouragement may retaliate. *Revenge* becomes a means of feeling significant and important. It implies that if one cannot belong, at least one can hurt back. Discouraged athletes are now convinced that they don't belong, aren't liked, and don't have any significance. They become mistakenly convinced that they will count only if they can hurt others as they believe others have hurt them.

The following list gives examples of types of athletes who use disruptive or revengeful behaviors.

- *The Destructive Athlete* feels a sense of hopelessness and believes that she has been rejected by everyone, so it doesn't really matter what she does. Nobody will like her regardless of how she behaves. She loses control over her impulses and acts out against others and the environment with destructiveness and aggressiveness.

- *The Defiant Athlete* strikes out against those who he believes have hurt him. He strikes back with fits of anger, temper tantrums, and defiance.
- *The Contemptuous Athlete* has so much mistrust of others that she seems to despise everyone. An athlete who feels that others have continually treated her unfairly will find it difficult to have a trusting relationship.

The fourth mistaken goal is used by completely discouraged athletes. These athletes demonstrate their *self-imposed inadequacy* by simply giving up. They believe that they have no way of succeeding by useful or destructive means and avoid the hurt of even trying to achieve what they mistakenly believe is not possible. These discouraged athletes believe that they lack the ability and stamina to perform competently; they have a low opinion of their athletic abilities. When they don't think they can be the best, they give up. The discouraged athletes do not believe that it is possible for them to belong, to be liked, and to have any significance. They give up and hope that people will leave them alone. Coaches generally feel despair and may also want to give up on the athlete. Coaches may actually come to agree that the athlete is incompetent and inadequate.

The following list gives examples of types of athletes who use self-imposed inadequacy behaviors.

- *The Socially Inept Athlete* is the severely withdrawn individual who has turned all of his negative feelings inside. He does not make eye contact, refuses to talk most of the time, and stays apart from others whenever possible. Fear, anger, and frustration are repressed and never expressed. He is a loner who is sometimes seen as a "good child" because he never causes trouble.
- *The Depressed Athlete* exhibits feelings of ineptness, hopelessness, and despair. She has no energy and has given up. She no longer wants to be involved.

Why the Mistaken Goals of Behavior Do Not Work

Unfortunately, the mistaken goals of behavior provide only temporary relief to the athlete and, in long run, worsen and compound the problem. There is a snowball effect because the athlete's inappropriate behavior increases the negativity and hostility in the coach and the environment; these in turn enhance the athlete's emotional neediness and the likelihood that the athlete will behave more and more inappropriately in the future.

Most people's natural reaction is to respond in a way that is precisely opposite to the actual response that the athlete needs. For example, one is usually tempted to ignore the athlete who is acting out for attention, but that usually causes the athlete to increase the behavior. One usually wants to "show who's boss" in a power struggle, but this usually makes the athlete feel more need to demonstrate his or her own power. One usually wants to punish the revengeful athlete, but that only makes the athlete want to seek greater revenge. Finally, the coach may want to give up on the inadequate athlete, and that only allows the athlete to sink deeper into his or her isolation.

To bring about real change, a coach must relieve the problems that cause the chronic misbehavior and find appropriate methods to meet the athlete's emotional needs. When a coach becomes aware that an athlete's chronic misbehavior is a consequence of one of the four mistaken goals, the coach has a basis for action. Once a coach identifies the "need" behind a behavior, the coach can understand the hidden purpose of the behavior. What seemed illogical now begins to seem logical and make sense. The coach is now in a position to act.

Athletes are usually not aware of their mistaken goal, except when the goal is revenge. Even when their goal is revenge, athletes do not know that they have decided that the only way to deal with feeling hurt is to hurt back. They are acting on an unconscious level. Nothing is gained by the coach telling the athlete what he or she suspects is the mistaken goal. This disclosure should be left to someone who is more professionally trained to deal with such matters. However, once the coach is aware of the mistaken goal, he or she can develop a plan of action.

It is also important to recognize that not all behavior is based on these four mistaken goals. Some antagonistic or senseless behavior of players and adults may be explained in terms of the four mistaken goals, but other forms of behavior may be linked to such things as financial gain and risk-taking behavior, which do not necessarily fall within the scope of these goals.

Identifying the Mistaken Goal

The only way for coaches to determine the mistaken goal of behavior is to identify their own feelings and the player's reactions to their attempts to correct the misbehavior. Jane Nelsen [1987] discussed two clues that can help coaches to identify the mistaken goal.

He that can have patience can have what he will.
BEN FRANKLIN

1. **Identifying the feelings of the coach as he or she responds to the misbehavior.** The following chart categorizes the coach's feelings followed by the athlete's mistaken goal.

Coach's Feelings	Athlete's Mistaken Goal
1. Irritation or annoyance	Attention
2. Threatened by the behavior	Power
3. Hurt	Revenge
4. Inadequate	Assumed inadequacy

2. **The athlete's response when you tell him or her to stop the misbehavior.** The following chart identifies the mistaken goal and athlete's response.

Mistaken Goal	Athlete's Behavioral Response
1. Attention	Behavior stops momentarily but usually resumes.
2. Power	Continues behavior and verbally defies or passively resists the coach's request to stop.
3. Revenge	Retaliation by doing something destructive or saying or doing something hurtful.
4. Assumed inadequacy	Passive, hoping the coach will soon give up and leave him or her alone. Simply quits.

Every man is a volume, if you know how to read him.
W. E.
CHANNING

Prescriptions for Each Mistaken Goal

When the coach realizes that an athlete is demanding undue attention, he or she can simply ignore the behavior. What is the point of demanding attention if the coach does not respond? When a coach is in a power struggle, he or she can withdraw from the contest. What is the point of being the victor of a noncontest? When an athlete seeks to hurt, the coach can become aware of the athlete's deep discouragement, avoid feeling hurt, avoid punishing and develop a plan of action. Finally, a coach can help the "helpless" athlete by structuring experiences that will lead to success and help the athlete to discover old and new abilities.

Obviously, there is no one simple way to solve such complex problems. The above paragraph is overly simplified. However, the coach needs to think out the solutions that best fit the situation. It is always reasonable and prudent to consult others. The important thing to remember is that these problems, like all other situations, should be approached with continued attitudes of encouragement, understanding, dignity, and mutual respect.

Some general guidelines for effective responses to each mistaken goal are outlined below. They are only possible suggestions based on the principles of this book.

Attention-Seeking Behavior

- Ignore the misbehavior. Do not acknowledge the misbehavior and, whenever possible, walk away from it. Be aware that ignoring the behavior may cause the athlete to increase his or her attention-seeking behavior. However, if a coach is consistent, over time the behavior will be extinguished. Give positive attention during cooperative, enjoyable, and agreeable times. This will help the athlete to reevaluate his or her methods.

- Schedule some "special" time with each athlete on a regular basis. Take a little extra time to help validate the athletes' feelings and needs. Be interested and learn to listen. This strategy should be a part of the solution for all mistaken goals.

- Redirect the misbehavior into some positive contributing behavior that reinforces participation. Give all athletes some genuine responsibility that is essential to the functioning of the team.

Most men are better than they seem to be.
UNKNOWN

Power Behavior

- Remove yourself from the power struggle to give yourself and the athlete some time to calm down or cool off. This gives you an opportunity to seek a respectful and friendly solution that will help you to decide what you will do, not what you will try to make the athlete do.

- Act in one of the following ways: (1) Remain calm and act thoughtfully, but firmly. (2) Follow up with a one-to-one problem-solving session. Remember to practice encouragement, understanding, and mutual respect. Learn to listen and be open-minded. Do not go in with a hidden agenda; the athlete will see through it, and the power struggle will be exaggerated.

- Do whatever has to be done to keep an athlete from harming others and the physical environment.

- Provide limited choices whenever possible. Allowing the athlete a choice is essentially saying, "You may make your own choices—within reasonable limits—but you must also live with the consequences of your choice.

- Avoid "head to head" confrontations. Aggressive behavior further establishes a model for this type of undesirable behavior.

Revenge Behavior

- Withdraw from the revenge cycle by avoiding retaliation or punishment. Withdrawal does not mean withdrawal from the athlete. Acceptance, respect, and friendliness still remain. Withdrawal from the revenge cycle helps to maintain a positive relationship. If coaches continue in the conflict, they feel more inclined to punish or retaliate. Punishment will only perpetuate the revenge cycle.
- After withdrawing from the conflict, remain respectful and friendly during the cooling-off period.
- Do whatever has to be done to keep an athlete from harming others and the physical environment.
- Follow up with a one-to-one problem-solving session. Maintain the same rules that were discussed above in the "power behavior" guidelines.
- Build cooperative relationships with defiant athletes, to become the athletes' ally and friend while refusing to participate in inappropriate interactions with them.
- Avoid overreacting to expressions of defiance such as vulgar language.
- When necessary, remove or restrain any athlete in extreme circumstances with firmness and resolve, not anger or punitiveness.

People are much more alike than they are on the surface.
UNKNOWN

- Earn the athlete's trust through consistent fairness, honesty, true acceptance and good modeling.
- Model trust by placing the athlete in situations in which the coach knows that the athlete is likely to succeed and, if he or she should fail, it can be easily overlooked.

Assumed Inadequacy Behavior

- Arrange nonthreatening experiences that result in success by creating small, achievable steps.
- Do not make assumptions about the athlete's abilities and knowledge. Take adequate time for training.
- Use encouragement.
- Special guidance from outside sources may be required.
- Reduce stress in the athlete's training by introducing nonthreatening activities and easing the athlete into more active involvement with things and people around him or her.

TIME OUT: IN THE COACH'S CORNER

Identifying the Athlete's Mistaken Goals

Quiz 1
Fill in the athlete's mistaken goal on the basis of the coach's feelings:

Athlete's Goal	Coach's Feelings
1. Power	Angry
2. _____	Hurt
3. _____	Despair
4. _____	Irritated
5. _____	Provoked
6. _____	Worried
7. _____	Threatened
8. _____	Disbelieving
9. _____	Hopeless
10. _____	Disappointed

When little men cast long shadows, it is a sign that the sun is setting.
WALTER LANDOR

Quiz 2
Fill in the what you believe is the athlete's goal on the basis of his or her behavior. Remember, the real clue is how you feel in response to those behaviors. You may not completely agree with the answers to Quiz 2 because each situation is different, and some of these behaviors may elicit a different response in you.

Goal	Example of Athlete's Behavior
1. Attention	Forgetting
2. _____	Clowning around
3. _____	Rude
4. _____	Quitting all the time
5. _____	Disobedient
6. _____	Truant
7. _____	Outlandish dress
8. _____	Minor mischief
9. _____	Defiant
10. _____	Arguing

Answers to Quiz 1

1. Power   2. Revenge   3. Inadequacy

4. Attention   5. Power   6. Attention or inadequacy

7. Power   8. Revenge   9. Inadequacy

10. Revenge

Answers to Quiz 2

1. Attention   2. Attention   3. Revenge

4. Inadequacy   5. Power   6. Inadequacy

7. Attention   8. attention   9. Power

10. Power

QUESTIONS AND ANSWERS

Question: It seems that Dreikur's four mistaken goals of behavior are somewhat limited. Are there any other reasons why athletes misbehave?

Answer: Yes. Eugene Kelly and Thomas Sweeney (as cited in *The Parent's Guide: Systematic Training for Effective Parenting (STEP)* [Dinkmeyer and McKay, 1983]) extended the list of goals to include excitement, peer acceptance, and superiority. These goals, of course, can be used in positive ways, but they can also be negative and destructive. However, they were not discussed with the four mistaken goals because they are usually more of an issue between parent and child than between athlete and coach. It is especially important that you know the basic four goals discussed in the chapter. The other three are briefly discussed below:

1. Excitement. Some young people use negative behavior to pursue this goal. For example, speeding in a car, taking drugs out of curiosity, and promiscuous sex are not acceptable to most adults.
2. Peer acceptance. Having a peer group is usually fine until the individual joins an "unacceptable" group. For example, joining a gang that is identified with crime would not be acceptable to most parents or coaches.
3. Superiority. Most adults will approve of kids who seek to be superior in achievement in school or sports. However, some young people seek superiority in destructive ways. For example, putting down others or consuming more alcohol than anyone else are destructive.

Major Points Discussed in Chapter 12

1. Dreikurs theorized that the true primary goal of most behavior is to:
   a. find a sense of belonging,
   b. feel that one has significance by having control over one's life,
   c. feel that one has been treated fairly, or
   d. avoid stressful and frightening situations.
2. The four mistaken goals of behavior are:
   a. attention,
   b. power,
   c. revenge, and
   d. self-imposed inadequacy.
3. Mistaken goals do not work.
4. Coaches can identify the mistaken goals by:
   a. identifying their own feelings as they respond to the misbehavior and
   b. recognizing how the athletes are responding when you tell them to stop the misbehavior.
5. There are specific strategies that a coach can utilize to help solve the problems associated with mistaken goals.

13

Coaching Responsible Behavior: Empowering Discipline

The moment we break faith with one another, the sea engulfs us and the light goes out.

James Baldwin

The Purpose of Discipline

The purpose of discipline is to help players develop an inner guidance system so that they can ultimately function responsibly by themselves. In the short term, coaches start building self-discipline through the little things that occur on a daily basis so that in the long term, the athletes can develop the inner strength to deal with the larger issues.

In the realm of athletics, discipline is training a player in mind and character to enable him or her to become self-controlled and a constructive member of the team. How one goes about achieving and maintaining discipline has been one of the questions of the ages. However, discipline is immeasurably easier when the player feels genuinely liked and accepted. It is easier to accept the coach's guidance without hostility. Without a relationship of mutual respect and dignity between coach and player, a player reacts to discipline with anger, resistance, and resentment. In addition, it is important for coaches to control their emotions when they discipline. Uncontrolled anger is especially detrimental to good discipline.

Coaches try to teach players to behave responsibly both on and off the field. Factors that influence how coaches go about disciplining players may include the way they themselves were disciplined as players, what they believe the needs of the players to be, what they observe other coaches are doing, and their own moral beliefs.

Good behavior is the result of inner willingness, not of outer compulsion.
UNKNOWN

Once coaches commit to teaching discipline to their players, they must discipline themselves to change any old destructive patterns and model new ones.

Good discipline is time-consuming because teaching players about discipline and responsibility requires planning and patience. Unfortunately, in the name of expediency, some coaches find that it is easier to control players than to teach them about discipline. However, in the long term the investment in teaching about discipline will give players a focused direction and a foundation on which a system of values can be built.

Styles of Discipline

Most coaches discipline according to one of the three basic models described below. Each model is based on a different set of beliefs about how players learn about discipline. Each model also teaches a different set of lessons about cooperation, responsibility, and the rules coaches use for acceptable behavior.

Hostile Discipline

Hostile discipline is based on punishment. Anyone can punish. It takes no sensitivity, no judgment, no understanding, and no talent. To depend on punishment to control people is to make the critical error of assuming that discipline equals punishment. *Discipline* is training that develops self-control, character, or orderliness and efficiency. *Punishment* is a method of maintaining discipline by imposing a penalty or retribution rather than correcting for a perceived or actual wrongdoing.

Let's examine a typical behavior problem in athletics, a verbal quarrel between two players. As the punitive basketball coach reaches the scene of a heated argument, two angry players are pushing and yelling at each other. An argument is about to become a fistfight.

Coach (almost screaming):"Hey, cut it out! What's going on? Can't you two jerks get along?"

Player 1: "He's got a big mouth and I'm going to shut it!"

Player 2: "Yeah? Just try it, wimp!"

Coach (clearly angered): "Both of you settle down. Who started this?"

Player 1: "He did with his big mouth."

Player 2: "He's been looking for a fight all practice."

Coach (clearly frustrated): "I've had enough of your fighting and lying. Both of you do 25 laps."

Player 1 (sarcastically) : "Just great! Thanks, coach."

Player 2: "Come on, coach, this isn't fair."

Coach: "Don't talk back to me. You two just earned 50 laps."

Players (turning their backs and walking away, and quietly mumbling): "Stupid coach."

People must never be humiliated—that is the main thing.
ANONYMOUS

Coach (needing to get the last punitive words in): "Get moving now, and don't let me catch you loafing."

Coaches who punish find themselves in the role of both policeman and judge. Their job is to investigate the crime, determine guilt, and impose penalties. Penalties are usually severe and unrelated to the misdeed. Players are viewed in terms of good or bad and right or wrong.

No passion so effectually robs the mind of all its powers of acting and reasoning as fear.
EDMUND BURKE

Punishment usually involves a threat that obligates the player to either obey or resist rather than to think constructively and respond. One may argue that punishment works. Very few people would disagree; punishment does usually stop misbehavior. Punishment can work in an immediate situation, but the cooperation that punishment achieves may come at a high price that includes hurt feelings, impaired relationships, and angry power struggles. Players who must operate in this type of environment are more likely to quit their teams than are players who do not live in constant fear of their coach.

Punishment degrades, dehumanizes, and humiliates players. Consequently, it hurts feelings, evokes anger, and incites resistance or withdrawal. When it comes to being humiliated, players respond much as adults do. They get mad. They rebel, seek revenge, and sometimes withdraw in fearful submission. The long-range effects of punishment can be devastating, resulting in a player feeling one or all of the following:

1. *Indignation/resentment.* Players feel anger or scorn resulting from the perception that they have been treated unfairly or out of meanness. Punishment creates distrust.
2. *Retaliation.* Players think about inflicting back some of the hurt and pain that has been inflicted on them. They want to get even for the meanness or injustice that has been imposed on them.
3. *Withdrawal.* Players think that they are deserving of punishment and will try to please through submissive compliance. Anxious docility along with a lack of confidence and spontaneity become part of the baggage that punishment creates.

One hostile athlete can be more destructive to a team than ten injuries. A hostile athlete can rip a coach's strategy to shreds.

Aside from the negative feelings and behaviors that might arise from punishment, coaches must ask themselves whether or not players will learn any new skills for resolving conflicts on their own. Will they learn anything about cooperation or responsibility? Will they learn how to solve problems? Punishment doesn't teach any of the above. Coaches who use punishment make all the decisions, have all the power and control, and do the problem solving. Punishment takes responsibility and learning opportunities away from players because it leaves them out of the process.

A tragic consequence of punishment is when the player imitates the aggressor. The players begin to identify with the punishing coach, coming to believe that being punitive is right. Then, of course, when players become coaches, they will treat their players as they themselves were treated. Coaches who use punishment were usually themselves ill-treated. The use of punishment or the threat of it consequently becomes part of a vicious cycle.

Permissive Discipline

Permissive discipline is at the opposite end of the continuum. It is a democratic process without limits, rules, or order. Permissive discipline gives the players control over the final decision. Such freedom without rules, limits, or order creates anarchy, and players will not learn to respect rules or authority or how to handle freedom responsibly.

The worst sin toward our fellow creatures is not to hate them, but to be indifferent to them.
GEORGE
BERNARD SHAW

Permissiveness gives the coach and players an equal voice in determining rules and privileges. When a player misbehaves, a permissive coach appeals to the player's intellect and sense of responsibility by explaining the difference between right and wrong. The player, with that information, then decides what to do. Most players will manipulate the coach into rescuing and protecting them from the consequences and results of their own behavior.

Let's return to the example of the player conflict and see how this problem is handled by the permissive coach.

Coach: "Hey, Cut it out! Someone is going to get hurt." (The fight stops momentarily. Then shoving and pushing erupt again.)

Coach: "Did you two hear what I said? Cut it out!"

Player 1: "Coach, tell him to keep his mouth shut! He's driving me crazy."

Player 2: "What's his problem?"

Punishment is the absence of reward.
ANONYMOUS

Coach: "Why don't you two guys try to get along? This is a team effort."

Player 1: "He's getting on my nerves. He's constantly telling everybody what to do."

Player 2: "I'm just calling the plays."

Coach: "Come on, you two, why don't you try to get along? This fighting doesn't help the team any. Remember, we've got a game tomorrow, and we need to be together."

Player 1: "Yeah, we'll get along when pigs fly."

Player 2: "Jerk."

Coach (exasperated): "You two do what you want, but don't do it here."

The reason that the players didn't cooperate was that they didn't have to. Cooperation was optional, not required. Neither player was accountable for his behavior, and the coach relied on reason or persuasion to get his message across. The coach did not support his words with any effective action or consequences.

Players who are trained with permissiveness will become accustomed to getting their own way and will become experts at ignoring, avoiding, arguing, and defying. Permissive coaches are constantly shifting from strategy to strategy (repeating, pleading, reasoning, etc.) to get their players to cooperate. The coach usually ends up frustrated and humiliated, giving up any hope of success, and the players end up getting their own way.

Can you imagine what a soccer game would be like if it were played in a permissive manner? Imagine the chaos that would result if, every time there was an infraction, the referee gave the players second and third chances without imposing penalties? Let's join such a game in progress.

A player on the yellow team is ready to kick a shot at the goal, but a player on the green team sticks a foot out to trip her. As play stops, the referee approaches the green player and says, "Was that an accident or was it intentional?" The green player apologizes but indicates that it was an accident and that she didn't mean to trip the yellow player.

Permissiveness is for disciplined people.
LEO TOLSTOY

"Well, okay," the referee says. "Be careful. I may call a foul on you the next time. Try not to let it happen again."

The next incident occurs when a ball hits the hands of the same green player. The whistle blows, play stops, and the referee confronts the player.

"You know it is against the rules for you to touch the ball with your hands. First you tripped the other player, and now you touch the ball with your hands. I can't keep letting you get away with stuff like that. If it keeps up, I'm going to call a penalty."

Soon another infraction occurs and another confrontation: "Didn't you hear what I said the last time? Why would you do it again?" the referee pleads in exasperation.

Although discipline and freedom seem antiethical, each without the other destroys itself.
DONALD BARR

The player looks down and sheepishly says, "I don't know."

The referee looks the player in the eyes and says, "You have had your final warning. The next infraction and I'm calling it." Pointing at the player, the referee says, "Do you understand?"

As the game goes on, the referee continues to reprimand, lecture, threat, complain, and everything else except to call a penalty. The game eventually is in shambles, and players are in a free-for-all.

Permissive coaches are a lot like the permissive referee. They give warnings and reminders and try to reason when their players break the rules. Without consequences to hold them accountable, the players have little cause to take the team rules or responsibilities seriously. Permissiveness doesn't usually stop behavior, nor does it teach anything about rules, cooperation, responsibility, or respect for authority.

Empowering Discipline

Hostile discipline is discipline with firmness but requires no respect. Permissive discipline is discipline with respect but requires no firmness. Empowering discipline is discipline that requires a balance between firmness and respect. It is a process that decides on rules for the mutual benefit of coach and players. It is a process that teaches about rules, cooperation, responsibility, and respect for authority.

Through empowering discipline, the coach does not direct, but guides the players' misbehavior through a problem-solving process. The coach provides clearly defined limits, acceptable choices, and clearly stated consequences that hold the players accountable for their behavior or actions.

Let's return to our familiar conflict and see how the problem is handled by an empowering coach.

Coach (in a clear, matter-of-fact voice): "Guys, stop the shoving and yelling. I'm sure there's a way we can solve your problem. Do you two need to take a little time to cool off first before we talk?"

Player 1: I'm ready to talk now."

Player 2: "Me too."

Coach: "What would be another way to handle this problem without all the shoving and pushing?"

Player 1: "I don't know. I just want him shut up. I'm just tired of him trying to boss everyone around and being a know-it-all."

Player 2: "Hey, I was just trying to make sure we were running the plays right. I wasn't trying to be bossy."

Coach: "Well, you guys can either stop fighting and shake hands or go home for the evening. Which would you like to do?"

Player 1: "I'll shake. I'm sorry I got so hot."

Player 2: "I'll shake. I'll try to control myself. I didn't realize I was coming off that way"

No teacher should ever punish a pupil when either is angry.
EDWIN BROWN

Coach: "Good choice guys. Shake hands, and let's get back to playing some basketball."

With empowering discipline, the coach is able to stop the misbehavior and teach the intended lesson. There was no power struggle or conflict. The first step was to give a clear, direct, and matter-of-fact message about the behavior he wanted stopped. Second, he sent a message of cooperation by using a "we" message expressing confidence in the players' ability to solve the problem. Third, the coach recognized that problems cannot be cooperatively solved in a climate of anger. The coach asked whether the players needed a cooling-off period before talking. This choice forced the players to be responsible for controlling their own angry feelings.

Next, the coach checked with the players to see whether they had the skills and information they needed to resolve the conflict on their own. They didn't. The coach then suggested solutions in the form of limited choices. By choosing the solution themselves, the players were responsible for their own problem solving. The conflict ended in an atmosphere of mutual respect and dignity.

In summary, the empowering discipline process includes:

1. communicating about expected behavior (firm limits),
2. communicating confidence in the players' ability to solve the problem,
3. offering a choice of a cooling-off period,
4. providing an opportunity for the players to solve the problem, and
5. if necessary, giving limited choices with a logical or natural consequence. (See Chapter 14 for a detailed discussion of natural and logical consequences.)

The following is a summary of the three discipline styles:

Hostile Discipline (Autocratic Method)
Order without freedom
No choices
Compliance through force

Permissive Discipline (No-Limit Method)
Freedom without order
Unlimited choices
Compliance through persuasion

Empowering Discipline
Freedom with order
Limited choices
Compliance through cooperation and accountability

I hold that the only discipline, important for its own sake, is self-discipline, and that this can only be acquired by a wide use of freedom.

ALFRED NORTH WHITEHEAD

TIME OUT: THE COACH'S CORNER

Twelve Helpful Hints to Reduce Discipline Problems

1. Dump the old notion that to make athletes do better, a coach must first make them feel bad. Don't say things to hurt feelings or create guilt with the idea that these statements will shame the athletes into better behavior. Nobody, not even the coach, likes to feel humiliated.

2. Give athletes meaningful team and individual responsibilities. Athletes feel a sense of belonging when they believe that they are making real contributions to the team.

3. Make decisions together. When athletes have input into important decisions, they take greater ownership of the decision. This will increase cooperative behavior.

4. Punishment works only in the short term. In the long term it creates negative feelings of anger and resentment.

5. If you are angry, cool off before you confront the athlete. Go someplace private and say all the negative things you feel like saying—but say them alone. When you have vented your anger and are ready to talk, approach the athlete in a respectful manner.

6. Use natural and logical consequences whenever possible. Allow the athlete to learn from the consequences of his or her choices.

7. Teach and model mutual respect. A coach can be kind and still be firm. When in conflict, maintain respect. Focus on correcting the behavior without attacking the athlete's personality. The athlete needs to know that he or she is still respected even though the behavior is not.

8. Encouraging athletes will make them feel accepted and capable and, consequently, more motivated to participate responsibly.

9. Make sure the environment is both physically and emotionally safe for the athlete. Fearful athletes are more likely to get hurt and become less cooperative.

10. Teach athletes what you want by being specific. For example, the phrase "a clean locker room" may mean different things to the coach and to the athletes. If a process or procedure is important, demonstrate it.

11. When one or more of the basic needs in life are not being met, athletes may adopt certain misbehaviors to try to get those needs fulfilled. For a detailed discussion of this issue, see Chapter 12.

12. Hold regular team forums to solve problems through

We must learn to stick to something we're not stuck on.

EDGAR DALE

cooperation and respect. See Chapter 16 for a detailed discussion of this issue.

QUESTIONS AND ANSWERS

Question: Sometimes my anger gets in the way of empowering discipline. How can I keep it under control?

Answer: Step back from the situation. Cool off before attempting to communicate. Remember, anger is a secondary response. Identify what made you angry in the first place and try the following steps:

The greatest freedom man has is the freedom to discipline himself.
BERNARD M. BARUCH

1. Determine what caused the anger. In most cases it revolves around (a) the frustration of needs and desires, (b) someone's failure to satisfy your expectations and wishes, resulting in loss of pride or self-esteem, and (c) someone's not acting in a socially approved manner. The more specific you are in identifying the cause, the easier it will be for you to deal with the problem.
2. Once you know why you are angry, tell the other person what you are angry about and how you feel about the situation. If you can't do this, get a third party to help.
3. Consider the other person's feelings. Ask how he or she feels about what you've said. This will help to clarify the situation so that each of you is aware of the other's perception of what happened.
4. Take steps to prevent the situation from being repeated.

Question: What effect does my anger have on my players?

There are no problem children, only problems in children.
UNKNOWN

Answer: Averill [1983] reported that most people experience negative consequences for their anger. The most commonly reported reactions to anger were: indifference or lack of concern, defiance, apology or other signs of contrition, anger or hostility, denial of responsibility, hurt feelings, surprise, rejection, jokes, frivolity, or silliness. These responses are usually not in the angry person's best interest.

Question: What do you believe are the most common discipline problems that a coach must deal with?

Answers: That's a tough question. Each coach and situation is a little different. However, I see five situations that can lead to potential discipline problems among many teams. The following are not listed in any particular order:

1. **Arguing.** Players often challenge the coach's beliefs and attitudes.
2. **Insults and vulgar language or gestures.** Players often swear to create excitement or to gain peer acceptance.
3. **Forgetting.** Some players will "conveniently" forget as an excuse for not fulfilling a responsibility. Sometimes players will forget to get attention.
4. **Arguing, put-downs, and fighting among teammates.**
5. **Players not being responsible.** For example, they may miss practices, be late for practice, or do not stay on task.

Each of these problems is unique, and each requires a different strategy that depends on the situation. Strategies for solving these problems are discussed throughout this entire book. Examples are reflective listening, setting firm limits, applying natural and logical consequences, conflict resolution strategies, and the use of I-messages.

TIME OUT: SELF-ASSESSMENT

Are You a Tolerant Coach?
Directions: Read each statement carefully. Circle the letter that corresponds to your response. **Treat the results as a guide only. There is a margin of uncertainty in all questionnaires of this kind.**

If you are currently not coaching, you may respond according to how you think you would respond to the situations, or you can choose a former or present coach and try to respond as you think he or she would respond.

1. An athlete has begun to show unsettled behavior just before a major competition, complaining of aches and pains that you suspect are caused by nerves rather than anything else. Do you
   A. Speak to the athlete firmly and say that he or she must compete, like it or not?
   B. Allow the athlete to "scratch" from the competition, and send him or her to the athletic trainer?
   C. Continue to prepare the athlete for competition but resolve to keep an eye on the situation?
2. How do you respond if one of your athletes openly swears at you?
   A. A stern reprimand at the instant the act is performed followed by punishment.

Evidently he had taken a lot of courses in insensitivity training.
EDGAR DALE

B. No punishment, but a quietly spoken reprimand.

C. A reprimand followed by a determined attempt to reward the athlete for positive behaviors.

3. If a player does something that is outside of the athletic arena (examples: drinking, sexual behavior) and that you very much disapprove of, do you

A. Remove the athlete from the team?

B. Tell the athlete how you feel but keep him or her on the team and keep your distance?

C. Tell yourself that the behavior is not a team issue and behave toward the athlete as you always did?

4. You are trying to concentrate on getting some important matters finished, but the noise of the players fooling around outside your office distracts and irritates you. How would you feel?

A. Feel that kids are kids and be happy that they are having a good time.

B. Feel furious with them.

C. Feel annoyed but acknowledge to yourself that kids do make noise.

5. Do you discuss an athlete's behavior critically with other athletes?

A. Often

B. Rarely or never

C. Sometimes

6. An athlete comes to you and confides that he is really unhappy with his life. Would you

A. Listen with empathy?

B. Tell him what to do?

C. Do things for him to try to cheer him up?

7. If an athlete openly questioned your authority, would you

A. Feel uneasy?

B. Think that it is okay to do so?

C. Feel very angry?

8. Do you believe

A. That some team rules are necessary, but the fewer the better?

B. That players must have specific rules because they need to be controlled?

C. That team rules are unnecessary?

9. Which statement do you most agree with?

A. Don't judge an athlete's actions because we can never fully understand his or her true motives.

B. Athletes are responsible for their actions and have to take the consequences.

C. People's actions must be judged.

Whoever preaches absence of discipline is an enemy of progress.

MAX NORDAU

10. State whether you strongly agree (SA), tend to agree (TA), tend to disagree (TD), or strongly disagree (SD) with each of the following.

A. SA TA TD SD   Athletes should be seen and not heard.

B. SA TA TD SD   The majority of misbehaviors and problems can be traced to a lack of firm discipline.

C. SA TA TD SD   It is better to reward good behavior than to punish bad behavior.

D. SA TA TD SD   A coach should never raise his or her voice in anger to an athlete.

E. SA TA TD SD   The best way to eliminate bad behavior is with severe punishment.

F. SA TA TD SD   Athletes will always take advantage of a coach who is not strict.

G. SA TA TD SD   When misbehavior begins to appear, stop it immediately before it becomes a pattern.

H. SA TA TD SD   "Spare the rod and spoil the child."

Unless we win our children's hearts today, they will break our hearts tomorrow.
UNKNOWN

Scoring:
Find your score by adding up the sum of your responses

1. A. 4   B. 2   C. 0
2. A. 4   B. 2   C. 0
3. A. 4   B. 2   C. 0
4. A. 0   B. 4   C. 2
5. A. 4   B. 0   C. 2
6. A. 0   B. 4   C. 2
7. A. 2   B. 0   C. 4
8. A. 2   B. 4   C. 0
9. A. 0   B. 4   C. 2

10.	SA	TA	TD	SD
A.	4	3	2	0
B.	4	3	2	0
C.	0	2	3	4
D.	0	2	3	4
E.	4	3	2	0
F.	4	3	2	0
G.	4	3	2	0
H.	4	3	2	0

The hardest faults to excuse in children are those they have observed in you.
UNKNOWN

Analysis:

Over 48   You are a very intolerant person. You are probably authoritarian, defensive, and opinionated. If you scored in this category, you may want to ask yourself why you are unable to accept faults in others.

32–47   You are not as tolerant as most other people are. You are probably bothered by little things and waste a lot of emotional energy. Try to focus on the significant problems rather than trivia. Try to have more genuine relationships with other people and experience more of life. If you do, your score will come down.

16–31   You are a reasonably tolerant person, and people will see you as one. You are accepting of the views of others.

Below 16   You are a very tolerant person. You are able to put yourself in another person's shoes and have empathy for their problems and difficulties. You are accepting even when you are offended.

Major Points Discussed in Chapter 13

1. In the realm of athletics, discipline is training players in mind and character to enable them to become self-controlled and constructive members of society.
2. Good discipline is time consuming because teaching players about discipline and responsibility requires planning and practice.
3. The three basic models of discipline discussed in this chapter are:
   a. hostile discipline, which is based on punishment;
   b. permissive discipline, which allows freedom without rules, limits, or order; and
   c. empowering discipline, which requires a balance between fairness and respect.
4. Anger can get in the way of empowering discipline.
5. Coaches must control their anger before they discipline.
6. Punishment usually involves a threat that obligates the player to either obey or resist rather than to think constructively and respond.
7. Punishment degrades, dehumanizes, and humiliates players. Consequently, it hurts feelings, evokes anger, and incites resistance and withdrawal.

14

Coaching toward
Self-Discipline:
Using Natural and
Logical Consequences

*Why do I so frequently need to be protected from those
who love me?*

Ashleigh Brilliant

Consequences are the second part of a rule. They speak louder
than the coach's words. Consequences support the rule. They
stop the misbehavior. Consequences should be kept simple and
are designed so that their implementation will not cause severe
disruption to ongoing athletic activities.

Athletes learn in a variety of ways. They learn by trial and
error, by being told things, by watching others, and through
experience. In life, one's actions are often followed by natural
or logical consequences. If a person is late getting to the bus
stop, he will miss the bus (natural consequence). If an athlete
goes out too quickly in the mile run, she will fade in the end
(natural consequence). If the employee does not attend work
regularly, he may be fired (logical consequence). If a player
commits five personal fouls in a basketball game, she is out of
the game (logical consequence). No one is trying to hurt or an-
noy anyone. These consequences are merely the way things
work. Through them, however, people learn to behave in certain ways if they want to avoid undesired results and achieve
their goals.

It is not recommended that coaches rescue athletes from the
logical and natural consequences of their actions and choices as
long as the consequences are reasonable and safe. However, a
coach would never risk a nonswimmer's being hurt as a natural
consequence of jumping into the swimming pool or permanently
dismiss an athlete from the team as a logical consequence of
missing practice due to sickness.

Natural Consequences

Natural consequences follow naturally after an event. If you play golf in the rain, you get wet. If you wear shoes that are too tight, you get blisters. If you don't drink water while running the marathon, you get dehydrated. If you don't water the plants, they will die. The connections are direct and clear. Natural consequences place the responsibility for the behavior directly on the athlete performing that behavior. A natural consequence is a natural lesson for the athlete and does not require any intervention on the part of the coach. Natural consequences are easy to use. Listed below are some situations in which you can use natural consequences.

1. When athletes keep forgetting. If athletes are in the habit of forgetting, the coach must allow the consequence of forgetting to occur. The coach cannot keep reminding players or rescuing them from their forgetting by doing things for them that they should be doing for themselves.

At a recent road game, John came running out of the locker room yelling, "Oh, no! I left my basketball shoes at home!" His coach angrily muttered, "John, this is the second time you have forgotten something. Why are you so careless? Get your street clothes on, and we will go down to the nearest sport store, and I'll get you a pair. We've got to hurry. The game starts in an hour."

The coach would have used natural consequences if he had said, "John, I'm sure you feel terrible about forgetting your shoes. Can you think of anything you can do to solve the problem?"

John might suggest that he would try borrowing a pair or that he would buy a pair at the nearest sport store. If neither of these suggestions was workable, the natural consequence of John's forgetting would be that he could not play in the game.

By helping John find ways to solve his own problem (rather than solving it for him), the coach guides John to focus on his problem of forgetfulness. John will realize that his discomfort results from the natural consequence of his forgetfulness. If John is not allowed to play because of his forgetfulness, he will probably never forget his shoes or anything else again in the future.

The decision not to let John play is a difficult one because the game is important not only to John but also to the coach and the team. If this were a first-time offense, the coach might decide to help problem-solve the situation with John and find a way to get a pair of shoes. However, if it is habitual for John to forget, the coach must let the consequences occur.

2. When athletes fail to live up to their responsibilities. Let the athlete experience the results of his or her actions.

Lisa was habitually late. There were numerous occasions

when the team had to wait for Lisa to arrive. The other players resented her being late and nicknamed her "Late Lisa." However, Lisa's behavior did not change.

The team was leaving for an away game at 7:30 A.M., and it was important that the bus leave on time. The coach suggested that everybody try to arrive a little early to avoid any problems. Lisa was nowhere in sight at the announced departure time. The coach ordered the bus driver to leave. Lisa arrived 20 minutes later and, consequently, missed the bus and the game.

In the beginning, Lisa was not learning from her experiences. However, missing the trip and the game caused Lisa to reevaluate her behavior. On the next occasion she was early. She was never late for another trip.

3. When athletes lose or damage equipment or clothes because of carelessness, misuse, or lack of responsibility. Do not repair or replace the damaged or lost item until enough time has passed for the athlete to experience its loss.

Within three days of receiving her new team volleyball uniform, Evelyn forgot her sweatshirt and left it on a chair in the school cafeteria, and it disappeared. She begged for another one and blamed the other students for their dishonesty in taking the sweatshirt. The coach recognized how important it is for young athletes to proudly wear team clothing in public. Sympathetic to Evelyn's pleading, the coach gave her another sweatshirt. One month later, Evelyn lost it.

The coach had learned her lesson, but Evelyn had not. After the first incident the coach could have offered another plan: "I'm going to give you an old team sweatshirt. When you show me you can be responsible for it, we will be ready to talk about how you might get a new one."

Logical Consequences

Logical consequences require the coach's intervention. They are the result of structured situations in which young athletes learn to be responsible within a social order. If an athlete skips practice without permission, the athlete doesn't play in the upcoming game. If a player breaks curfew, the player doesn't make the next road trip. If a basketball player commits a fifth personal foul, the player is out of the game.

The law of consequences has not been repealed.
ANONYMOUS

The connection between the situation or the behavioral act and the consequence must be logically related. It is important that the athlete see the connection between cause and effect. Fighting, for example, causes the coach to remove the player from the game.

When players know what is expected and do not comply with the rules, they learn from the consequences of their behavior. A logical consequence is not punishment. For example, if a player knows that he is going to have to run ten laps around the track for finishing last in a drill, that is not a logical consequence. Nelsen [1987] suggests that consequences must be *related* to the behavior, *respectful,* and *reasonable* to both the coach and player. In addition, logical consequences should be agreed on in advance by both the coach and players. Therefore, it must be *revealed.* If a misbehavior occurs that was not previously discussed, player(s) and coach should problem-solve the situation. Logical consequences can then be determined for future reference.

> *Every failure teaches a man something if he will learn.*
> DICKENS

Unfortunately, some coaches think of logical consequences as a way to punish athletes for what they have done instead of focusing on solutions for the future. What happens if a logical consequence for a particular behavior is not obvious? The answer is that a logical consequence is not appropriate if it is not obviously related to the behavior.

There is not a logical consequence for every problem or behavior. If there is no logical consequence, look for a solution. This situation gives the coach a tremendous opportunity to work together with the athletes to find a solution through problem solving. Getting athletes to help in deciding on the consequences is a wonderful learning opportunity for all.

The following are situations in which coaches can use logical consequences.

1. Purposeful destruction of equipment. Make the player repair, replace, or pay for the item.

In a fit of anger, Kyle threw and broke his batting helmet against the dugout wall. After Kyle calmed down, the coach calmly asked him how he might vent his anger more constructively. After getting a reasonable response, the coach added, "How do you want to pay for a new batting helmet?" Kyle never threw a helmet again.

2. When athletes make a mess. Make the athletes clean up the mess.

The exuberant athletes leave the locker room in a mess after an important playoff win. The coach announces, "Nobody leaves until the mess in the locker room is cleaned up." Shawna replies, "We promise we will do it after the celebration party." "There won't be any celebrating until it's done," the coach responds. Everyone wants to attend the celebration party. The locker room is picked up within five minutes.

3. Misuse of athletic equipment. Temporarily take the item away from the athlete.

Tim, a college javelin thrower, noticed that the archery targets had been left out on the athletic field. Perceiving this situation as a new challenge, Tim started throwing the javelin at the target. The coach said, "Tim, that's not what the javelin or the archery target is used for. You can have the javelin back tomorrow if you use it right."

4. When athletes misuse or abuse any of their team privileges. Temporarily withdraw or modify the privilege.

Sarah borrowed a volleyball to practice her setting skills at home. She forgot to bring it to practice the next day. On its return the following day, the coach said, "You may not bring the volleyball home for the rest of the week. You can try again next week."

A little experience often upsets a lot of theory.
CADMAN

Helping Athletes to Learn From Their Behavior

Coaches often interrupt the natural process of learning from consequences by rescuing athletes from adversity. When coaches rescue, the athletes miss out on important lessons. The undesirable behavior is therefore more likely to be repeated. For example, the logical consequence for an athlete's failing a class is ineligibility. However, if the coach rescues the athlete by asking the teacher to make special allowances, it teaches the athlete that rules can be bent and that his or her athletic ability has precedence over scholastic responsibilities.

A coach must make a strong commitment to help athletes learn about life from their own behaviors and from the social system. This must be done in an atmosphere of dignity, respect, and firmness. The choice not to rescue is a difficult one. The choice must be appropriate to the age and maturity level of the athlete and the situation. Obviously, if an athlete is being abused and does not have the resources to deal with it, a coach must choose to rescue. When the situation endangers an athlete's emotional or physical safety , the coach has the moral obligation to intervene.

The memory strengthens as you lay burdens upon it.
THOMAS DE QUINCEY

However, when an athlete's safety is not at issue, a coach must be careful not to step in too quickly. If a coach steps in too quickly, the athlete will not have the opportunity to develop the tools that are necessary for positive growth.

Rather than rescuing, it is more appropriate to help the athlete learn from the experience. By reflecting on the experience, athletes can learn to make decisions on how to handle future situations. Explore the situation with thoughtful questions such as, "What is your understanding of what happened? Why do you think that happened? How do you think you might handle the situation differently the next time?" By exploring the experiences, a coach will help young athletes to develop good judgment skills.

Time-Out as a Logical Consequence

Time-out is the removal of the athlete from the situation. It stops the misbehavior by removing the athlete from the problem environment. Generally, time-outs are applied for aggressive, hurtful, disrespectful, or defiant behavior.

This method uses a time-out room or area that is devoid of interesting objects so that during this period the athlete talks to no one and has nothing to play with or to occupy his or her attention.

A time-out should not be used as punishment. It is not a prison sentence to force the athlete into compliance. Punitive time-outs are not constructive and cause aggression on the part of the athlete. A punitive time-out sounds like this: "Sit on the bench and keep your mouth shut until I'm ready to deal with you." The athlete is to remain on the bench for a lengthy period of time until he or she "learns his or her lesson." The value of any lesson is now lost.

Time-outs should simply be removal of the athlete from the environment in which the misbehavior is occurring. They are brief and used to help the athlete calm down and learn the rules. Once calm, the athlete and coach can communicate in a friendlier atmosphere to resolve the problem and learn from the situation.

The following are guidelines for using time-outs.

1. Select the appropriate time-out area in advance. Make sure it does not contain any stimuli that will hold the athlete's attention.

Second thoughts are even wiser.
Euripides

2. Keep the time-outs brief. Use a timer if necessary. Time-outs should not exceed 15 minutes. Older athletes can usually be given the option of returning when they feel they are ready to discuss the issue.

3. Time-outs should be applied immediately after a rule has been violated. For example, fighting is not okay, and the players should be given a time-out directly. If the athlete refuses to go to the time-out area, limited choices or consequences are applied to the situation.

4. Once the time-out is over, it is over. If the athlete is no longer misbehaving, do not use the incident as ammunition in future conflicts or as grounds for punishment in later incidents.

5. Apply time-outs every time they are required. Do not hesitate to use time-outs when they are needed. Over time, the athletes will learn the appropriate behaviors.

The Difference Between Punishment and Consequences

The following chart lists the differences between punishment and natural and logical consequences.

Wisdom is the scar tissue of experience.
UNKNOWN

Punishment	Natural and Logical Consequences
Makes coaches responsible for their players' behavior. They become policeman and judge.	Makes players responsible for their own behavior
Decisions are made by the coach. Players must obey or resist.	Players must decide which actions they want to take. Players must think constructively and respond.
Penalties are usually severe and unrelated.	Teaches that behavior results in a natural order of events rather than results that are based on the coach's mood.
Players are degraded, dehumanized, and humiliated.	Players feel powerful and secure in the outcome of events.
Creates anger and hurt feelings and invites resistance or withdrawal.	Creates less guilt and hostility in the coach, since he or she is not directly involved in the decision.

Coaching Beyond Consequences

It is important to use logical consequences as a way of focusing on solutions rather than punishment. Nelsen, Lott, and Glenn, [1992], have given the following seven suggestions for going beyond consequences and/or making sure consequences are not disguised punishment.

1. If a consequence is not obvious, it is not appropriate. If an athlete kicks the ball over the fence in anger, it would be logical (also related, respectful, and reasonable) to have that athlete retrieve it. It would not be logical to have the athlete run ten laps around the track.

2. Focus on solutions. Rather than looking for consequences, look for solutions.

3. Involve athletes in solutions. The players can be your greatest resource. Tap into their wisdom and talent for solving problems when you are looking for a solution.

4. Logical consequences might be appropriate when opportunity = responsibility = consequence. For every opportunity (such as new equipment) there is a responsibility (such as taking care of equipment). When athletes choose not to take care of equipment, the consequence is to lose the opportunity of having new equipment. However, consequences are effective only if they are enforced respectfully and athletes have another chance when they are ready for the responsibility.

5. Focus on the future. Look for solutions that will help athletes to learn instead of focusing on the past.

6. Avoid piggybacking. Coaches must avoid following a consequence with punishing statements or acts. For example, the coach piggybacks a consequence with such statements as "Maybe you'll think twice the next time!" or "Just sit there and think about what you've done." Do not make athletes "pay" for their actions. Help athletes learn from their experiences with dignity and respect.

7. Plan ahead. Enlist the aid of your athletes in deciding on consequences in advance. For example, the coach might say, "What would be a logical consequence for coming to practice late?" Team forums (discussed in Chapter 16) and problem-solving sessions are excellent opportunities to ask players for their help.

Prelude to disaster: "We have done everything for that boy."
ANONYMOUS

TIME OUT: IN THE COACH'S CORNER

Experience is knowing the effects which follow one's acts.
UNKNOWN

What Happens When There is No Rule?

During the track meet, Mohammed approaches Coach Chin and says that he has to leave the track meet immediately after he competes in his only event. He needs to get home early to get ready for a concert that he and his friends are attending that evening.

Coach Chin, surprised by this request, says, "Absolutely not! You need to stay for the entire meet and support your teammates."

Mohammed pleads, "But, coach, everyone doesn't support me when I'm competing. They're off doing their own thing. You have never said we couldn't leave early. This isn't fair. Besides, I've already paid for the tickets."

Turning his back and walking away, Coach Chin says sternly, "End of discussion, Mohammed. You should know you're supposed to stay for the entire meet. If you decide to leave, don't bother to come to practice because you will be off the team."

Multiple Choice

If you were Coach Chin, what would you have done?

A. I would have done the same as Coach Chin.

B. I would have allowed Mohammed to go home after explaining to him that no athlete will be allowed to leave early in future meets.

C. I would have explained to Mohammed why he needs to stay and support his teammates and let him make his own decision about leaving early.

D. I would have allowed Mohammed to leave but told him that the next time, he must let me know at least one day before the meet.

Responses B and D are both correct. There was no rule about leaving a track meet early. Coach Chin cannot assume that all athletes have the same supportive attitude that he has. Mohammed, of course, cannot always know what coach Chin is thinking. If it is an issue that is important to Coach Chin, he must incorporate it into team rules and regulations, but not spring it on the player at the moment the issue arises. In other words, it must be revealed ahead of time.

If Coach Chin doesn't mind an athlete's leaving under unique circumstances, he must establish a policy that clearly states when the request for early departure must be made. Coach Chin must also define what he means by unique circumstances.

Another approach is to put this issue on the agenda during the next team forum. The procedure for team forums is discussed in Chapter 16.

Response A is not fair to Mohammed. You cannot punish someone if they don't know what you are thinking. Mohammed would always feel that he was unfairly punished. Punishment will always create a barrier in any relationship.

It is easy to be in tune with the past; it is tough to be in tune with the future.
ANONYMOUS

Response C is a strategy to create guilt. Of course, Mohammed is going to leave early. He has spent money to get his tickets and is looking forward to the concert. If Coach Chin has strong feelings about this issue, this approach will change nothing for the future. No rule or policy has been established.

QUESTIONS AND ANSWERS

Question: I have to constantly repeat and remind a particular athlete to do things. What can I do to avoid this routine?

Answer: Repeating and reminding is exactly what the athlete wants you to do. It is a form of passive-aggressive behavior (power) in which the athlete ignores or tunes you out, and it is easy to fall into his game. One simple method to overcome this situation is to use a simple "check-in" procedure by saying one of the following: "Do you understand what I said?" "Were my directions clear?" or "What did you hear me say?" If the athlete chooses to ignore the message after checking in, he is testing your limits. You must apply the consequences.

A man must become wise at his own expense.
Montaigne

Question: What should I do when I apply a logical consequence and my player says she doesn't care?

Answer: Nothing. It is her problem, not yours. Applying the consequence still makes the player accountable for her unacceptable behavior.

Question: Are there any specific rules that I should consider when applying consequences?

Answer: Yes. Here are four rules to consider:
1. Consequences must be effective. A consequence is a consequence only if it works. If the behavior does not stop or diminish, the consequence is not working. A more effective consequence must be used.
2. Consequences must be applied immediately. If the consequence cannot be delivered promptly, its effect will be weakened.
3. The consequence must be controlled or made contingent on the behavior. A reinforcer that has been arranged to be contingent on the occurrence of a particular behavior must be delivered when the misbehavior occurs. A consequence that cannot be delivered after the behavior should not be used.
4. A consequence must be consistent. It must be consistently applied from one occasion to the next. It must also be consistently applied to all players.

Major Points Discussed in Chapter 14

1. Consequences support the rules.
2. Natural consequences follow naturally after an event.
3. Logical consequences require the coach's intervention and are the result of structural situations in which young athletes learn to be responsible within a social structure.
4. Logical consequences must be:
   a. related to the behavior,
   b. respectful,

    c. reasonable to both the coach and player, and

    d. revealed or agreed on in advance.

5. Time-outs should simply be the removal of the athlete from the environment in which the misbehavior is occurring.

6. A time-out should not be used as punishment.

7. Punishment and natural and logical consequences are not the same.

8. Rather than always looking for logical consequences, a coach should look for solutions. In this way, coach and player can be working together for the common good.

15

Conflict Resolution

If the blind lead the blind, both shall fall into the ditch.

Matthew 15:14

Coaches who are dictators don't have to be concerned about conflict or solving problems because they make all the decisions. They take the position that they are right and if the player doesn't like it, "tough." However, most coaches don't operate completely in that manner, so, like it or not, a coach must be a negotiator when conflict occurs. Negotiation is a basic means of getting what the coach wants from others. It is a process in which a coach and player(s) reach an agreement when both sides have some interests that are shared and others that are in conflict.

The process of negotiation has become an important tool in the lives of most people who work with others. Players want to participate in decisions that affect them; most are unwilling to accept decisions that are dictated to them. Over time, autocratic coaches will lose control.

Negotiating a conflict, of course, is not easy. If a coach doesn't have the tools or strategies for effective negotiation, both players and coach will usually end up frustrated, tired, and/or alienated. Typically, coaches approach negotiation from one of two typical positions: (1) Afraid of personal conflict, the coach makes amicable compromises that leave him or her feeling exploited and angry. (2) The coach must win because the coach feels that if he or she doesn't, control and authority are lost. Some coaches may also find themselves fluctuating somewhere between these two positions because they do not have a clear perspective of which is right. Both positions are wrong.

Before specific steps for resolving conflict are discussed, it is important to discuss certain principles that set the foundation for fair negotiations. Negotiating conflict in a fair and dignified manner requires the following prerequisites: (1) caring and respect and (2) the seven operating assumptions defined by Gerstein and Reagan [1986].

Caring and Respect as the Foundations of Negotiations

Understanding basic human needs and how they become frustrated or satisfied is the first step in understanding how conflicts between individuals can be resolved. Most everyday conflicts have either a psychological or a social basis rather than a physical or material foundation. Conflict usually results from unfulfilled psychosocial needs such as the desire to feel accepted, significant, and capable. Most conflicts that coaches have with their athletes and others can be resolved through improving human relations and satisfying each other's basic needs.

Cooperation is spelled with two letters—WE
GEORGE VERITY

Most conflicts cannot be completely resolved or prevented if respect and empathetic caring do not exist between the individuals who are in conflict. Only when people respect each other and care about each other's basic needs can conflict be turned into mutual respect and cooperation with lasting agreement and order. Consequently, caring and respect are the most important ingredients in conflict resolution in all aspects of one's life.

Operating Assumptions for Approaching Conflict

Gerstein and Reagan [1986], in their book *Win-Win: Approaches to Conflict Resolution,* listed the following seven operating assumptions for approaching conflict:

1. **All needs are legitimate and important and must be attended to.** When all needs are considered to be of equal importance, the task shifts to a search for options to meet all needs instead of seeing the task as having to prove which need should be addressed. For example, a coach may feel that the gymnast is ready to advance to a more difficult trick while the athlete argues against it because he or she is focused on the fear of injury. At this point it is exceedingly difficult for either side to hear the needs of the other.

2. **There are enough resources to meet all needs.** There is no limitation on the human potential to create new ideas and resources. The concept of human synergy tells us that all of us collectively know more than any one of us.

3. **Within every individual lie untapped power and capacity and people in conflict know better what they need than outside experts can.** Coaches cannot impose their own solutions based on their own idea of what they believe is the athlete's problem. Imposing solutions without recognizing the need will create unwilling athletes.

4. Process is as important as content because it provides direction and focus. Process is the flow of feelings, thoughts, and events. If one becomes too fixed on particular details of content, one misses important valuable clues and information about what is going on and what people are doing. Often the intended listener is so caught up in specific pieces of content, either rehearsing an attack or thinking of evidence to support a position, that the process that is going on is totally missed.

5. Improving situations is different from solving problems. It focuses on the underlying causes rather than just eliminating the problem or symptom. For example, physical exercise may relieve the tension that arises from the stresses in people's lives, but it does not focus on what causes the stress or the problem.

6. Everyone is right from his or her own perspective. Therefore, if it is possible to move inside the situation to see it from the other person's perspective, a coach can come up with a resolution that is more favorable to both parties. In many conflict situations, people spend an inordinate amount of time defending or supporting their own positions and points of view. This can be exhausting and wasteful. Continual arguing only teaches people more ways to argue and leads to lose–lose outcomes.

7. Solutions and resolutions are temporary states of balance and are not absolute or timeless. They depend on the flux of circumstances and human changeability. That is why contracts are renegotiable and not irrevocable. When circumstances change, we also expect an adult to recognize those changes and alter his or her actions so that a dynamic balance can be reached.

Successful collaborative negotiation lies in finding out what the other side really wants and showing them a way to get it— while you get what you want.
HERB COHEN

The Four Steps to Problem Solving

It is important to remember that problem solving and negotiation are not debates or trials. They are processes of building relationships. They require a coach to focus on the problem and separate the people from the issue. The basic approach to problem solving is to deal with people as human beings who deserve the respect and dignity that you expect from them. A coach should negotiate the problem or conflict only on its own merits. The following four steps are useful in resolving conflict.

1. Self-perception. A coach must believe that "I can solve the problem." The first step in successful problem solving is for the coach to develop the belief that he or she is a problem solver and can negotiate a fair and honest settlement. A problem solver accepts the fact that problem situations are a normal part of life and that it is important to face such challenges calmly and rationally, not impulsively.

Some coaches despise personal conflict and make concessions to try to reach quick and amicable resolutions that leave them feeling exploited and angry. A true problem solver knows that he or she can rely on his or her problem-solving skills to decide on a reasonable and fair course of action.

In addition, some coaches have attitudes that reflect the opposite extreme. They feel that "Someone has to suffer," "This can't make a difference," "You really can't trust anyone," or "I can't let you win, so I'm going to argue." These are examples of negative beliefs that obstruct progress in conflict resolution. "It is possible to make a difference," "It is possible for everyone to win," and "It is possible to learn to trust ourselves and others" are examples of positive beliefs that can lead to fair resolutions.

2. What's wrong? Identify the problem or situation to be improved. The first thing to do when faced with a challenge or conflict is to understand exactly what is happening by defining the problem. The process of identifying the true problem is extremely important because your emotions often distort objective thinking.

Unfortunately, many coaches try to argue or defend their position rather than focusing on the underlying concerns of all parties. Consequently, fair resolution is unlikely, and less satisfactory decisions are usually made.

To avoid taking positions, a simple process is to have each party write in one sentence, on a separate sheet of paper, what he or she thinks the problem is. This simple procedure will often solve the problem without any further steps. Viewing the problem from the other person's perspective often creates an immediate understanding of the situation. Seeing the problem from the other person's point of view puts the problem into a mutual perspective. Then together, describe the situation on one single sheet of paper.

3. What could be done? Brainstorm to generate options to improve the situation. The procedures for brainstorming are as follows.

Life cannot subsist in society but by reciprocal concessions.
SAMUEL JOHNSON

A. List all options that could be taken to improve the situation. All ideas are valid and welcomed. They are not judged, criticized, or commented on. Write down each option on a blackboard or large sheet of paper so that all concerned can see. This process gives the parties involved a tangible sense of collective achievement, encourages greater participation and creativity, reduces the tendency to repeat, and helps to stimulate other ideas.

B. Whenever appropriate, consolidate ideas by joining or combining one with another. After viewing them, mark the most promising ideas that may be worth developing further.

C. Select a plan of action. Become selective by evaluating each of the ideas. Through a process of discussion without criticism, choose the best of the listed options. Be willing to invent ways to make some of the more promising ideas better or more realistic. If more than one option is going to be used, make a rank-ordered list of what you will do first.

No man will work for your interests unless they are his.
DAVID SEABURY

4. Get commitments from each party and follow through on accountability. This final step is to carry out the appropriate option(s) to improve the situation. The selected option is then evaluated after a predetermined period of time to determine whether it is working. If it is not working, the brainstorming process is started over.

Regardless of the conflict, the process of problem solving is consistent, and the basic steps do not change. Problem solving can be used whether there is one or several issues and whether there are two or more individuals. This simple process is a great equalizer because it eliminates two major factors that may be perceived as advantages: experience of individuals and dominating personalities. Most important, conflict resolution through problem solving becomes easier with practice.

QUESTIONS AND ANSWERS

Question: What if I am trying to resolve a conflict and the player doesn't want to participate in the spirit of fair negotiation and begins attacking me or my proposals?

Answer: If the player attacks you or your proposals instead of the problem, Fisher and Ury [1983] suggest three basic approaches to resolve this problem.

1. Focus on what you shouldn't do and what you can do. Do not push back. If the players attack your ideas, don't defend them. If they attack you, don't counterattack. If they assert their position, do not reject them. Break the vicious cycle by refusing to react. Instead of pushing back, sidestep the attack and deflect it against the problem by using these three maneuvers:

   A. Don't attack the players' position; look behind it by seeking out the principles that it reflects, and think about ways to improve it. Instead of making statements, ask questions. Statements usually generate resistance, whereas questions generate answers. Questions allow the players to get their point across and help you to understand them. If you ask respectful and honest questions, wait in silence to allow the player to respond. If the answer is insufficient, just wait. People who have doubts about what they have just said are uncomfortable with silence. When you ask questions, pause. Some of the most effective negotiating is accomplished when you are not talking.

It might be just as offensive to be around a man who never changed his mind as one who never changed his clothes.

Country parson

B. Don't defend your ideas; invite evaluation and advice. Instead of asking the athletes to accept or reject your idea, ask them what's wrong with it. Say for example, "What concerns of yours do my suggestions fail to take into account?" Rework your ideas in light of what you learn from them, and turn criticism from an obstacle into a working solution to the problem.

C. Remember that an attack on you is really an attack on the problem. Listen to and show the players that you understand what they are saying. When they are finished, redirect their attack on you and focus on the problem. Use constructive communication to help the athlete rechannel or refocus their verbal energies toward solutions to the conflict.

Question: What if I realize that I am the guilty party and that it was my behavior that caused the conflict between myself and the athlete? Is there anything that I can do to resolve the situation and still maintain my dignity?

Answer: Nobody is perfect. We all make mistakes. Sometimes we do or say things that we truly regret. We tend to criticize ourselves and make negative judgments about our behaviors. However, instead of viewing mistakes as negative elements in our lives, if we see them as opportunities to learn, we can grow and change in more positive ways.

Lott and Nelsen [1988] recommend that by using the "Four R's of Recovery (Recognition, Responsibility, Reconciliation and Resolution)," you can make your relationship with your players better than it was before you made a mistake.

1. **Recognition.** Nobody is perfect, and we all make mistakes. Admit that you made a mistake and that what you did or said was inappropriate. It is important to be comfortable with saying, "I made a mistake."

2. **Responsibility.** Responsibility means describing what you did. Your description should be void of any guilt as well as any accusing remarks that may have provoked your outburst. Take responsibility for your part in the conflict that was created by your mistake. Be specific in telling your athlete the nature of your mistake: "I am sorry for swearing at you. My language was entirely inappropriate, and there really is no excuse for what I said."

3. **Reconciliation.** Apologize. Say, for example, "I apologize for making fun of you in front of your teammates. I treated you disrespectfully, and I'm sorry for any hurt that I may have created." One of the wonderful aspects of young athletes that you may have already discovered is their readiness to forgive when we are willing to apologize.

4. **Resolution.** When appropriate, take action to fix any damage that might have occurred from your actions. Also, if necessary, design a strategy that you and the players are satisfied with in case the problem occurs again.

Of course, athletes make mistakes too. You can teach them the Four R's of Recovery. The best way to teach this skill is to model it with your own behavior when working with your athletes.

TIME OUT: IN THE COACH'S CORNER

What Happens When the Coach is Disrespectful?
It was the bottom of the ninth inning, with one out, runners on first and third bases, and the score tied. The rest of the infield was pulled in, but Reggie stayed close to first base to keep the base runner from stealing second base. Reggie held his breath as the pitcher released the ball toward the batter.

With the crack of the bat, Reggie moved in to catch the slowly bouncing ball. As he leaned down to cradle the ball in his glove, he saw the runner on third hesitate slightly and begin to turn back toward third. In a moment of excitement and confusion, Reggie turned and threw the ball toward second base just as the runner on third stopped, turned, and broke full speed toward home plate. There was no hope of getting a double play. In that moment of confusion, Reggie could only watch the ball sail toward second base as the runner sped toward home plate. The moment Reggie released the ball, he realized his mistake and knew that the runner had tricked him and would easily score the winning run.

It was a very frustrating season for Coach Martinez. It was the first time in his career that he had a losing season and the first time that he had ever lost three games in a row. He was putting

We are judged by what we finish, not by what we start.
ANONYMOUS

pressure on himself and the team to turn the season around. If they won this game, the team still had an outside chance of making the playoffs. A loss would surely end the season short of any tournament play.

Coach Martinez felt his frustration and anger rise as he watched the runner cross home plate. Reggie stood for a moment and turned toward the dugout. He could see the fury in the face of Coach Martinez. Reggie jogged tentatively toward the dugout.

As he threw his hat to the ground in disgust, Coach Martinez shouted, "Reggie, how could you have been so stupid? Any lame-brained idiot would have known to throw the ball home. Your bonehead play cost us the game and any chance of making the play-offs."

Reggie, embarrassed by his mistake as well as being the object of the coach's rage, with head down, sheepishly responded, "Coach, I'm sorry. I don't know what happened."

"I know what happened. You screwed up. Now, get out of my sight."

Reggie, near tears but comforted by some teammates, slowly turned away. With his back to the coach, he could hear the coach's final words:"Stupid (bleep) idiot!"

Can This Relationship Be Saved?
Until Coach Martinez recognizes that he made a mistake in the language and attitude that he displayed to Reggie and the other players, he will not be able to repair the damage that was done. However, if Coach Martinez recognizes the error of his behavior, he can follow the Four R's of Recovery recommended by Lott and Nelsen. This process can be the starting point to recovery.

Nothing relieves and ventilates the mind like a solution.
JOHN BURROUGHS

1. *Recognition:* "Reggie, I made a mistake."
2. *Responsibility:* "I lost my temper and used vulgar language and made unkind and uncalled for remarks. I am truly sorry. There is no excuse for what I said."
3. *Reconciliation:* "I am sorry if I hurt you in any way, and I will also apologize to your teammates for the way I treated you in front of them. I was wrong. I will try to keep my temper under control."
4. *Resolution:* "Reggie, if there is anything more that I can do to mend this situation, please tell me."

How Could Coach Martinez Have Handled the Situation in the First Place?
A perceptive Coach Martinez would already have known that Reggie was embarrassingly aware of his mistake and emotionally devastated by it. Any further negative comments would

serve no purpose except to punish Reggie. There would be no value in punishing him. Coach Martinez could offer a supportive gesture by placing a comforting hand on Reggie's shoulder and talk with him a little later.

It is not who is right but what is right.

ANONYMOUS

Once the emotions were somewhat dissipated, Coach Martinez could help Reggie to eliminate the same mistake in future. He might ask, "Reggie, what happened?"

"Coach, I don't know. I was confused, and I wasn't sure what to do. It wasn't until I threw the ball that I knew I had really screwed up."

"Can you think of anything that we could do to prevent something like this from happening again?"

"Yeah, Coach, I've had a little time to think about it. Maybe in tight situations like that, a communication system can be set up so everyone knows exactly what to do."

"You mean, like calling a time out and bringing everybody together or having some type of communication or relay system where the players spread the word to each other?"

"Yeah, something like that."

"Great idea! The team can talk about it at our next practice."

In this process, Coach Martinez treats Reggie with respect, and together they develop a system to prevent similar errors in the future. Both individuals profit from this experience.

Major Points Discussed in Chapter 15

1. Negotiating a conflict is not easy.
2. A coach should not be afraid of personal conflict.
3. Don't use power in negotiating
4. Caring and respect are the foundations of negotiation.
5. The operating assumptions for approaching conflict are that:
   a. all needs are legitimate;
   b. there are enough resources to meet all needs;
   c. within every individual lie untapped power and capacity;
   d. process is as important as content;
   e. improving situations is different from solving problems;
   f. everyone is right from his or her own perspective; and
   g. solutions and resolutions are temporary states of balance.
6. The four basic steps to problem solving are:
   a. one must believe that "I can solve the problem";
   b. identify the problem;

   c. brainstorm solutions; and

   d. get commitments from each party.

7. The Four R's of Recovery are:

   a. recognition;

   b. responsibility;

   c. reconciliation; and

   d. resolution.

PART

V

Putting It All Together

16

The Team Forum

We must all hang together, else we shall all hang separately.

Benjamin Franklin
(on signing the Declaration of Independence)

The team forum was designed to help coaches and players make plans and decisions, provide encouragement, and solve problems. It provides an opportunity for all to be heard on issues arising within the team. The topics that can be discussed in a team forum cover a wide range of issues such as beliefs, values, wishes, complaints, plans, questions, and suggestions. An empowered team thrives on making decisions together. Team forums improve communications, cooperation, and responsibility and, most important, reflect how fortunate the athletes are to have each other.

Most coaches will be surprised when teams take the time to meet together to decide what needs to be done and how to do it. Coaches will discover that players are likely to be more responsible and cooperative in following through when they have input into the decision-making process. Successful forums help team members learn to share responsibility and solve problems together.

What a Team Forum Is

The team forum is a regularly scheduled meeting that is designed to provide an opportunity for the coach and the players to learn the democratic procedure of cooperation, mutual respect, emotional honesty, and responsibility. These forums:

- promote team harmony through the establishment of rules;
- help to solve problems in a cooperative manner;

- help team members to make decisions through a democratic process;
- encourage team members by recognizing the good things happening within the team and pointing out strengths of individual members;
- allow everyone to be listened to—not just heard, but understood;
- allow individual members to express concerns, feelings, and complaints;
- enable teams to practice honest dialog;
- provide leadership opportunities by providing each team member the chance to chair team forums;
- allows each team member to be taken seriously—not just understood but accepted and respected;
- allow each team member to feel genuinely appreciated for his or her own personal worth, contributions, and significance.

*A committee is
a group that
does together
what's tough or
even impossible
to do alone.*
EDGAR DALE

What a Team Forum Is Not

A team forum is not a meeting in which the coach can lecture and moralize to the players. Nor is it an opportunity for the coach to exercise excessive control. Players will see through this behavior and will not cooperate. The coach is simply an equal member within the group. He or she has equal input and one equal vote.

The Team Forum Foundation: Mutual Respect and Emotional Honesty

Two of the most exciting aspects of the team forum are working with the established ground rules of mutual respect and emotional honesty. Dr. Jane Nelsen [1987] in her book *Positive Discipline*, said that mutual respect incorporates attitudes of (a) faith in the abilities of yourself and others, (b) interest in the point of view of others as well as your own, and (c) a willingness to take responsibility and ownership for your own contribution to the problem. Thus mutual respect means that coaches must allow for differences, staying away from judgments of right or wrong and blaming stances, and respect their own feelings as well as the feelings of others.

Lynn Lott, in an article about "family" meetings [in Lott and Nelsen, 1988], viewed emotional honesty as a learned skill. She defined the word *emotions* as feelings that happen inside of us. She used such words as *angry, happy, irritated, joyful,* and *hopeless.* Feelings aren't judgments about others and are different from thoughts. Feelings are neither good nor bad, and they aren't actions or behaviors. The feeling of anger is very different from a display of anger. We cannot always tell how a person is feeling from just observing his or her behavior. For example, people can smile even though they are angry. To really know how someone is feeling, we must ask them how or what they are feeling.

Communicating the "honesty" part of your feelings can be very frightening. When we communicate feelings, we are vulnerable, and sometimes the people around us do not listen sensitively but take things personally and react defensively. Listeners may try to explain our emotions away or correct them. But without emotional honesty there is little growth in the acceptance of oneself and others.

Emotional honesty works in both directions. We are emotionally honest when we communicate our feelings; on the other side, we are emotionally honest when we hear another's feelings without judging, criticizing, defending, assuming, explaining, or fixing. A major concern is that emotional honesty will hurt someone else's feelings. In an environment of mutual respect and cooperation the exact opposite is true. Emotional honesty opens communication and invites closeness and respect.

The Team Forum Structure

Team forums should be held at least once a week at a regularly scheduled time. This assures all members of a specific time at which they can discuss the issues that are important to them. These forums become an important ritual and tradition when they are regular and predictable.

Establish an appropriate amount of time for the forum. Thirty minutes to a maximum of one hour is the recommended time. Any issue that has not been concluded by the end of the meeting can be the first item on the agenda for the next forum. Stick to time limits.

> *The chief problem of this generation and succeeding generations is to put people in touch with each other—in mind and heart.*
> EDGAR DALE

A specific agenda is discussed at each forum. The agenda can be as simple as a list on a sheet of paper on a clipboard. The agenda is kept in a designated but easily accessible place, and team members add items to it during the week as issues arise that involve anyone on the team. The items are discussed in the order in which they were written on the agenda.

Each team member should have the opportunity to chair the meeting. A rotation schedule should be determined. The coach can chair the first few meetings to model the procedures. The chairperson starts and closes the forum at the times agreed on. He or she makes sure that all points of view are heard and tries to keep the discussion focused on the issue.

Keep minutes for each team forum so that a record of issues, plans, and decisions is kept. Some teams may find it helpful to post the minutes of each meeting so that team members can check on the agreements that were made. The role of the secretary should also be rotated.

How to Have Effective Team Forums

The following steps provide helpful guidelines that coaches can use for successful team forums.

1. Meet in a circle for team forums. Meeting in this fashion reduces some of the physical barriers that prevent dialog.
2. Begin with compliments, appreciations, thank-yous, or acknowledgments. This step is important because it sets the tone for pleasant communication. Since criticism and complaints are common in most teams, starting the meeting with appreciations helps to focus on the strengths and positives of individuals. Individuals who want to give a teammate or the coach a compliment will raise their hands, and the chairperson should go around the circle in a specific order and call on everyone who has a hand raised. The chairperson must not call on individuals randomly or arbitrarily choose when to stop. Instead of raising hands, an object such as an eraser may be used. The person who has the object in his or her hands may either speak or pass it on. Sometimes, especially in the beginning, individuals will have difficulty verbalizing compliments, and the coach may have to model this behavior by giving several compliments, such as "I would like to compliment (a person's name) for (something specific that person did)" or "I appreciated it when (name of person) because (something specific that person did)" or "I want to thank (a person's name) for (some specific action)."

   During the first few forums, everyone should give at least one appreciation. After this, appreciation can be optional. It is also a good idea to teach players to say thank you after receiving a compliment or acknowledgment.
3. Read and, if necessary, discuss the minutes from the previous forum.
4. Discuss old business (items left over from previous agenda).
5. Read the first item on the agenda. Ask the individual who wrote the item whether it is still an issue. If the problem no longer exists, simply move on to the next

item. If the problem still exists, ask the person to briefly explain the item on the agenda.

6. If another person is involved, asked the "accused" if he or she has a suggestion for a solution. If the "accused" does, ask the group to vote on the suggestion. If the majority vote agrees with the suggestion, go on to the next item.

7. If the "accused" has no suggestion or the suggestion is voted down, go around the circle twice for comments and suggestions. Start with the person who wrote the agenda item and end just before this person after going around the circle twice. All team members should be given the opportunity to make suggestions.

> *We cannot expect children to learn democracy unless they live democracy.*
> WILLIAM H. KILPATRICK

Especially in the early stages of team forums, it is important that the coach withhold his or her suggestions until the team members have finished giving theirs. Jumping in too quickly may be interpreted incorrectly, and some team members may think that the coach is trying to force his or her ideas on them.

8. The secretary writes down every suggestion exactly as it is stated.

9. After the list of suggestions has been completed, evaluate each suggestion in the order in which they were given. If this brainstorming process is done with mutual respect, it will encourage the willingness to participate in generating solutions. If a member's suggestion is rejected as soon as it is said, the person will probably stop giving ideas. When evaluation is postponed until all suggestions have been given, a member's idea may be seen as one of many that are not accepted by the team.

10. Read all suggestions before asking for a vote. Instruct individuals to vote for only one suggestion. Read the suggestions again, one at a time, and have the secretary record the number of people voting for each suggestion. Some issues may require a secret vote if some individuals are reluctant to vote publicly or there is a potential for individuals to be influenced by the way other team members vote.

> *Responsibility walks hand in hand with capacity and power.*
> JOSIAH HOLLAND

11. If a majority vote is not reached, table the item until next week with the words "It looks as if we're not ready yet to agree on a solution. Let's think of some other ideas this week and talk about them at our next forum." If it is an issue that needs immediate attention and a majority vote cannot be reached, the coach may have to make a temporary decision until the issue can be discussed again at the next forum. Obviously, a coach needs to be cautious with this procedure. A coach should never make such a decision in anger or revenge.

Smaller teams may choose to make decisions by consensus. By using consensus instead of voting, they develop group solidarity and teach cooperation. When decisions are made by majority rule, factions may develop, and competition may divide the group. Consensus can demonstrate that, no matter how difficult the problem, if a team persists, they can come up with a solution that will be acceptable to all. If consensus cannot be reached, the making of a decision is put off until a solution that is mutually satisfactory is reached.

12. When the final vote is in, ask the person for whom the solution was suggested when he or she would like to do it, and give two possibilities to choose from, such as today or tomorrow, or before or after practice. The reason for allowing choice is to give the individual some sense of power and commitment.

13. A final summary settles the decisions and commitments that were made during the forum: "Today, we decided _____. Is that the way everyone understands it?"

14. Post the meeting notes in an appropriate place that is accessible to all team members.

Ground Rules for Team Forums

The following rules were taken from *Preparing for the Drug (Free) Years* by Developmental Research and Programs, Inc. [1988]*:

Everyone gets a chance to talk.
One person talks at a time and doesn't get interrupted.
It's okay to say what you feel without attacking someone.
No one has to talk.
Everyone has to listen.
No one puts anyone else down.

Getting Started

It is amazing how much people can get done if they do not worry about who gets the credit.
SANDRA
SWINNEY

Betty Lou Bettner and Amy Lew, in their book *Raising Kids Who Can* [1992] have a chapter called "Getting Started." Some of their "family meeting" ideas have been modified for a team forum and incorporated below. One way to get started is to

*Permission to use selected information from the book, *Preparing for the Drug (Free) Years* © 1987, 1988 Developmental Research Programs and Comprehensive Health Education Foundation (C.H.E.F.®) was granted by C.H.E.F.®, Seattle, WA. All rights reserved.

have the coach introduce the idea of the team forum by saying, "I read this article about a process that teams can use for organizing themselves, making plans, and working out problems. I would like to try this plan with our team, maybe for a month, and see whether it can work for us."

Some coaches, excited about the idea of team forums, expect that their players will also share their excitement and see the value in it. However, some players may be suspicious of the coach's motives and may be resistant to the idea.

By uniting we stand, by dividing we fall.
JOHN DICKINSON

Start Slowly

One way to circumvent this problem is to start off slowly. Instead of introducing the team forum all at once, coaches can introduce the idea of team problem solving and decision making by simply asking everyone to get together for a specific purpose, such as planning a team social activity. The main point is that the topics should be of interest to the athletes. When fun is involved, most players are intrigued and are usually willing to take a chance. Other issues such as team curfews and missing practice could also be introduced. As these issues are being discussed, coaches can slowly introduce some of the ground rules of a team forum.

To introduce the idea of future expanded forums, coaches can ask the players for their input and feedback about how the planning session went. Some useful questions might be "Do you think this decision-making process worked well? What would you change? What made it fun? Was there anything that you didn't like? What other topics do you think we could discuss at future forums?"

The Team Goal

Teams may need several planning sessions before they develop the trust and skills that are necessary to add further agenda items. However, as the team members begin to recognize the advantages of establishing a regularly scheduled team meeting, they will be ready to develop it more fully. The coach can then introduce the idea of establishing a "Team Goal." The coach can introduce the idea of the Team Goal by asking the players to write down their answers to the following questions:

- "What would our team be like if it was the way you wanted it to be?"
- "Can you think of what this new and improved team might be like?"
- "If you were a coach, how would you like your team to be?"

It is important that everyone have the opportunity to come up with his or her own ideas before sharing with the others. It is important to make sure that everyone knows that nobody's ideas will be put down or judged. Coaches will be surprised to hear what is of real value to their players.

Be sure to remind the players to focus on what they would like, not what they don't like. This process will eliminate put-downs and defensiveness.

(don't like)	"I hate the way John is always yelling at people."
(would like)	"I would like people to speak respectfully to others."
(don't like)	"I can't stand it when Susie loafs during practice."
(would like)	"I would like everyone to give 100% during all the practice drills."

It is better to talk it out in a forum than to fight it out in an arena.

TOM LEHRER

After everyone has finished writing, it is time for sharing. Each person takes a turn reading his or her ideas. After the person shares his or her ideas, the other members of the team may respond in the form of "what I agree/disagree with," "what surprises me," "what I don't understand," and so on.

Bettner and Lew recommend that all the ideas then be separated into two categories: (1) qualities, how we would like the team to be, and (2) actions, what the team needs to do to be that way. Examples of qualities are closeness, respect, and cooperation. Examples of actions are listening to someone's concern, being on time to practice, and maintaining good study habits.

Since the Team Goal serves as a guideline or ideal to be striven for, it should be a statement of qualities. A Team Goal might be something like the following:

- "We will respect each other, and we will do what we mutually agreed to do."
- "Our team is a place where everyone can feel safe and respected. Everyone will help each other and make others feel important."

Once the Team Goal is established, the next step is to put the action statements into practice. Each team member is to think about what he or she could do to reach the Team Goal. Each team member can make an unpressured choice and pick one thing to work on during the coming week.

A house divided against itself cannot stand.

ABRAHAM LINCOLN

At the next forum, each team member will review his or her own action and evaluate how it worked. New actions may now be chosen and/or old ones worked on for another week. The statement of the Team Goal should also be reviewed. Any changes to the Team Goal should be mutually agreed on. Once established, the Team Goal should be put in a prominent place such as the locker room, the gymnasium, or a specified meeting room. In the future, when disagreements or conflicts occur, the team can refer to the Team Goal to determine whether their solutions and/or actions conform to the Team Goal ideals.

TIME OUT: IN THE COACH'S CORNER

The Obnoxious Individual

Situation 1

Sherri, the number one tennis player on the local high school team, has become somewhat "high on herself," and her obnoxious behaviors are irritating her teammates. She has elected herself the "know-it-all" and commander-in-chief of the team. She is constantly telling her teammates what to do and how to do it.

During practices, she stops her teammates in the middle of drills and tells them what she believes they are doing wrong. During practice matches, it is not unusual to hear her shouting such phrases as "Come on, you're being lazy!" "Don't just stand there." "Move to the ball." "Remember! Early racket preparation." "That's it. You're hitting the ball much harder." "Keep focused!" "Keep those feet moving all the time." "Toss your ball higher on your serve." "Come on! Charge the net." "Don't be a baby! Be aggressive."

Some of the players have become so frustrated that they got together and decided to come to you, the coach, for help. They said, "Please get Sherri to stop acting like a jerk. Her bossy behavior is driving everyone crazy."

Multiple Choice

Would you:

- A. Tell the players, "Don't worry, I'll have a talk with Sherri"?
- B. Tell the players to put it on the agenda for the next team forum?
- C. Tell the players to talk with Sherri themselves?
- D. Do nothing and ignore the whole issue (1) maybe it will go away or (2) they will just have to learn to live with the situation?

Coming together is a beginning; keeping together is progress; working together is success.

Henry Ford

Situation 2

A number of players on the high school soccer team are disgruntled by the coach's favoritism. He is coddling and catering to only the starting players. In the coach's eyes, these star athletes can do no wrong. He pays little attention to the less skilled players. On many occasions he has even forgotten the players' names or has called them by the wrong name. Even at games he has a tendency to talk only with the parents of his star players and ignore the parents of the lesser skilled players. In fact, some parents have attended every game, and the coach has no idea who they are.

Multiple Choice

The players are frustrated and don't know how to handle the situation. Should they:

A. Get the athletic director, another coach, or an outsider to confront the coach about his problem?.
B. Put the problem on the agenda for the next team forum?
C. Confront the coach about their concerns?
D. Do nothing and ignore the whole issue and (1) maybe it will go away or (2) they will learn to live with the situation?

Answers

There are two possible answers for both situations.

Response B is the easiest way to deal with both situations. The team forum is the logical place for these kinds of problems to be addressed.

Response C is also a possibility. Of course it depends on the individuals' ability to use constructive communication techniques. If these techniques have been learned and modeled by the coach and players, this procedure is probably the quickest and most efficient way of dealing with these kinds of situations. However, if the individuals do not know how to communicate constructively, face-to-face confrontations will, in all likelihood, lead to further conflict.

Response A is appropriate only when both parties have reached an impasse and a third-party mediator is needed to facilitate a solution. The "accused" individuals in the above situations are not even aware that there is a problem. Calling in a third party would, in all probability, create an immediate barrier based on the logic: "Why didn't they come and see me first and talk about it instead of going around my back and bringing in someone else to confront me?"

Response D will only bring on more frustration. If the individual doesn't know that a problem exists, he or she will probably continue the behavior.

QUESTIONS AND ANSWERS

Question: Are their some issues that should not be discussed at a team forum?

Answer: Individual coaches will probably have items they don't think should be discussed at a team forum. Although final responsibility for making certain decisions may lie with the coach, the opinions and concerns of others may provide additional possibilities or valuable insights and may even influence the final choice.

Question: What about teams that have a large number of players such as a football team? Wouldn't it be almost impossible to run a team forum?

Answer: Having a large group does make a team forum more difficult. One of the problems of large groups is that it becomes difficult for team members to really communicate on a personal level. In addition, if you use the suggested format, time becomes a critical factor with large groups. With extremely large groups, one suggestion is to divide the team into smaller groups (such as defense and offense). Each group can discuss its own agenda. Periodically, both groups can meet together in a total team forum to discuss total team issues. The purpose of meeting together, of course, is not to take sides, one against the other, but to try to work together with mutual respect and dignity and come to acceptable team solutions. The dividing of the team is not the most desirable solution, but it is workable.

Question: What are the most common administrative mistakes in team forums?

Answer: Starting late, meeting for too long, allowing one or more people to dominate the meeting, overemphasizing or focusing on the negative, such as complaints and criticism, and not putting agreements into action.

Question: What happens when the team forums merely become gripe sessions?

Answer: If griping becomes chronic, establish a rule that complaints will be heard only if the complainer is willing to seek a solution. This can be done by asking the person who raises the problem whether she or he wants to solve it or only complain about it. Be sensitive to the complainer's feelings, and keep the

There is a little difference in people, but that little difference makes a big difference. The little difference is attitude. The big difference is whether it is positive or negative.
CLEMENT STONE

The world must learn to work together, or finally it will not work at all.
DWIGHT EISENHOWER

focus on solutions. Say, "Do you have any suggestions that may solve this problem?"

Question: What happens if no one writes anything on the agenda?

Answer: Still hold the team forum and go through the other aspects of the agenda such as the minutes and giving compliments. When the agenda has been completed, end the forum. This lets players know that no matter how angry we got at each other during the week, we can always find a few good things to say.

Creative minds are like parachutes... they work only when they are open.
Anonymous

Question: Don't individuals need immediate solutions to their problems? I don't think some of my players can wait until the next team forum.

Answer: The purpose of waiting is to provide a cooling-off period in which the individual has time to get control of his or her temper and calm down. Discussion of the problem will then be much more rational, helpful, and, most important respectful. Incidentally, just the simple act of writing the problem on the agenda usually provides some immediate gratification for the individual.

Question: How receptive will athletes be to this concept?

Answer: Young athletes don't usually trust that adults are ready to listen to them or to take them seriously and are usually skeptical of the idea of a team forum. At first, things will often get worse before they get better because some individuals will use this newly acquired power to be hurtful and revengeful. For many individuals this is the only model they know. Don't forget the long range goals of the team forum and don't quit. In the long run, you will be rewarded for your efforts.

Question: What if a consequence that has been decided on isn't working?

Answer: The decision stays in effect until someone puts it back on the agenda. The item then will be discussed at the next team forum.

Question: What if someone feels that a consequence is unfair?

Answer: He or she can put it on the agenda, and it can be discussed at the next meeting. Logical consequences should be used whenever possible. When punishment is used, it is very easy to get into a revenge cycle.

Question: What if an individual does not follow through on the agreement?

Answer: The time when agreements are made is the best time to discuss and settle on what will happen if they're broken. Try to build in logical consequences whenever possible, not punishment.

Question: What if someone puts something on the agenda that is inappropriate?

Answer: Do not censor agenda items. If a coach censors agenda items, players will lose faith in the process. What may seem inappropriate to you may not be to the athlete. The important thing to remember is that the process is even more important than the solution. In addition, it is important to find the positive intent behind every behavior. This enables individuals to feel validated and respected.

Question: Can the coach put something on the agenda?

Answer: Of course. The coach is an equal member within the group.

Question: Can athletes put the coach on the agenda?

Answer: Yes. This is a perfect opportunity for the coach to model appropriate behavior. Coaches should feel comfortable discussing their own mistakes and view them as opportunities for learning. Remember, a coach who values open and direct communications, is giving his or her players permission to disagree. The consequences (not punishments) should be equivalent to what other team members might receive.

TIME OUT: SELF-ASSESSMENT

Rate Your Team's Strengths

Listed below are strengths that are commonly found in an empowered team. To assess your team, consider the degree to which you think that each statement is true for your team. If you are not coaching please assess a team of which you were a participant and determine its strengths. **Treat the results as a**

United we stick; divided we are stuck.
Unknown

guide only. There is always a margin of uncertainty in all assessments of this kind.

1. Never   2. Rarely   3. Sometimes   4. Often   5. Always

1. _____ Players spend time together and do things with each other outside of team activities.
2. _____ Players have input into many team decisions.
3. _____ Players have good communication (talking, listening, and sharing of feelings with each other).
4. _____ All players are treated fairly.
5. _____ Players practice in a safe environment (equipment, facilities, rules, etc.).
6. _____ Players are kept informed about what is going on in the team.
7. _____ The team deals with crises and change in a positive manner.
8. _____ Players easily manage the pressure of competition.
9. _____ Team rules and policies are fair.
10. _____ Players and coaches express appreciations to each other.
11. _____ Individual and team efforts are recognized and rewarded.
12. _____ There is a closeness of relationship between coach and athletes.
13. _____ Individual differences in lifestyle and culture are appreciated.
14. _____ There is a closeness of relationship between coach and athletes.
15. _____ There is a spirit of enthusiasm, excitement and camaraderie during practices.

Success should be a journey, not a destination.
UNKNOWN

Scoring:

66–75   Congratulations! You have a winning team. High scores should be celebrated but shouldn't lead to complacency. Continue to nurture your team, and it will continue to grow in strength.

50–65   You are in the average range, and your team has a combination of both positive and negative traits. Your team still has room for improvement.

Below 50   Your score indicates below-average team strengths. Low scores on individual items identify areas that teams can profitably spend time on. You are undermining your most valuable assets. Take an honest look at your approach to leading your young athletes.

Major Points Discussed in Chapter 16

1. Team forums provide opportunity for open and honest communication. They establish a structure through which coach and players can treat each other with mutual respect. They provide a process and a reflection of how we want to relate to each other. It's the working out that is important, and in team forums, that working things out takes place in an atmosphere of mutual respect and emotional honesty in which we may think and feel openly and listen openly to what others think and feel. Team forums are forums for problem solving, cooperative planning, and shared encouragement.
2. The team forum has a specific structure.
3. Effective team forums follow specific guidelines within the designated structure.
4. Team forums have specific ground rules.
5. Setting a specific team goal is a good way to start the team forum process.

References

Chapter 1

Brundage, A. *The Olympic Games.* New York: Amateur Athletic Union of U.S., 1948.

California Task Force to Promote Self-Esteem and Personal and Social Responsibility. *Toward a State of Esteem.* Sacramento, CA: California State Department of Education, 1990.

Engh, Fred. "National Youth Sports Coaches Association (NYSCA)—More Than Just a Certification Program." *Journal of Physical Education, Recreation and Dance,* September 1992, pp. 43–45.

Katz, Robert. "Skills of an Effective Administrator." *Harvard Business Review,* No. 74509 Sept.–Oct. 1974.

Maritain, J. True Humanism. *Reflections of America.* New York: Charles Scribner's Sons, 1938.

Martens, Rainer. *Coach's Guide to Sport Psychology.* Champaign, IL: Human Kinetics Publishers, 1987.

Seefeldt, Vern and Brown, Eugene (Editors). *Program for Athletic Coaches' Education (PACE).* Dubuque, Iowa: W.C. Brown, 1992.

Chapter 2

Goode Vick, C. *You Can Be a Leader: A Guide for Developing Leadership Skills.* IL: Champaign, IL: Sagmore Publishers, 1985.

Hart, L. *The Winning Family.* Oakland, CA: Lifeskills Press, 1990.

Tiedemann, Russ. "Psychological Factors in Coaching," *Coaching Clinic,* Vol. 14, No. 2 (Feb. 1976), pp. 13–15.

Chapter 3

Browner, Paul. "The Power to See Ourselves." *Harvard Business Review,* No. 64602, Nov.–Dec. 1964.

California Task Force to Promote Self-Esteem and Personal and Social Responsibility. *Toward a State of Esteem.* Sacramento, CA: California State Department of Education, 1990.

Conklin, Robert. *How to Get People to Do Things.* New York: Ballantine Books, 1979.

Payne, W. and Hahn, D. *Understanding Your Health.* St. Louis, MO: Times Mirror/Mosby College Publishing, 1989.

Rosenburg. M. *Society and the Adolescent Self-Image.* Hanover, NH: Wesleyan University Press, 1986.

Van Ekeren, G. *The Speaker's Sourcebook: Quotes and Stories.* Englewood Cliffs, NJ: Prentice Hall, 1988.

Warren, William. *Coaching and Motivation: A Practical Guide to Maximum Athletic Performance.* Englewood Cliffs, NJ: Prentice Hall, 1983.

Youngs, Bettie. *The 6 Vital Ingredients of Self Esteem and How to Develop Them in Your Child.* New York: Rawson Associates, 1991.

Chapter 4

Clarke, J.I. *Self Esteem: A Family Affair.* New York: Winston Press, 1978.

Tutko, T.A. and Richards, J.W. *Psychology of Coaching.* Boston: Allyn and Bacon, 1971.

Van Ekeren, G. *The Speaker's Sourcebook: Quotes and Stories.* Englewood Cliffs, NJ: Prentice Hall, 1988.

Chapter 5

Van Ekeren, G. *The Speaker's Sourcebook: Quotes and Stories.* Englewood Cliffs, NJ: Prentice Hall, 1988.

Rutter, M. "Resilient Children," *Psychology Today*, March 1984, pp. 77–65.

Wehlage, Gary (editor). *Reducing the Risk: Schools as Communities of Support.* Philadelphia, PA: Falmer Press, 1989.

Bernard, B. *Fostering Resiliency in Kids.* A paper prepared for the Western Regional Center for Drug Free Schools and Communities, August 1991.

Sarason, S. *The Predictable Failure of Educational Reform.* San Francisco: Jossey-Bass, 1990.

Kurth-Schai, R. "The Roles of Youth in Society: A Reconceptualization." *Educational Forum*, Vol. 52, No. 2, Winter 1988, pp. 131–132.

Chapter 6

Staff reporters. "Lucas," *Los Angeles Times*, Sunday, Feb. 14, 1993, p. C1, Sports Section.

Dreikurs, R. *Children: The Challenge.* New York: Penguin Books, 1964.

Glenn, H. Stephen. *Raising Self-Reliant Children in a Self-Indulgent World.* Rocklin, CA: Prima Publishing & Communications, 1989.

Chapter 7

Gordon, T. *Teaching Children Self-Discipline at Home and at School.* New York: Times Books, 1989.

Surler, C. "Hey, I'm Terrific," *Newsweek*, Feb. 17, 1992, pp. 46–52.

Chapter 8

Kleinke, Chris. *Coping with Life Challenges*. Pacific Grove, CA: Brooks Cole, 1991.

Marks, I. *Living with Fear: Understanding and Coping with Anxiety*. New York: McGraw-Hill 1978.

Yost, C. editor. "The Injury Problem in Sports," *Sports Safety*. Washington DC: Division of Safety Education of the AAHPER/National Education Association, 1971.

Chapter 9

Mayer, David and Greenberg, Herbert. "What Makes a Good Salesman," *Harvard Business Review*, No. 64411, July–Aug., 1964.

Rogers, Carl and Roethlisberger, F.J. "Barriers and Gateways to Communication," *Harvard Business Review*, No. 52408, July–Aug. 1952.

Weinberg, Robert and Richardson, Peggy. *Psychology of Officiating*. Champaign, IL: Leisure Press: 1990.

Chapter 10

MacKenzie, Robert. *Setting Limits: How to Raise Responsible, Independent Children by Providing Reasonable Boundaries*. Rocklin, CA: Prima, 1993.

Chapter 11

Gordon, Thomas. *P.E.T.: Parent Effectiveness Training*. New York: Peter H. Wyden, 1970.

Chapter 12

Dreikurs, R. *Children: The Challenge*. New York: Penguin Books, 1964.

Dinkmeyer, Don and McKay, Gary. *The Parents Guide: Systematic Training for Effective Parenting (STEP)*. Circle Pines, MN: American Guidance Service 1983.

Chapter 13

Averill, J. R. "Studies on anger and aggression: Implications for theories of emotion." *American Psychologist*, No. 38, 1983. pp. 1145–1160.

Chapter 14

Nelsen, Jane, Lynn Lott, and Stephen Glenn. "Beyond consequences." *Capable People Quarterly*, Summer 1992.

Nelsen, J. *Positive Discipline*. New York: Ballantine Books, 1987.

Chapter 15

Fisher, R. and Ury, W. *Getting to Yes: Negotiating Agreement*

Without Giving In. New York: Penguin Books, 1983.

Gerstein, A. and Reagan, J. *Win-Win: Approaches to Conflict Resolution.* Salt Lake City, UT: Gibbs M. Smith, 1986.

Lott, L. and Nelsen, J. *Teaching Parenting.* Fair Oaks, CA: Sunrise Press, 1988.

Chapter 16

Bettner, B. and Lew, A. *Raising Kids Who Can.* New York: Harper Perennial Publications, 1992.

Lott, L. and Nelsen, J. *Teaching Parenting.* Fair Oaks, CA: Sunrise Press, 1988.

Nelsen, J. *Positive Discipline.* New York: Ballantine Books, 1987.

Developmental Research and Programs, Inc. *Preparing for the Drug Free Years: A Family Activity Book.* Washington, DC: Comprehensive Health Foundation, 1988.

A Guide to Facilitating the Power of Positive Coaching

A manual of selected experiential activities

Contents

Introduction   207

Warm-Ups   1. Name Tags   2111
              2. The Scouting Report   212
              3. Who or What Am I?   214
              4. Getting Acquainted   215
              5. Likes and Dislikes   216
              6. Introduction Skits   218
              7. The Auction   219
              8. "Tell Me" Questions   221

Each of the following activities relates to content of a specific chapter in the book. The chapter number and title are listed with the corresponding activities.

Chapter 1   The Coach's Challenge
            1. The Players' Dilemma   222
            2. Prioritizing Your Athletic Values   227
            3. The Equality Demonstration   229

Chapter 2   What Kind of Coach Are You?
            1. The Giant Coach   230
            2. Who's Changing?   232

**Chapter 3   Building Strong and Independent Athletes
            from the Inside Out**
            1. Nurturing the Athlete   234
            2. Behavioral Characteristics of a Good Coach   236

Chapter 4   Emotional Affiliation: Acceptance and Belonging
            1. Recognizing Uniqueness   238
            2. Putting Labels on People   239
            3. The Porcupine   240

**Chapter 5   Emotional Significance: Helping Each Athlete
            Feel Important**
            1. Goal-Setting Exercise   242
            2. Relabeling: Turning Negatives into Positives   245

Chapter 6   The Capable Athlete: Structure for Success, Not Failure
            1. How to Destroy an Athlete's Self-Concept   247
            2. Learning from Mistakes   249

Chapter 7   The Capable Athlete: Encouragement
1. The Encouragement Circle   252
2. Encouraging Personal Growth   254

Chapter 8   The Need to Feel Safe
1. Dealing with Fear   256
2. Perception of Barbs   257

Chapter 9   Effective Communication: Listening to and Acknowledging the Athletes' Thoughts and Feelings
1. Active Listening   258
2. Sending Nonverbal Messages   260

Chapter 10   Sending Firm Messages and Establishing Team Rules and Procedures
1. Sending Firm Messages   262
2. What Do I Value?   264

Chapter 11   Coaching Without Anger: Communicating Your Needs in Words
1. "I Feel ...." Statements   266
2. Assessing Anger   268

Chapter 12   Athletes in Conflict: The Mistaken Goals of Behavior
1. The Mistaken Goals of Behavior   270
2. Needs in the Coach-Player Relationship   272

Chapter 13   Coaching Responsible Behavior: Empowering Discipline
1. The Circle of Power   274
2. Punishment Exercise   275

Chapter 14   Coaching Toward Self-Discipline: Using Natural and Logical Consequences
1. Alternatives to Punishment   277
2. Which Discipline Method Encourages Responsibility?   278

Chapter 15   Conflict Resolution
1. Seeing Both Sides of a Conflict   280
2. No-Postage Letter   282

Chapter 16   The Team Forum
1. Coming to Consensus   284
2. The Team Goal   286

Introduction

A Guide to Facilitating the Power of Positive Coaching: An Activity/Discussion-Based Program

This guide is designed to help instructors direct and facilitate students' learning; the activities are student-centered rather than teacher-centered. Student-centered activities are powerful learning tools when done in a consistent and structured format. Following are some positive reasons for adopting a student-centered activities approach:

- Actively participating in an activity and processing that experience are a powerful perceptual method of learning and consequently help students retain the information.
- Activities are more interesting, stimulating, and entertaining then typical classroom lectures.
- Student-centered activities encourage active rather than passive participation.

The activities are designed with a consistent format or structure to help students know what to expect, how to behave, and what is expected of them. Each activity follows the same format. Most important, most of the activities can be done with little advance preparation. The person facilitating the activities does not have to be an expert in the content area.

The design of the activities is simple and sufficiently detailed that a student can easily follow the step-by-step directions and lead a successful class. Each activity is designed in the following manner.

The Activity Format

Title: Each activity has a title that is intended to capture the basic principle involved.

Time: The time statement provides an estimate of the minimum time needed to conduct the activity. It does not account for any spontaneous extension of the activity or the discussion period that follows.

Objective: The objective defines the intended teaching point, purpose, or principle.

Materials: The preparation statement provides the necessary preclass preparations and the list of materials that are needed before the class begins.

Procedures: The procedure subheading gives step-by-step instructions for actually conducting the activity.

Suggested Discussion Questions: Some possible questions to be discussed are listed at the end of each activity.

The Facilitator's Role

The person in charge of any of the activities is really a facilitator. He or she provides a structure for the learn-by-doing or experiential activities by supplying materials, organizing time, giving directions, and facilitating interactions.

The activities in this guide are designed to help classroom participants to understand their own values and ideas through their participation in the activities. For this to occur, the facilitator must do the following:

- Establish the appropriate classroom atmosphere. It should be one built on trust and a feeling of warmth and acceptance in the classroom. It is a place where differences of opinion are accepted—in fact, desired. Participants and facilitator must be supportive of each other and sensitive to each other's needs. It must be an atmosphere in which everyone feels comfortable with his or her privacy and voluntary self-disclosure. It is a place where participants are not forced or pressured to explain their positions nor to defend their choice not to participate in a discussion.
- Not force his or her values, ideas, or perceptions on the group. He or she can only provide possible alternatives but be accepting of the participants' values, ideas, or perceptions.
- Provide an emotionally safe environment in which there are no putdowns, criticisms, or insults. No person's growth can be gained at the expense of someone else's. It is an atmosphere in which all students and facilitators are treated with mutual dignity and respect.

The learn-by-doing or student-centered educational process requires that students learn human relation skills. Many of the activities are designed to help students learn these skills. For the class to function effectively as a group, the students must become acquainted with group dynamics and be able to operate as productive group members. This manual provides many warm-up activities to help students develop the requisites for student-centered learning.

Some of the requisite skills developed through the warm-ups and activities for student-centered learning are:

1. Familiarity with and trust of other students in the class.
2. Listening skills.
3. Knowledge of and experience with the decision-making process.
4. Cooperation and participation among all members of the class.
5. An understanding and appreciation of both one's own feelings and the feelings of others.
6. Open communication among disagreeing factions and empathy with people who have opposing viewpoints.
7. Appreciation of individual differences and unique potentials.

Warm-ups as an Aid for Developing the Requisite Skills

Warm-ups are used in the first portion of a class when people are arriving. Warm-ups contribute to the development of the requisite skills; they also serve to help people move from their busy lives into a frame of mind in which they can focus on the class.

Warm-ups are nonthreatening and are conducted in an informal manner. They are designed to help students verbally interact in an open and trusting atmosphere. Warm-ups help to build trust among classmates.

Group Leadership Skills

The facilitator's role is not to present information. The activities and discussions that follow each activity will accomplish that. The leader is to facilitate the learning process so that participants learn to apply that information in their own lives and in their future coaching behaviors and philosophy. Following are some helpful hints:

1. Become Acquainted with the Activity. Although the activities are reasonably simple, the facilitator should allow a short time to acquaint himself or herself with the activity. This should be done at least one day before the activity is presented.

2. Be Prepared. Prepare all materials a day before you plan to do the activity. Be aware of the importance of thinking out beforehand how to divide participants into groups.

3. Explaining the Activities. Each activity has detailed directions on how it should be run. The leader should read it over carefully, have a full understanding of the activity, and be prepared to answer any questions that might arise.

4. Facilitating Discussion. The discussion phase is critical. It processes the activity and puts some closure to it. It is here where the real meaning of the activity or experience is internalized and, it is hoped, becomes part of the participants' lives.

Although each activity has a list of discussion questions, facilitators are encouraged to ask their own based on the make-up of the group.

5. Some Helpful Hints for Facilitating.
   a. When someone asks a question, open it up to the group. (For example, "How do the rest of you feel about that?")
   b. Facilitators must listen to all participants—even those you don't agree with.
   c. When students are working in small groups, the facilitator should not sit in the groups.
   d. To remember what a participant has said, you can either repeat what the person said, or take notes to refer to it later.
   e. Be sure to use open-ended questions rather than yes/no questions.
   f. Nonverbal messages are very important.
   g. Give the participants time to think and answer. Be comfortable with silence.
   h. How comfortable are you with sharing feelings? You need to be comfortable if you expect participants to be.
   i. Hold back your own response to understand the speaker's feelings.

Explore, repeat what you think she or he said, then check for understanding.

j. When asking participants to share a situation, problem, or feeling, be ready to share an example from your own life to clarify what you are asking of them.

k. Invite participants to let themselves be learners instead of experts.

l. Let participants decide what fits for them. There is no absolute right or wrong way to coach.

m. Be aware of cultural differences, if this applies to your group.

A Final Note to the Instructor of the Class

Before assigning any of the activities to your students, please read all of the activities in this manual. Select only those activities that you believe will be most beneficial to your class.

Name Tags

————————●————————

Time: 10 to 20 minutes

Objective: Warm-up or ice breaker to help students become acquainted. It also helps students to increase their awareness of their own uniqueness as a person, with different ideas, likes, values, and opinions.

Materials: Large index cards or colored paper
Tape, paper clips, or pins to hold the tags on participants' shirts or blouses.
A variety of colored large felt-tip pens

Procedure:

1. Distribute cards and pins to participants.

2. Ask each person to write his or her first name in the middle of the card, using a large felt-tip pen. Tell the participants to leave some space around the outside of the card for additional information.

3. Tell students to write:
   a. above their name, the name of the athlete or coach they most admire;
   b. below their name, the animal that best describes them;
   c. along the right border in a vertical column, what they feel is their most important virtue;
   d. along the left border in a vertical column, their greatest athletic accomplishment.

4. When the students have completed their cards, they are to move freely around the room and become acquainted with each other.

Suggested Discussion Questions:

1. What made this exercise pleasant or unpleasant?

2. What did you learn about other people in the group?

3. What, if anything, surprised you about this activity?

The Scouting Report

————————●————————

Time: 15 minutes

Objective: To get acquainted and begin to disclose personal information.

Materials: None

Procedures:

Members are to fill out the Scouting Report. Each student is to match other students who fit the descriptions on the worksheet. A student may use a name only once. However, more than one person may be named for the same item. After completing the report, members may share things that they learned.

Suggested Discussion Questions:

1. What elements make this exercise pleasant or unpleasant?

2. What did you learn about people in the group?

3. After looking over your list, do you have any questions that you would like to ask people in the group?

4. How do you feel about being a member of this group?

The Scouting Report

Find someone who:

1. Played on a high school athletic team.

2. Was the captain of an athletic team.

3. Was voted the most valuable player on an athletic team.

4. Had a serious season-ending athletic injury.

5. Was on a championship team (conference, district, state, etc.) or won an individual championship.

6. Maintained better than a 3.50 GPA in high school or college.

7. Played in a televised sporting event.

8. Traveled to another country to participate in a sporting event.

9. Is playing on an athletic team right now.

10. Is currently maintaining a regular fitness program.

11. Is left-handed.

12. Is currently coaching an athletic team.

Who or What Am I?

————————●————————

Time: 10 to 15 minutes

Objective: To help participants relax, get acquainted, and get actively involved with each other.

Materials: 1. Index cards and tape or computer mailing labels.

2. Thick felt-tip pen

Procedure:

1. Assemble at least one index card or computer mailing label for each participant.

2. On each card, write the name of an athlete or coach, a college mascot, a piece of sports equipment, the name of a professional sports team, or some other specific category related to athletics. For example:

   Athlete: Babe Ruth, Wayne Gretsky, Dominic Dawes, Pat Summit
   Mascot: Duke Blue Devils, Tennessee Vols (Volunteers), Notre Dame Fighting Irish
   Equipment: Shuttlecock, Vaulting horse
   Professional team: Florida Marlins, San Jose Sharks, Toledo Mudhens

3. Tape one label on the back of each participant without letting him or her see what it says. Make a few extras for students who may want to participate more than once.

4. Instruct the participants to try to guess what is written on their label by asking the other participant only yes/no questions. Each participant can ask only three yes/no questions of any one individual. After three questions have been asked, he or she must move to another participant. The participant continues asking questions until he or she guessed the name on the label correctly.

5. Continue until everyone has succeeded. If time is a factor, the leader can announce that the other group members can give clues to the participants.

6. When the participant guesses correctly, he or she removes the label.

Suggested Discussion Questions:

1. What made this exercise pleasant or unpleasant?

2. What did you learn about the people in the group?

Getting Acquainted

————————●————————

Time: 10 to 15 minutes

Objective: To allow participants an opportunity to learn some things about each other and to provide an environment in which people practice good listening skills.

Materials: None

Procedure:

1. Have participants pair off with someone that they do not know very well. Instruct them to find a place where they will not interfere with other pairs.

2. Allow each participant at least 5 minutes to talk about himself or herself to his or her partner.

3. Bring the group back together in one large circle with each student sitting next to his or her partner.

4. Ask each participant to introduce and speak about his or her new friend. Remind the group that no one else should talk while the speaker has the floor.

5. After everyone has made introductions, the facilitator can moderate a question-and-answer period.

Suggested Discussion Questions:

1. What did you like about this activity?

2. What did you learn about others that surprised or pleased you?

3. How did you feel during this activity?

Likes and Dislikes

---•---

Time: 25 to 30 minutes

Objective: To help participants share some of their values and experiences.

Materials: None

Procedure:

1. Divide the class into groups of four to six participants.

2. Tell each group that they are to come to a consensus about each of the categories found on the Likes and Dislikes List. It is important that honesty be stressed in this activity (10 to 15 minutes).

3. The groups then complete The Common Experiences List (5 minutes).

4. Each group shares its Common Experiences List (5 minutes).

5. After completing both lists, each group must choose three items from each list to share with the entire class (5 to 10 minutes).

Suggested Discussion Questions:

1. What were some items about which you had difficulty coming to consensus?

2. What did you like about this activity?

3. What did you learn about others?

Likes and Dislikes LIst

The object of this activity is for each group to reach a consensus.

	Like	Dislike
1. Sport	_____	_____
2. TV show	_____	_____
3. School subject	_____	_____
4. Athlete	_____	_____
5. Coach	_____	_____
6. Food	_____	_____
7. Drink	_____	_____
8. Exercise	_____	_____
9. Animal	_____	_____
10. Summer vacation	_____	_____

The Common Experiences List

Participants are to search for experiences they have had in common.

1. A time when they felt uneasy during athletic competition

   _____

2. A time when they got away with something they should not have

   _____

3. Something they have done with their friends about which they are very proud

   _____

4. A pleasant childhood memory

   _____

5. Something that they did for someone that really made a difference in that person's life

   _____

Introduction Skits

Time: 20 to 30 minutes

Objective: To help participants build trust by working together in a fun activity.

Materials: None

Procedure:

1. Divide the class into groups of five or six.

2. Allow each group 15 minutes to put together a three-minute skit that will serve to introduce the members of that group.

3. Allow the students to be creative as possible. If groups are stuck, suggest some ideas:

   A police line-up with a police officer asking questions.

   A sportscaster interviewing some athletes.

   Television show formats such as quiz shows or *The Dating Game.*

4. At the end of the skits, all participants gather together.

Suggested Discussion Questions:

1. What pleased you about the activity?

2. What did you learn about others in the group?

3. What did you learn from this activity?

The Auction

—————●—————

Time: 15 to 20 minutes

Objective: To help participants examine their priorities and make choices on the basis of those priorities.

Materials: Play money (from a game or any teacher-made currency)

Procedure:

1. The class is divided into groups of three or four participants.

2. Each group refers to the Auction List and receives a predetermined amount of money (such as 500 dollars).

3. Explain to the groups that each item will be auctioned off in order of appearance on the Auction List to the highest bidder.

4. Once a team runs out of money, its members can no longer bid.

5. Only groups can make purchases; individual students within the groups cannot make independent decisions.

6. The money cannot be divided among the members of the group.

7. Gather all the groups together.

Suggested Discussion Questions:

1. Was your group happy with what it received?

2. Why was your selection important to you?

3. If you didn't receive what you wanted, how did that make you feel?

4. Were there any members in the group who were unhappy with the group's decision?

5. What did you learn from this activity?

Note: This activity works well when the facilitator gets into the spirit of the activity and has fun auctioning off the items. He or she should keep trying to raise the price without dwelling too long on any one item. The instructor can also choose an outgoing student to be the auctioneer.

Auction List

1. Winning the individual/team championship in your chosen sport.

2. A feature article in *Sports Illustrated* about you.

3. A chance to spend a day with your teammates at Disney World.

4. A chance to be your coach's special guest at a sports banquet at which he or she is being honored.

5. A guarantee that you will have whatever coaching position you want when you graduate from college.

6. Participation as an athlete in the Olympics.

7. Perfect health for your entire life.

8. The promise to have a perfect friendship for life.

9. The chance to solve the problems (such as racism, cheating, and professionalism) in college sports.

10. To have others accept you for who you are and not what they want you to be.

11. A perfect transcript of earned straight A's.

12. A coaching position in which you are liked and respected by your players, colleagues, and community.

"Tell Me" Questions

————————●————————

Time: 10 minutes

Objective: To help participants get to know each other on a more personal basis.

Materials: None

Procedure:

1. Divide the class into groups of four.

2. The participants refer to the "Tell Me" Questions. Remind the participants that the "tell me" questions should relate to their feelings and there are no right or wrong answers.

3. Tell the participants that they are to designate a person to be the starting point for the activity.

4. That person directs the first statement to each individual in the group.

5. After each person has completed the first statement, the next person to the right directs the next statement to each of the individuals in the group.

6. This process continues until all statements have been read and answered.

7. Gather all participants into one group.

Suggested Discussion Questions:

1. What did you like about the activity?

2. What did you learn about others?

3. How did you feel during this activity?

4. Did you learn anything about yourself through this activity?

"Tell Me" Questions

1. Tell me something about your most memorable athletic moment.

2. Tell me something that frightens you.

3. Tell me something that really makes you happy.

4. Tell me something that really irritates you.

5. Tell me something about a favorite childhood memory.

6. Tell me something about your first love.

7. Tell me something that makes you laugh.

8. Tell me something that_____ .

The Players' Dilemma

————————●————————

Time: 30 to 45 minutes

Objectives: To teach participants about the importance of establishing trust and honesty and how difficult both of these traits are to recover if they are ever lost in a relationship.

Materials: Small squares of paper to represent ballots

Preparation: This activity is the most difficult to understand, and it will require a little more preparation time than the others. Carefully review the rules of the game and be prepared to explain how the Players' Dilemma is played. This is a fun activity. The directions may appear a little lengthy, but stick with it. You and your students will enjoy the outcome.

How the Game Is Played:

1. Tell the participants that the purpose of this game is to win as many points as they can.

2. There will be six rounds of play.

3. Each team will consist of two to four players.

4. Team 1 will compete against Team 2, Team 3 will compete against Team 4, and so on.

5. The strategy is simple: Each team has to select either the letter A or the letter B. The letter that each team chooses will determine how many points the team will receive.

6. Since there are only two teams competing against each other and only two letters, the number of combinations is very limited.

7. Consult the following grid. It shows that

   a. If both Team 1 and Team 2 choose the letter A, both teams receive 3 points.
   b. If Team 1 chooses the letter A and Team 2 chooses the letter B, Team 1 receives 6 points and Team 2 loses 6 points.
   c. If Team 1 chooses the letter B and Team 2 chooses the letter A, Team 1 loses 6 points and Team 2 receives 6 points.
   d. If both Team 1 and Team 2 choose the letter B, both teams will lose 3 points.

Team 1

	A	B
T A **e**	+3	−6
a **m**	+3	+6
2 B	+6	−3
	−6	−3

8. Each team chooses its letter in the following manner:

   a. A representative from each team negotiates a strategy (out of hearing distance from the rest of the teammates) for each of the six rounds of play. The representatives from each team will discuss what is the best strategy for both teams and how each should cast their ballots (choosing either the letter A or B).

   b. After the representatives discuss the best strategy for both teams, each representative goes back to his or her team and discusses with the other members the strategy that was agreed on.

   c. Each team then discusses its strategy, whether or not to write the letter agreed on or change it.

   d. Finally, each team makes its decision and writes the team name and the letter A or B on a piece of paper (ballot).

   e. The ballots are then given to the class facilitator.

9. After receiving both ballots, the instructor reads out loud the letters that the teams have written on their ballots. The scores are recorded on the score sheet and the blackboard.

10. The leader then instructs the group to repeat the same process for the next round, except that a new representative should be chosen to negotiate the strategy.

11. As you can see on the Players' Dilemma Tally Sheet, some rounds multiply the points so that if the scoring box indicates you won 3 points, for instance, you would multiply the amount by the round's multiplication factor.

Procedure:

1. Have participants refer to the Players' Dilemma Tally Sheet.

2. Divide the class into small teams of two to four players. At least one male and one female should be in each group. Give each group at least six small pieces of paper (ballots).

3. Pair each team with another team. Designate which is Team 1 and which is Team 2. The teams may name themselves if they desire.

4. Explain the game and tell the paired groups that they will be competing against each other and that the purpose of the game is for each team to try and win as many points as they can.

5. Tell each team to choose a negotiator for the first round. Send them both out of the room to negotiate the best strategy for both teams (2 minutes).

6. When each negotiator returns to his or her team, each will have three minutes to consult with their team about what was negotiated and decide whether they will stick to the agreement or be dishonest and change the decision by putting another letter on their ballot and try to gain more points at the expense of the other team.

7. At the end of the three minutes, tell each team that they must now write the name of their team on the ballot and their chosen letter, fold the ballot, and give it to you. Be sure you keep the ballots from the two competing teams together, especially if you have many teams competing.

8. Read out loud each team's name and the letter the team submitted on its ballot.

9. Record the scores.

10. Move to the next round. After the first three rounds, the same teams will compete against each other.

11. In the last three rounds, teams may negotiate with any team that is willing to negotiate with it. Therefore some teams may negotiate with more than one team in each of these latter rounds. If that is the case, scores for each individual negotiation will be scored and the total sum will be recorded. A team must therefore submit a ballot for each negotiation. If no team is willing to negotiate with a particular team, that team must sit out the round.

12. Add up the total scores for all groups, and declare the winners.

Suggested Discussion Questions:

1. What did the Players' Dilemma mean to you?

2. What lessons can be learned from this game?

3. How did you feel when the competition became intense?

4. How did you feel when the other team changed the agreed on letter and you lost points?

5. How did you feel when your team changed the agreed on letter and you gained points through your team's dishonesty?

6. How did you feel if your team went ahead and changed the agreed on letter even though you protested this strategy?

7. In the latter rounds, how did you feel if you were on a team that no one was willing to negotiate with?

8. How can you apply the lessons from this game to your coaching philosophy?

Players' Dilemma Tally Sheet

Objective: Get as many points as you can

		Team 1	
		A	B
Team 2	A	+3 / +3	+6 / −6
	B	−6 / +6	−3 / −3

Scoring:

a. If both Team 1 and Team 2 choose the letter A, both teams receive 3 points.

b. If Team 1 chooses the letter A and Team 2 chooses the letter B, Team 1 receives 6 points and Team 2 loses 6 points.

c. If Team 1 chooses the letter B and Team 2 chooses the letter A, Team 1 loses 6 points and Team 2 receives 6 points.

d. If both Team 1 and Team 2 choose the letter B, both teams lose 3 points.

Time for each round

Round(s)	Time for negotiating with opposing team(s)	Time for consulting with own team
1 through 3	2 minutes	3 minutes
4	3 minutes	5 minutes
5	3 minutes	5 minutes
6	3 minutes	5 minutes

Point Totals

Round	Choice		Cumulative Points
	A	B	
1.			
2.*			
3.**			
4.			
5.*			
6.**			

* Payoff points are doubled for this round.
** Payoff points are tripled for this round.

Prioritizing Your Athletic Values

———————●———————

Time: 5 to 10 minutes

Objective: To help the participants recognize how their values will affect their coaching philosophy and behavior.

Materials: None

Procedure:

1. Have the students complete "Prioritizing Your Athletic Values."

2. Have students form triads to discuss their rankings.

3. Have all students gather together.

Suggested Discussion Questions:

1. What did you learn about yourself?

2. What did you learn about others?

3. What about the activity surprised you?

4. How can this activity be of value to you as a future coach?

Prioritizing Your Athletic Values

A value is:

1. something that is desirable or worthy of esteem for its own sake.

2. something you include in your life even when you have to give up something else.

Pretend that you are a coach. What values would you model and, ideally, instill in your players? Prioritize the following list as well as any other values that you would care to include. Number from the most important to the least important, beginning with the number 1 as the most important.

_____ Doing whatever you can to win

_____ Trustworthiness

_____ Having fun

_____ Fairness

_____ Caring for others

_____ Hard work

_____ Courage

_____ Aggressiveness

_____ Skill

_____ Honesty

_____ Safety

_____ Doing what is right

_____ Self-respect

_____ Independence

_____ Responsibility

_____ Losing isn't fun

_____ Discipline

The Equality Demonstration

————————●————————

Time: 3 to 5 minutes

Objective: To help participants learn that equality does not mean sameness.

Materials: A one-dollar bill, one dollar in coins (3 quarters, 2 dimes, and 1 nickel), 100 pennies, a silver dollar (if available), 10 dimes, 20 nickels, and 4 quarters.

Procedure:

1. Select one volunteer for each of the different dollar amounts.

2. Have the volunteers sit at a desk or table, and place a different one-dollar amount in front of each volunteer.

3. Ask the volunteers whether any of them has an amount that is more valuable then another.

4. Ask the class which dollar would be of more value if you wanted to enclose a dollar inside a birthday card for a child.

5. Ask the class which dollar would be of more value if you wanted to get a 65-cent beverage from a coin-operated vending machine.

6. Ask the class which dollar would be of more value if you wanted to play the quarter slot machines in Las Vegas.

7. Ask the class which dollar would be of more value if you took a child to a carnival where she could try to pitch pennies onto a plate to win prizes.

8. Ask the class which dollar would be of more value if you needed to make a telephone call from a public phone booth.

9. Ask the class which dollar would be of more value if you needed to park your car at a metered spot.

10. Ask the class which dollar would be of more value if you wanted to give a child a "special" dollar (the silver dollar if you have one).

11. Comment that the dollars are equal in one sense, but that each still retains its own unique properties and strengths.

Suggested Discussion Questions:

1. In what ways are the two amounts of money equal or not equal?

2. If you establish an egalitarian relationship with your athletes, will you lose your uniqueness? Why or why not?

3. How can you apply this demonstration to your coaching philosophy?

The Giant Coach

————————●————————

Time: 15 minutes

Objective: To help the participants understand the effects of a controlling and/or hostile coach.

Materials: One chair for each pair of participants

Procedure:

1. Participants pair up and decide who will be A and who will be C.

2. Instruct C to stand on a chair facing forward with the back of the chair behind C. It can now be revealed that C stands for "coach."

3. Instruct A to stand very close to and facing the coach. It can now be revealed that A stands for "athlete." Tell A to now look up at the coach.

4. The facilitator now reads the following script to the participants:

   "You are looking at the Giant Coach. This coach knows everything. This coach is smarter than you, can think faster than you, knows more than you do, and can do almost everything better than you. That Giant Coach knows all the answers and solves all problems and does everything right. You can't do anything right! Almost everything you do is wrong and imperfect and needs to be corrected by that Giant Coach."

5. Scolding exercise: Instruct the Giant Coach to stand straight and tall on the chair, extend one arm and point his or her index finger with a tapping motion. Tell the Giant Coach something like this:

   "In 10 seconds you are going to lower that finger and wave it in front of that athlete's face and give him or her insults and criticisms such as "You are really incompetent. You're the worst player on this team. Can't you ever do anything right? Why do I have to tell you everything?" Be stern, and no smiling. Ready—lower that finger and give it to the athlete. (Allow about 20 seconds.)

6. Head-patting exercise: Next, instruct the Giant Coach to bend over and very gently pat the athlete's head and give patronizing and sugary comments such as: "You're so nice and sweet. You always do such a great job. I wish everyone behaved like you. You are just super." Remind the coach not to rub or stroke too hard. (Allow about 20 seconds.)

7. Have the students switch roles and repeat the exercise (steps 1 through 6).

Suggested Discussion Questions:

1. How did you feel during this exercise?

2. How often is this situation a reality in coaching?

3. How does humiliation or patronizing behavior affect relationships?

4. How many of you, when you were standing on that chair, felt that you were in complete control. (The leader should point out that most coaches are feeling out of control when they are acting controlling.)

5. How many of you have noticed that when you hear others humiliating a youngster, it sounds so terrible, but when you are doing it, it is because that person "darn well deserves it"?

6. What did you learn about the long-term effects of humiliation?

7. What are some sources of inferiority feelings?

Adapted from an activity (The Competent Giant) by John Taylor from his book *Person to Person: Awareness for Counselors, Group Leaders, and Parent Educators*. San Jose, CA: R&E Publishers, 1984. By permission of the publisher.

Who's Changing?

——————●——————

Time: 10 to 15 minutes

Objective: To acquaint the students with how both coaches and athletes have changed over the years.

Materials: None

Procedure:

1. Ask participants to fill out the Historical Perspective Chart.

2. After all students have finished their lists, have them compare their responses by discussing some of the responses on the board.

Suggested Discussion Questions:

1. Do you see any significant changes in the methods that coaches have used over the years? If so, what changes?

2. Do you see any significant changes in the attitudes of the athletes over the years? If so, what changes?

3. How do you think athletes typically responded to coaches during each of the periods? Why do you think they responded the way they did?

4. Do you see any parallels in the way both coaches and players have changed over the years? If so, what are these parallels?

5. How do you think some of the famous athletes that you listed would respond to some of the famous coaches of the past? Why?

6. Do you think some of the past coaches that you listed would be as successful today as they were before? Why?

7. What other things do you notice as you compare the two lists?

Historical Perspective Chart

Select the coaching method (autocratic, permissive, or democratic) that you believe was the dominant style used during each of the following periods.

Today _____

1980s _____

1960s _____

Before 1950 _____

List some famous coaches (both past and present), and select what you believe was his or her coaching style.

Coach	**Style of Coaching**
1. _____	_____
2. _____	_____
3. _____	_____
4. _____	_____
5. _____	_____
6. _____	_____

List the typical characteristics of athletes (compliant, assertive, aggressive, wishy-washy, etc.) for each of the following periods.

Today _____

1980s _____

1960s _____

Before 1950 _____

List some famous athletes of today whom you admire.

1. _____ 2. _____ 3. _____

4. _____ 5. _____ 6. _____

Nurturing the Athlete

————●————

Time: 20 minutes

Objective: To help the participants recognize people's basic needs.

Materials: A small variety of plants, including some that look great, some that are wilted, some that are in bloom, a cactus, and perhaps a weed. A plant for each participant is ideal but not absolutely necessary. (Pictures of different plants can be substituted but are not quite as impressive as real plants.)

Chalkboard and chalk or a flipchart with marking pens

Procedure/Suggested Discussion Questions:

1. Pass out a plant to each participant or one plant to a small group of participants.

2. Each participant or group is then requested to make some comments about their plant. Have the participants compare their plant with the others. Ask the participants which plant they would choose if they were able to keep one and why. How many got their favorite plant? If you received a petunia but wanted a rose, is there anything you can do to turn your petunia into a rose?

3. Record responses to the following questions on the blackboard. Since you got the plant that you got, what do you need to do to help your plant develop its full potential? (Possible answers: water, light, good soil, sunshine, shade, tender loving care, quiet music.) What happens when any of these needs is neglected?

4. Ask whether all of these plants need the same amount of water, sunlight, etc.

5. Ask what teenagers need to develop their full potential. Record the responses.

6. Ask what athletes need to develop their full potential. Record the responses.

7. Ask whether all athletes need the same amount of nurturing. Why?

8. Ask what the participants have learned from this exercise to help their athletes.

9. Ask how the participants think coaches violate a young athlete's needs (for example, try to change an athlete into the coach's own image, like trying to change a petunia into a rose).

10. Have the participants take a few minutes to think about something specific they would like to do differently due to the increased insight they gained from this activity. They should be specific about what they want to do, why they want to do it, and exactly when they will do it.

11. Allow time for any who would like to share his or her commitment.

Adapted from an activity by Lynn Lott and Jane Nelsen, *Teaching Parenting: A Step-by-Step Approach to Starting and Leading Parenting Classes.* Provo, UT: Sunrise Press, 1988. By permission of the publisher.

Behavioral Characteristics of a Good Coach

Time: 20 to 25 minutes

Objective: To help the participants understand that good coaching requires a coach to be respectful, trusting, and accepting.

Materials: Two large sheets of butcher paper for each group
Different-colored felt-tip pens
(A blackboard and chalk can be used if butcher paper and pens cannot be obtained.)
Masking tape for each group
A pair of scissors for each group

Procedure:

1. Divide the class into groups of four to six participants

2. Distribute two large sheets of butcher paper and felt-tip pens to each group.

3. Using one sheet of butcher paper, each group is to brainstorm a list of adjectives that they think best describes the positive behavioral characteristics or traits that they think are required for good coaching.

4. After each group brainstorms the list, they are to prioritize the list by choosing what they believe are the six most important traits.

5. On the other sheet of butcher paper, each group is to draw a coach's shield (see the example below) and divide it into six parts. Tell the groups to be creative in their art work.

Example of a Coach's Shield

6. After the six traits have been chosen, the group is to write one trait in each of the six sections on the coach's shield.

7. The coach's shields should be taped on a wall in the room.

8. The groups join together for the discussion.

Suggested Discussion Questions:

1. Why did you choose to list those six specific characteristics as qualities that a good coach needs?

2. Can you recall any personal experiences that are related to the characteristics you listed?

3. Were you surprised by any similarities or differences of opinions between the people in your group?

4. Were you surprised by any similarities or differences of opinions between the different groups within the classroom?

5. If you were to do the opposite and list the worst traits of a coach, what words do you think would you list?

6. How do you think these worst traits would affect the team?

7. What other words or statements can you add that will contribute to developing positive behaviors in athletes?

8. What have you learned from this lesson, and how can you apply it to your coaching career in the future?

Recognizing Uniqueness

—————●—————

Time: 20 minutes

Objective: To help the participants learn to appreciate similarities and differences.

Materials: One old tennis ball per participant. (Any common object will do.) If you can afford them, apples or oranges are really fun because the participants can eat them afterward.
A basket to hold the tennis balls
Chairs placed in a circle

Procedure:

1. Give one old tennis ball to each participant.

2. Ask each participant to study his or her tennis ball carefully for 30 seconds.

3. Ask each participant to describe one characteristic of his or her ball. Urge the participants to use all of their senses. Participants take turns making their observation. Go around the circle twice.

4. After the participants share their observations, place the basket in the middle of the circle and ask the participants to put their ball in a basket. Mix the balls up.

5. Tell the participants to retrieve their balls. Wait until all balls have been retrieved.

Suggested Discussion Questions:

1. What did you learn from this experience?

2. Can what you learned from this experience be applied to people?

3. Which is more basic and primary: similarities or differences?

4. Although there are marks or blemishes on your tennis ball, they helped you to identify it. What does this fact teach you about people?

5. What did you learn about the long-term effects of recognizing similarities and differences in people?

Adapted from activity ("Tutti-Fruitti") by John Taylor in *Person to Person: Awareness Techniques for Counselors, Group Leaders, and Parent Educators.* San Jose CA: R&E Publishers, 1984. By permission of the publisher.

Putting Labels on People

———————●———————

Time: 20 minutes

Objective: To help the participants understand the damage that labeling can do to athletes' development.

Materials: Sticky labels such as computer mailing labels or index cards with tape. One label or card for each participant. Each label will have a positive or negative descriptive word(s) on it. Some examples are: dumb, shy, smart, captain, clumsy, coach, forgetful, star, mean, HIV-positive, injured, aggressive, gay, loud-mouth, stuck-up, speaks little English, deaf.

Procedure:

1. A label is placed on the back of each participant. The participant, of course, does not know what is written on the label.

2. Tell the group that they are gathered in the gym and waiting for the bus to arrive to take them to the conference track meet. While they are waiting, they are to mill around responding to people's labels (10–15 minutes).

Suggested Discussion Questions:

1. What were you feeling when people were talking to you?

2. Were you able to guess your label? What were some of of the clues?

3. Did you find yourself changing your behavior in any way as people talked with you?

4. Do you think there are any good labels? Why?

5. In your own life, do you think you have labeled certain people?

6. If so, what can you do differently?

7. Do you think you have been labeled? Is there anything you can do to make people see you differently? What?

8. If not, what can you do?

9. What have you learned from this activity that you can apply to your future coaching philosophy and behavior?

The Porcupine

———————●———————

Time: 2 minutes

Objective: To help the participants learn that acceptance involves honoring one's own needs without having to like everything about another person.

Materials: None

Procedure:

1. Walk slowly around the room, explaining that you are a porcupine and that you are happy and satisfied with being a porcupine. Thrust out your arms several times as you walk, each time thrusting in a new direction, with your index fingers extended in a pointing position. Explain that these thrusts are your quills, which stick out in all directions. Point out that the quills are an important part of you and they help define who you are.

2. As you come to a certain participant, thrust your finger into his or her shoulder area, exerting enough force to cause constant, firm pressure.

3. Ask the participant "Do you have anything to say to me?" (Get him or her to ask you to remove your quill.)

4. When the participant makes the desired request, say, "Oh, you don't want me to be a porcupine? You won't let me be who I am?" (Get the participant to say that he or she just wants you to remove your quill and does not wish you to be something else.)

5. Following the participant's clarification, say, "Oh, you just want me to move my quill, but it's okay with you if I remain a porcupine!"

6. Thank the participant for accepting you and honoring your uniqueness.

Suggested Discussion Questions:

1. What is the difference between "Move your quill" and "Don't have quills"?

2. If someone's quill is sticking you, do you have to like it to be accepting of that person?

3. What does acceptance mean?

4. In what ways do you give nonacceptance messages to others?

5. In what circumstances do others give you nonacceptance messages?

6. In what ways does this activity apply to your experiences as a coach or athlete?

7. What will you start or stop doing after this experience?

Adapted from John Taylor, *Person to Person: Awareness Techniques for Counselors, Group Leaders, and Parent Educators*. Saratoga, CA: R&E Publishers, 1984. By permission of the publisher.

Goal-Setting Exercise

——————●——————

Time: 15 minutes

Objective: To help the participants set goals for themselves.

Materials: None

Procedure:

1. Ask each participant to refer to the Goal-Setting Plan.

2. Explain the difference between a long-term (general) goal and a short-term (measurable) goal, and explain that the short-term goal is the basic action plan that is going to help to achieve the long-term goal.

3. Explain that research has indicated that specific small daily goals or specific action plans (I will shoot 100 free throws at each practice) are more effective than general long-term goals (I will improve my free throw shooting this year).

   More examples:
   Long-term goal: "I will get better at my backhand."
   Short-term goal: "I will practice my backhand drills for 30 minutes at every practice."

   Long-term goal: "I will lose some weight before our first game."
   Short-term goal: "I will complete a daily food diary each day for the next two weeks."

   Long-term goal: "I will warm up better before each game."
   Short-term goal: "I will complete the recommended stretching exercises and jogging plan one hour before each game."

   Long-term goal: "I will improve my jumping skills."
   Short-term goal: "I will do the coach's recommended plyometric jumping drills after each practice."

   Long-term goal: "I will improve my skills to make the first team this year."
   Short-term goal: "I will keep a daily log of my improvements."

4. Have the participants fill out parts A and B of the Goal-Setting Plan (5 minutes).

5. After parts A and B have been completed, explain that short-term goals must be reasonably flexible because potential barriers can keep the best plans from being accomplished. For example, what do you do if it rains or the gym is closed for repairs?

6. Have participants fill out part C of their Goal-Setting Plan (5 minutes).

7. Have participants get a witness signature.

8. Gather everyone together for group discussion.

Suggested Discussion Questions:

1. What did you learn from this experience?

2. Do you think a coach should help each athlete set goals for the season? Why?

3. Do you think a coach should set goals and share them with their athletes? Why?

4. Do you think athletes should periodically give themselves rewards as they accomplish their short-term goals? Why?

5. If so, what kinds of rewards do you want to give yourself for achieving your short-term goals?

Name _____

Date _____

Date of beginning action plan(s) _____

Date long-term goal will be accomplished _____

Witnessed by _____
                                      (Signature)

Goal-Setting Plan

A. Long-term goal: _____

_____

B. List one or two short-term goals (action plan) to help achieve the long-term goal:

1. _____

_____

2. _____

_____

C. Keep your goals reasonably flexible. Think about potential barriers that can affect your action plan.

Barriers   **Strategies for overcoming barriers**

_____   _____

_____   _____

_____   _____

_____   _____

Relabeling: Turning Negatives into Positives
————————●————————

Time: 15 to 20 minutes

Objective: To help the participants recognize that the negative views that they hold about certain people can also be seen as positive traits if one is willing to look past one's bias and see the behavior from another view.

Materials: None

Procedure:

1. Ask participants to refer to the Relabeling Exercise and read section A.

2. Ask participants to think about individuals that they believe have negative behaviors and/or traits and list these behaviors or traits (5 minutes).

3. After the list has been completed, ask the participants to determine whether the listed behavior or trait is really their problem or the other person's. For example, is the thing you listed a matter of your own personal taste?

4. Next, ask the participants to study the listed behaviors and ask them to reevaluate the list and label the behaviors more positively (5 minutes).

5. If the participants cannot relabel the behaviors, ask them to list the behaviors on the blackboard.

6. Ask the rest of the participants to make suggestions for the traits that are listed on the blackboard (2–10 minutes).

7. Gather all participants together.

Suggested Discussion Questions:

1. What did you learn about yourself?

2. What were you thinking during the experience?

3. Did you have trouble relabeling? Why?

4. What will you start or stop doing after this experience?

Relabeling Exercise

Section A

A person who ...	could be called ...	or could be called ...
changes his or her mind a lot	wishy-washy	flexible
isn't orderly	sloppy, piggish	spontaneous
gets anxious	weak, cowardly	self-protective
is emotionally sensitive	sick, fragile	caring
isn't good at a task	stupid, inferior	hasn't practiced
pleases others	passive	likable
believes what others say	gullible	trusting
takes risks	impulsive	brave
gets excited	hysterical	exuberant
sticks to projects	compulsive	determined
gets depressed sometimes	neurotic	normal human being
is sure of something	conceited	self-confidence
expresses his or her opinion	egotistical	honest, assertive

Section B

List some negative behaviors or traits of individuals that you know, but do not list people's names.

1. _____

2. _____

3. _____

4. _____

List the negative labels that you have given these behaviors:

1. _____   2. _____

3. _____   4. _____

Relabel the behaviors with positive labels:

1. _____   2. _____

3. _____   4. _____

How to Destroy an Athlete's Self-Concept

———————●———————

Time: 20 to 25 minutes

Objective: To help the participants understand that sending negative messages
has destructive consequences for both the sender and the receiver.

Materials: None

Procedure:

1. Divide the class into groups of six or seven students.

2. Ask for a volunteer from each group who is willing to play the role of an
   "athlete."

3. Take the volunteers to another area outside of the classroom, and explain
   to them that this exercise will involve their receiving critical remarks from
   the other members of their group and that the purpose of the exercise is to
   help students understand the feelings that occur when negative messages
   are sent. Allow any of the volunteers to change their minds about participating if they feel they are too sensitive to critical remarks. Make substitu-
   tions if necessary. Tell the athletes that they are going to make two separate
   statements and that they should practice the following lines while you go
   back into the classroom to prepare the other group members:

   "I am really working hard and trying to get better."
   "Coach, I'm really glad I'm part of this team."

4. Tell each group that they are going to line up side-by-side and that their
   responsibility in this exercise is to make critical remarks to the "athlete"
   who comes back to their individual group.

5. Tell each group member that each of them will be approached by the athlete, who will make a statement. After listening to the statement, each
   group member will reply with a negative response such as a criticism, rejection, discouraging remark, insult, or lecture.

6. Ask the participants to role-play the situation and not to smile. Tell them
   to use body and facial gestures to emphasize their remarks. For example,
   they may point their fingers, raise their voices, frown, put their hands on
   their hips, or whatever is appropriate to enhance the remark. However,
   they may not touch the "athlete."

7. Tell them that the "athlete" will move from one person to the next until
   he or she reaches the end of the line. The process will then be repeated.
   The first time, the athlete will say, "I am really working hard and trying
   to get better." The second time, the athlete will say, "Coach, I'm really
   glad I'm part of this team."

8. Reassure the group that the "athletes" are aware of what is going to happen and that they have agreed to participate.

9. Return to the "athletes" and tell them that they are to return to their respective groups and start at the beginning of the line, face the first person, and say, "I am really working hard and trying to get better."

10. They are to listen to that person's remark and then move on to the next person and repeat the same statement. After going through the entire line, return to the beginning of the line.

11. The "athletes" should repeat the process, except say, "Coach, I'm really glad I'm part of this team."

12. Bring the "athletes" back into the room and to their groups. On your signal, tell all "athletes" to start.

13. When all groups are finished, reassemble everyone together and have the group members welcome the "athletes" back to reassure them that they are really cared for and that the group members are sorry for any discomfort they may have caused the "athletes."

Suggested Discussion Questions:

1. How do the "athletes" feel about what just happened to them?

2. How do the group participants feel about what just happened to them?

3. Did any of the "athletes" feel any physiological changes taking place during this experience? If so, what?

4. What about the activity surprised you?

5. Can anyone relate this activity to any real-life situations?

6. In what ways does this experience apply to your experience as a coach or athlete?

7. How are you going to be different after this experience?

Learning from Mistakes

———————●———————

Time: 20 minutes

Objective: To help the participants understand that mistakes provide opportunities for learning.

Comment: Coaches usually mean well when they try to motivate their athletes to do better by making them feel bad about their mistakes. However, we fail to check out the results of our good intentions. When we see the fallacy of our misguided intentions, we are then open to seeing how empowering it is to treat mistakes as wonderful opportunities to learn.

Materials: None

Procedure:

1. Participants pair up and interview each other using the Mistakes Interview Form. (Allow 5 minutes for each partner.)

2. After the interviews, discuss the following questions with the total group.

Suggested Discussion Questions:

1. What insights did you gain from participating in this activity?

2. Are you willing to make some new decisions about mistakes?

3. What are they?

Adapted from Lynn Lott and Jane Nelsen, *Teaching Parenting: A Step-by-Step Approach to Starting and Leading Parenting Classes*. Provo, UT: Sunrise Press, 1988. By permission of the publisher.

Mistakes Interview Form

1. What do mistakes mean to you?

2. Think of a time during your athletic career when you made a mistake and your coach was supportive and encouraging. (If you can't think of an athletic experience, use any experience from your childhood and think how supportive and encouraging your parent or parents were.)

   What did you do?

   What was the result of what you did?

   What did your coach do to support or encourage you?

   What did you learn from this experience?

3. Think of a time when you made a mistake and your coach was not supportive or encouraging but punitive or verbally abusive.

What did you do?

What was the result of what you did?

What did your coach do to punish or verbally abuse you?

What did you learn from this experience?

4. How have you changed from these experiences?

5. Did you see yourself as capable or incompetent after these experiences?

The Encouragement Circle

Time: 10 to 15 minutes

Objective: To help the participants understand that to be an effective encourager, one must be comfortable with encouraging oneself.

Materials: None

Procedure:

1. Ask students to complete the Encouragement Profile. (Allow 5 minutes for completion.)

2. Break class into groups of four to five participants and have them sit in a circle.

3. Explain to the participants that to be an effective encourager, you must feel comfortable encouraging yourself. Ask participants to take turns reading their Encouragement Profile to their group (3–5 minutes).

4. Explain to the group that they will now have the opportunity to practice encouraging each other and to experience what it feels like to be encouraged. Each person will be given the opportunity to be encouraged by the person on his or her left. Go around the circle until everyone has been encouraged. Each person is to begin by saying, "I think that it is great that you _____." The person who is encouraged should say, "thank you" after being encouraged (5–10 minutes).

5. Gather all participants together.

Suggested Discussion Questions:

1. What did you learn about yourself?

2. Why do you think it is difficult for some people to accept praise or encouragement?

3. What pleased you about the experience?

4. How did you feel when others were encouraging you?

5. How did you feel when you read your "Encouragement Profile?"

6. How did you feel when you encouraged others?

Encouragement Profile

I do very well at ——————————————————————————

One of my greatest strengths is ———————————————————

What I like best about myself is ———————————————————

Something nice that I did for someone else was ————————————

One of my greatest accomplishments was/is —————————————

I really enjoy ————————————————————————

I'm turned on by ——————————————————————

One of my most meaningful possessions is —————————————

My primary life goal is ——————————————————————

I am most proud of ————————————————————————

Encouraging Personal Growth

———————●———————

Time: 20 minutes

Objective: To help the participants understand how encouragement affects an athlete's feelings about himself or herself.

Materials: None

Procedure:

1. Ask the participants to complete Encouraging Personal Growth (5–10 minutes to complete).

2. Ask participants to share their responses.

Suggested Discussion Questions:

1. What is meant by encouragement?

2. What is the difference between praise and encouragement? When can praise be encouraging or discouraging?

3. Which do you believe is more effective: encouragement or praise? Why?

4. Why is it important to recognize effort and improvement as well as accomplishment?

Encouraging Personal Growth

The following situations require encouragement. What might each of the individuals believe about himself or herself? How would you respond?

1. Maria complains that the workouts are too difficult.

   _____

   _____

2. Alicia teaches Margaret a new gymnastics skill.

   _____

   _____

3. Andre plays his best golf but still loses his match.

   _____

   _____

4. Carlos is worried that he will not do well in the next race.

   _____

   _____

5. Although Avery is ranked as the number one seed, he loses in the first round and is eliminated from the conference tennis championships.

   _____

   _____

6. Josh is discouraged because he was not elected as next year's team captain.

   _____

   _____

Dealing with Fear
———————●———————

Time: 15 minutes

Objective: To help the participants experiment with different ways of dealing with their fears that are related to sports.

Materials: A variety of different art supplies such as paper, pens, color markers, and paints. Remind the participants ahead of time to bring art supplies.

Procedure:

1. The facilitator begins the activity by asking group members to share some of the fears that they encountered while participating in athletics.

2. After the sharing, the facilitator explains to the group that by confronting their fears, they will be more successful in overcoming them.

3. The facilitator explains that there are many ways to confront fears. By talking, writing, or drawing what is frightening, people can confront the things they fear instead of denying or avoiding them.

4. Ask the group members to choose two or more of the following ways to deal with their fears in sports:

   a. Draw a picture of something in sports that frightens you. The drawing might include a person, thing, or situation that touches off fear. Draw a second picture in which there is a happy ending.
   b. Write about all the things in sports that scare you.
   c. Write a poem or essay about being afraid.
   d. Write about what you do when you're afraid.

5. If members feel comfortable, invite them to share their drawings or writings.

Suggested Discussion Questions:

1. What were you feeling during the activity?

2. What physical reactions did you feel?

3. What did you learn about yourself?

4. What about the activity surprised you?

5. What will you stop or start doing after this activity?

Adapted from J. Devencenzi and S. Pendergast, *Belonging: Self and Social Discovery for Children of All Age.* San Luis Obispo, CA: Belonging, 1988. By permission of the publisher.

Perception of Barbs

———————•———————

Time: 5 minutes (discussion time not included)

Objective: To help participants cope with common barbs heard or felt.

Materials: None

Procedures:

1. Ask the participants to refer to their Barb Perceptions chart.

2. The participants are instructed to write down any barbs they or people they know have experienced or heard (allow 3–5 minutes).

3. While the participants are completing their charts, the facilitator draws a larger version of the chart on the blackboard or uses chart paper.

4. Ask the participants to share their barbs with the rest of the class. List them on the blackboard or chart paper.

Suggested Discussion Questions:

1. How have you tried to handle these barbs in the past?

2. How did you feel about what was said or done?

3. Why do you think the barb affected you the way it did?

4. What do you think the other person was really trying to say? (For example, "You fool!")

5. How can you protect yourself from similar happenings?

Barb Perceptions	
Physical	**Verbal**

Adapted from J. Devencenzi and S. Pendergast, *Belonging: Self and Social Discovery for Children of All Ages*. San Luis Obispo, CA: Belonging, 1988. By permission of the publisher.

Active Listening

———————●———————

Time: 15–20 minutes

Objective: To help participants learn to be active listeners.

Materials: None

Procedure:

1. Ask students to refer to the Qualities of an Active Listener sheet.

2. The facilitator explains each of the qualities of an active listener, demonstrating appropriate eye contact, body language, and other aspects. Modeling is an essential component of learning appropriate listening skills.

3. Group members form triads. Members are asked to choose the role of listener, speaker, and observer. There will be three timed sessions. The facilitator asks the speaker to choose a personal issue and talk for 3 to 4 minutes. During this time, the listener practices the qualities of an active listener as previously presented. The observer watches the listener and checks listening behaviors noted on the Qualities of an Active Listener sheet. At the end of the timed session, there is a two-minute sharing. Positions are traded until each member has had an opportunity to try each role.

4. If members have a difficult time choosing a talk topic, the following are suggested:

   A unique athletic experience
   A special coach or teammate
   A memorable game or contest
   An embarrassing moment

Suggested Discussion Questions:

1. What pleased you about the experience?

2. What did you learn about yourself?

3. How did you feel during this experience?

4. In what ways can this experience apply to the coaching profession?

5. How are you going to be different from this experience?

Adapted from J. Devencenzi and S. Pendergast, *Belonging: Self and Social Discovery for Children of All Ages.* San Luis Obispo, CA: Belonging, 1988. By permission of the publisher.

Qualities of an Active Listener

1. Use eye contact and listening body language.

   - Look directly at the speaker.
   - Lean slightly toward the speaker, but not too close.
   - Nod head slightly to show understanding.

2. Provide encouragement.

   - "Uh-huh."
   - "That sounds good."
   - "Yes, I see what you mean."

3. Listen attentively.

   - Remain silent when someone speaks.
   - Give the speaker complete attention.

4. Tell back/paraphrase.

   - "What I heard you say was ...."

5. Reflect feelings.

   - "It sounds as if you're feeling ...."
   - "You sound ..."

6. Be empathetic and nonjudgmental.

   - Value the speaker and what he or she says.
   - Accept the speaker's feelings.
   - Forgo judgments.

Sending Nonverbal Messages
————————●————————

Time: 10 minutes

Objective: To help the participants understand that body language is an important part of the message. Sometimes it speaks louder than the
words.

Materials: None

Procedure:

1. Participants choose one partner and decide who will be the speaker and
   who will be the listener.

2. Partners face each other about 4 to 6 feet apart.

3. The speaker is to convey his or her message by using only facial or body
   movements. Emphasize that the speaker may not touch the listener. The
   listener may not move from the spot in which he or she is standing.

4. Tell the speaker to display the following feelings to the listener as you
   describe them. Allow about 10 seconds for each message.

   Frustrated: I am frustrated with you.
   Anger: I am angry at you.
   Bashful: I am very shy.
   Admiration: I admire you.
   Scared: I was really scared.
   Joy: I am happy for you.
   Support: I am rooting for you.
   Empathy: I understand your feeling.
   Sad: I am really sad.
   Optimistic: I am optimistic about our chances.
   Puzzled: I don't understand.

5. Reverse the procedure and have the speaker become the listener and the listener become the speaker. Again, allow about 10 seconds for each message.

> Disappointment: I am disappointed in you.
> Guilty: I feel guilty about what I did.
> Hurt: You hurt me.
> Disapproval: I really disapprove of what you did.
> Like: I like you.
> Envy: I am really envious of you.
> Helpfulness: I want to help you.
> Boredom: I am bored with you.
> Shame: I am ashamed of you.
> Discomfort: I am too cold.
> Loaded: I had too much to drink.

Suggested Discussion Questions:

1. What did you learn about yourself?

2. How did you feel during this experience?

3. What physical reactions did your body show?

4. What did this experience remind you of?

5. What did you think your partner was thinking or feeling?

Sending Firm Messages

———————●———————

Time: 15 to 20 minutes

Objective: To allow the participants to practice sending firm messages.

Materials: A set of role-playing cards for each group on which the following are written or printed:

> An angry Joe has just shoved Matt to the floor because he thought Matt fouled him on purpose. You are the coach and must give Joe a firm message.

> Maria is talking to a teammate and disturbing your concentration while you are trying to explain a new strategy to the team. You are the coach and must give Maria a firm message.

> Tyrone has been very lazy during practice and has not been completing his required drills and warm-ups. You are the coach and must send Tyrone a firm message.

> Mitsuko cheated on her score card to qualify for the upcoming golf tournament. You are the coach and must send Mitsuko a firm message.

> Miguel called a teammate "an S.O.B." You are the coach and must send Miguel a firm message.

> Laura throws her tennis racquet in anger and kicks the ball off the court after losing a point. You are the coach and must send Laura a firm message.

Procedure:

1. Ask students to refer to the Firm Message Checklist.

2. The facilitator explains each of the qualities of sending a firm message, demonstrating appropriate eye contact, body language, and other aspects. Modeling is an essential component of learning appropriate listening skills.

3. Group members form triads. Members are asked to choose the role of listener, speaker, and observer.

4. The role-playing cards are equally distributed among each group.

5. The speaker reads aloud his or her role-playing situation and then delivers a firm message to the listener while the observer and listener evaluate the firm message.

6. The listener and observer share their thoughts about the firm message with the speaker.

7. The process is repeated as the group members rotate their roles and a new role-playing situation is read and another firm message is sent. Continue the process until all six role-playing cards have been processed.

Suggested Discussion Questions:

1. What did you learn about yourself?

2. Is it difficult for you to send firm messages? Why?

3. How did you feel during this experience?

4. Why is it important to focus on the behavior instead of the person?

5. What happens when the messages are "soft"?

6. In what ways can this experience apply to the coaching profession?

7. How are you going to be different because of this experience?

Firm Message Checklist

1. Use appropriate body language.

   - Maintain eye contact.
   - Uncross your arms and/or legs.
   - Sit or stand erect.
   - Make sure you are close but not too close.

2. Use a clear but normal tone of voice.

   - The fewer the words, the better.
   - Keep calm, and keep your voice under control.
   - Be matter-of-fact.

3. Focus your message on the behavior, not on the player.

   - "Joe, please stop interrupting."
   - "Mary, you cannot miss practice again."

4. Be direct and specific.

   - "I want everyone here at two o'clock, dressed for practice."
   - "Start your wind-sprint drills now."

What Do I Value?

─────────●─────────

Time: 20 minutes

Objective: To help the participants determine what behaviors are acceptable and not acceptable to them.

Materials: None

Procedure:

1. Ask students to refer to the values statements sheet.

2. Explain to participants that there are 16 cells in the values grid. At the top of the columns are the following labels: "Very Strong," "Strong," "Mild," and "No Opinion."

3. The students are to categorize the 16 statements by how strongly they feel about the statement, regardless of whether they approve of it or oppose it. Each cell must contain only one of the key italicized words from the statements. It is important to remember that whether a participant feels very strongly in favor of or very strongly opposed to a statement, the key word describing that statement should be placed in one of the four cells in the "Very Strong" column.

4. When all statements have been categorized, the grid will contain four key words in each of its four columns.

5. The class is divided into groups of four, who are to discuss the grids of each of their group's members. Reasons for choices should be stressed, and personal experiences relative to the statements should be recalled.

Suggested Discussion Questions:

1. What did you learn about yourself from this activity?

2. What surprised you about the activity?

3. What did you think the people in your group were thinking or feeling?

4. What did you learn from others?

Values Statements and Grid

Place the key words from each of the following 16 statements into the values grid. Only one key word is allowed for each of the 16 cells.

1. A coach calls an athlete *dumb* in front of his or her teammates.

2. A player *steals* some valuable team equipment

3. An athlete asks a teammate to *lie* for him.

4. A female athlete is harassed because of her *lesbian* orientation.

5. An athlete is suspended for getting *drunk*.

6. An athlete is removed from the team for *cheating* in a class.

7. A player on the team uses *cocaine*.

8. *Parents* verbally abuse their daughter if she makes mistakes in a game.

9. The coach verbally *abuses* the players if they make mistakes in in a game.

10. The coach plays *favorites* by overlooking inappropriate behaviors of his or her star athletes.

11. The coach pays little attention to the *third-string* players.

12. A star male athlete is using his athletic popularity as a tool to seduce and have *sex* with many girls.

13. A male athlete openly announces that he is *gay*.

14. A group of athletes physically and verbally harass a group of students whom they view as *"nerds."*

15. A coach inappropriately *touches* one of the athletes.

16. A player uses a *racial* slur in referring to a teammate.

Very Strong	Strong	Mild	No Opinion

"I Feel ...." Statements

————————●————————

Time: 15 minutes

Objective: To help participants practice "I feel ...." statements.

Materials: None

Procedure:

1. Ask participants to refer to the "I Feel ...." Statements sheet.

2. The facilitator directs participants to complete the "I feel ...." Statements sheet.

3. On completion of the statements, the participants form triads to discuss their feelings about the activity.

4. The participants gather into one large group for discussion.

Suggested Discussion Questions:

1. Did you find it difficult to make "I feel ...." statements? If so, why?

2. What did you learn about yourself?

3. How are you going to be different as a result of this experience?

"I Feel ...." Statements

Rewrite the following statements into "I feel ...." statements.

Restate each sentence so that the speakers take responsibility for their own feelings.

1. My teammates make me angry when they poke fun at my running style.

   I feel _____

   when _____

   because_____

2. All this emphasis on winning really bothers me!

   I feel _____

   about _____

   because_____

3. Learning this new defense is frustrating.

   I _____

   _____

   _____

4. The coach doesn't pay any attention to me.

   _____

   _____

5. Today's practice was perfect. Everything we did worked.

   _____

   _____

6. Heather is really irritating when she brags about her number one ranking.

   _____

   _____

7. Jake plays so recklessly and aggressively during practice, he is scary.

   _____

   _____

   _____

8. The way Jason sweet-talks the coach makes me sick.

   _____

   _____

   _____

Assessing Anger

Time: 5 to 10 minutes

Objective: To help the participants assess how they deal with anger.

Materials: None

Procedure:

1. Ask students to refer to the Assessing Anger sheet.

2. Instruct participants to complete anger assessment as honestly as possible and to carefully read the evaluation that follows the assessment (3 to 5 minutes).

Suggested Discussion Questions:

1. What did you learn about yourself?

2. What about the activity surprised you?

3. How do you feel when others express their anger at you?

4. What physical reactions does your body show when you get angry?

5. What physical reactions does your body show when someone expresses their anger at you?

6. Do you think that expressing anger at someone is good or bad?

7. Are there ways of dissipating your anger before confronting someone?

8. What will you try to change about yourself as a result of this activity?

Assessing Anger

Check how much you agree or disagree with the following statements.

	Strongly Agree	Agree	Disagree	Strongly Disagree
1. I tend to get angry more frequently than most people.	_____	_____	_____	_____
2. It is easy to make me angry.	_____	_____	_____	_____
3. I am surprised at how often I feel angry.	_____	_____	_____	_____
4. I get angry when something blocks my plans.	_____	_____	_____	_____
5. I get angry when I am delayed.	_____	_____	_____	_____
6. I get angry when people are unfair.	_____	_____	_____	_____
7. People can bother me just by being around.	_____	_____	_____	_____
8. When I get angry, I stay angry for hours.	_____	_____	_____	_____
9. I get angry when I have to work with incompetent people.	_____	_____	_____	_____

These statements come from the Multidimensional Anger Inventory (Siegel, 1986). Statements 1, 2, and 3 measure anger arousal. Anger arousal refers to the intensity, duration, and frequency of your anger. Statements 4, 5, and 6 measure the range of things you get angry about. Statements 7, 8, and 9 measure your tendency to have a hostile outlook. Another dimension measured by the inventory is the ease with which you express your anger. People who express their anger very readily tend to agree with these statements:

"When I am angry with someone, I let that person know."
"It is not difficult for me to let people know I'm angry."

Those who keep their feelings of anger to themselves tend to agree with these statements.

"I feel guilty about expressing my anger."
"I harbor grudges that I don't tell anyone about."

The Mistaken Goals of Behavior
———————●———————

Time: 25 to 30 minutes

Objective: To help the participants understand that the four mistaken goals of behavior can be examined through both positive and negative behaviors.

Student preparation: Read Chapter 12: "Athletes in Conflict: The Mistaken Goals of Behavior."

Materials: None

Procedure:

1. Ask students to refer to the Athlete's Mistaken Goal Chart.

2. Divide the class into triads.

3. Review the four mistaken goals of behavior and the negative behaviors associated with them:

Goal	Negative Behavior	Prescriptions
Attention	Undue attention seeking	
Power	Rebellious, stubborn	
Revenge	Retaliation or hurting others	
Withdrawal	Giving up, despair	

4. Briefly explain that many individuals try to fulfill the four mistaken goals of behavior through negative behaviors instead of positive ones because it is usually an easier approach and most coaches respond to it. In other words, most misbehaviors have a payoff.

5. Ask the class to brainstorm and list prescriptions for each mistaken goal (10 minutes).

6. Briefly explain that there are ways of achieving the same mistaken goals through positive behaviors instead of negative ones.

7. For each of the mistaken goals, brainstorm as many positive behaviors as possible, and list them in the positive behaviors category on the Athlete's Mistaken Goal Chart (5–7 minutes).

Prescription	Positive Approach	Goal
	Example: contribution	Attention
		Power
		Revenge
		Withdrawal

8. Ask the groups to list as many prescriptions or strategies as possible that can be used to encourage the positive approach to achieving the goals (10 minutes).

9. Bring the groups together.

Suggested Discussion Questions:

1. Is anyone willing to share a past experience that she or he now sees is related to the mistaken goals? What happened? Could it have been handled differently?

2. What positive behaviors did you list for each of the mistaken goals?

3. What about the activity surprised you?

4. How can you apply this activity to your future or present coaching philosophy?

5. What will you stop or start doing after this experience?

Athlete's Mistaken Goal Chart

List as many prescriptions as you can for each goal.

A.	Goal	Negative Behavior	Prescriptions
	Attention	Undue attention seeking	
	Power	Rebellious, stubborn	
	Revenge	Retaliation or hurting others	
	Withdrawal	Giving up, despair	

List as many positive approaches and prescriptions for each of the goals.

B.	Prescriptions	Positive Approach	Goal
		Example: contribution	Attention
			Power
			Revenge
			Withdrawal

Athletes in Conflict:
Needs in the Coach–Player Relationship

————————●————————

Time: 5 to 10 minutes

Objective: To help the participants recognize that relationships are based on trust, acceptance, respect, and dignity.

Materials: None

Procedure:

1. Ask the participants to refer to the Needs in the Coach-Player Relationship checklist, and allow participants a few minutes to complete it.

2. Have participants form triads to discuss and share their thoughts and answers on the survey.

3. Gather all the participants together.

Suggested Discussion Questions:

1. What did you learn about yourself?

2. What did you learn about others?

3. How do you feel when others treat you in respectful ways?

4. What were you feeling or thinking as you were filling out the survey?

5. How can you apply what you learned from this activity to your coaching philosophy?

6. How can you apply what you learned from this activity to your everyday life situations (for example, between boyfriend and girlfriend, husband and wife, parent and child)?

Needs in the Coach–Player Relationship

For this activity, think about your present or a past athletic experience. Please check any of the following statements that apply or applied to you in your athletic experience, and prioritize them according to the needs you felt most strongly about.

I want(ed) my coach to:

_____ 1. Treat me in a warmer and friendlier manner.

_____ 2. Allow me to make more decisions.

_____ 3. Allow me more freedom.

_____ 4. Expect less accomplishment from me.

_____ 5. Have more confidence in my abilities.

_____ 6. Feel more strongly that I am an important member of the team.

_____ 7. Have more respect for my judgment.

_____ 8. Be more interested in me rather than in my athletic abilities.

_____ 9. Give me more praise for my accomplishments.

_____ 10. Have more respect for my ability to solve problems.

_____ 11. Criticize me less.

_____ 12. Be more confident that I can be trusted with responsibilities.

The Circle of Power

————————●————————

Time: 5 to 10 minutes

Objective: To help the participants recognize their feelings when they are controlled and controlling.

Materials: None

Procedure:

1. Divide the class into groups of four participants.

2. In each group, one person is placed in the center of the ring formed by the remaining participants.

3. The participants hold hands to form an enclosed ring, trapping the person in the middle.

4. On a signal from the facilitator, the person in the middle attempts to escape from the ring while the other participants attempt to prevent that from happening. The facilitator must warn the group to avoid being overly aggressive and use caution in this activity. (Allow 30 seconds for the escape.)

5. Rotate positions until each person has experienced being in the middle.

6. After the activity, gather all participants together.

Suggested Discussion Questions:

1. What were you feeling during the activity?

2. What did you notice about your behavior?

3. What were you thinking as the activity progressed?

4. What did you think the others were thinking or feeling during the activity?

5. What kinds of tactics did the person in the ring use in attempting to escape?

6. Do you see any correlation in real-life situations when people are controlled or controlling?

Punishment Exercise

———————●———————

Time: 10 to 15 minutes

Objective: To help the participants understand the feelings that are generated in the person who is being punished.

Materials: None

Procedure:

1. Ask the participants to form dyads.

2. One partner will play the coach; the other will play the athlete.

3. The coach is going to play the role of the punisher and verbally admonish the athlete with strong words (scolding, insults, threats, criticisms, name-calling, etc.) and exaggerated body language (finger pointing, hands on hips, glaring at the athlete, etc.). However, touching the athlete is not allowed.

4. Read the following role-playing situation. Give the coach a few seconds to think how he or she is going to play the scene.

   Your athlete left his new football helmet on the field after practice. It has now disappeared and is probably gone forever. Coach, do your scolding, and be sure to insult the athlete good. Don't forget to get in his or her face.

5. Allow about 15 to 30 seconds for the scolding.

6. Repeat the scolding process for the second role-playing situation:

   Punish your athlete for missing the two free throws that would have won the big game.

7. Ask the participants to reverse roles and repeat the same process for the third and fourth role-playing situations.

   Now coaches, you are going to punish your athlete for starting a physical and verbal fight with one of his or her teammates.

   You are now going to punish your athlete because you notice he or she doesn't seem to be putting in a strong effort during practice.

8. Assemble all the participants together again.

Suggested Discussion Questions:

1. How did you feel during this experiment?

2. Why do you think people punish?

3. How did you feel when others treated you in this manner?

4. What physical reactions did your body show?

5. What did you think your partner was thinking or feeling?

6. In what way does this experience apply to you as a coach or athlete?

7. Did this experience remind you of anything?

8. What will you start or stop doing after this experience?

9. Reviewing each situation, how would a democratic or empowering coach handle them?

Alternatives to Punishment

—————————●—————————

Time: 30 minutes

Objective: To help the participants understand that there are more effective discipline methods than punishment.

Materials: Role-playing cards on which the following are written or printed:

  • A player has been fooling around and disturbing others during practice.
    • A player deliberately tries to hurt an opposing player during a game.
    • Your players have been leaving the locker room in a terrible mess after practice.
    • A player says something derogatory to you.
    • A player keeps disturbing you while you are trying to talk with others.

  Have participants list some of their past or present discipline experiences and add the new cards to the above list.

Procedures:

  1. Ask the participants to form triads.

  2. Divide the role-playing situations equally among the groups. Ask them to choose an alternative to punishment and set up a demonstration of how they would handle the problem situation without using punishment.

  3. Allow time for each group to demonstrate its role-play.

Suggested Discussion Questions:

  1. What did you learn from this activity?

  2. What did you learn about yourself from this activity?

  3. How do you feel when others treat you fairly or unfairly?

  4. What will you try to change after this activity?

Which Discipline Method Encourages Responsibility?

———————●———————

Time: 10 to 15 minutes

Objective: To help the participants become aware of the differences between the different discipline methods.

Materials: None

Procedures:

1. Ask for four volunteers to play Coach Natural Consequences, Coach Logical Consequences, Coach Punishment, and Coach Reward.

2. Take the volunteers out of the room, and give each of them their specific roles.

   Coach Natural Consequences: Show empathy and understanding, listen actively, but don't do anything to help.

   Coach Logical Consequences: Provide limits. Tell the athlete what options are available.

   Coach Punishment: Use threats, punishment, and verbal abuse.

   Coach Rewards: Offer bribes and rewards if behavior will change.

   Let the volunteers know that they are going to interact with an athlete who is continually coming to practice late.

3. Return to the group and ask a volunteer to be an athlete who is continually coming to practice late. According to team policy, the player may not participate in the next game.

   Other situations can be used, and the process can be repeated with different volunteers. Examples of other situations:

   - An athlete who is physically abusive to his or her teammates. Abusive behavior will result in an indefinite suspension from the team and appropriate counseling from the counseling office.

   - An athlete who has lied to you about attending class. Not attending class will result in a one-week suspension from the team.

   - An athlete who violated team rules by getting drunk. Violation of this rule will result in dismissal from the team.

   - An athlete who is failing classes.

4. Each of the four coaches takes a turn interacting with the athlete. After each interaction, the facilitator should ask both the athlete and the coach how they are feeling.

Suggested Discussion Questions:

1. Ask the rest of the class what they were feeling during this activity.

2. What did you learn from this activity?

3. What were you thinking as the activity progressed?

4. Did you feel any physical reactions?

5. What do you think you will do differently as a result of this activity?

Seeing Both Sides of a Conflict

———————●———————

Time: 10 to 15 minutes

Objective: To help the participants learn to perceive both sides of a conflict.

Materials: None

Procedure:

1. Divide the class into groups of three or four participants.

2. Each group pairs up with another group and is designated as group A or B. Each group should elect a secretary.

3. Designate group A as the coaches and group B as the athletes.

4. Instruct each group to compose a list of faults, shortcomings, and aggravating traits of people in the opposite group. State that you are asking for traits about people in general, not for specific traits of specific people in the opposite group (5 minutes).

5. Instruct each group to compose a second list. This list is to contain that subgroup's guess about what is on the opposite group's list. For example, athletes would develop a list of characteristics that they think the coaches have included on their list about "most athletes" (allow 5 minutes).

6. Have all groups read their lists in the following manner:

   a. Group A reads its second list, then group B reads its first list.

   b. This process continues until all paired groups have read their first lists.

   c. Group A reads its first list, then group B reads its second list.

   d. This process continues until all paired groups have read their second lists.

7. Gather all participants together.

Suggested Discussion Questions:

1. What were the similarities between the guess lists and the original lists?

2. Were you surprised by any similarities or differences? If so, what surprised you and why?

3. What can you do to help reverse the negative opinion others may have of you as a result of your membership in a specific group or class of people?

4. How is your group different from the opposite group?

5. How is your group similar to the opposite group?

6. What do you want most from the opposite group?

7. How will you be different after this activity?

Adapted from John Taylor, *Person to Person: Awareness Techniques for Counselors, Group Leaders, and Parent Educators*, San Jose, CA: R&E Publishers, 1984. By permission of the publisher.

No-Postage Letter

————————●————————

Time: 10 to 15 minutes

Objective: To help the participants learn to use humor and exaggeration to deal with a no-win situation.

Materials: None

Procedure:

1. The facilitator introduces the idea that humor and exaggeration can provide release when people are feeling up-tight or angry about a conflict.

2. The facilitator asks each group member to think of a person with whom he or she has a one-sided conflict. If the participants don't have any current conflict, ask them to refer to a past unresolved conflict. Each participant writes a letter to that person, exaggerating feelings about the conflict. Members know that this letter will never be mailed. Encourage silliness, overstatement, and dramatizing.

Suggested Discussion Questions:

1. How did you feel during this activity?

2. What did you learn about yourself while doing this activity?

3. Did the results of this activity please you or frustrate you?

4. What physical reactions did your body show?

5. What will you start or stop doing after this experience?

Adapted from J. Devencenzi and S. Pendergast, *Belonging: Self and Social Discovery for Children of All Ages.* San Luis Obispo, CA: Belonging, 1988. By permission of the publisher.

No Postage Letter

(never to be mailed)

Dear _____

_____

_____

_____

_____

_____

_____

_____

_____

_____

_____

_____

_____

_____

_____

_____

_____

Fondly,

P.S. _____

_____

Coming to Consensus

————————●————————

Time: 10 to 15 minutes

Objective: To help the participants experience cooperative decision making to arrive at a consensus and demonstrate to group members that it is possible to make decisions and to interact with others from positions of equal power.

Materials: $1 or less from each group member. Play money can be used.

Procedure:

1. Tell the group that you would like each member to contribute $1 to form a group fund, and ask students to refer to the What Consensus Means and Does Not Mean sheet.

2. Pose the question: "What shall we do with our group fund?"

3. Group members brainstorm possibilities, which are recorded on the blackboard.

4. Next, each suggestion is highlighted, and members are polled as to whether they agree or disagree on whether to spend money for that item. Members also indicate whether or not they want to speak about an issue. For example:

   Suggestion: We can use the money to have a party on the last day of class.

   Member 1: I agree.

   Member 2: I disagree.

   Member 3: I agree and would like to speak about this choice.

5. Each suggestion is handled until a consensus is reached as to which choices are eliminated and what the final choice is.

Suggested Discussion Questions:

1. What were you thinking during the experience?

2. What did you think other group members were thinking or feeling?

3. In what ways can this experience apply to your experiences as a coach or athlete?

Adapted from J. Devencenzi and S. Pendergast, *Belonging: Self and Social Discovery for Children of All Ages.* San Luis Obispo, CA: Belonging, 1988. By permission of the publisher.

What Consensus Means and Does Not Mean

1. Consensus **does not** mean that everyone thinks the decision is the best one possible.

2. Consensus **does** mean that those who are opposed to the decision can choose to:

   a. **stand aside** ("I don't want this, but I won't block others from doing or having it.")

   b. **block** ("I won't support this and won't allow the group to have it.")

   c. **withdraw** ("I see everyone else wants this and I can't accept it. I'm willing to leave the group.")

3. Consensus **does** allow for creative solutions, considering that collective energy often discovers more options than does an individual.

4. Consensus **does not** mean that the majority rules.

5. Consensus **does not** mean win/lose. If people leave the group session feeling as though they lost, the process needs to be discussed again.

6. Consensus **does** mean more of a time commitment than does voting.

7. Consensus **does** mean that group members need to have a commitment to negotiate compromise and present their positions assertively for the process to work well.

8. Consensus **does** mean that group members need to encourage others to present their positions and demonstrate respect for individual ideas.

9. Consensus **does** require that the group setting remain safe with only quality feedback given, that is, there must be no barbs or coercion.

10. Consensus **does** mean that the facilitator monitors an equal-time policy, usually 1 minute per person to speak about the issue.

The Team Goal

Time: 30 minutes

Objective: To allow the participants the experience of making a team goal.

Materials: None. However, the facilitator should review Chapter 16, "The Team Forum."

Procedures:

1. Ask the participants to pretend that they are a high school athletic team.

2. The facilitator pretends that he or she is the coach and introduces the idea of the team goal by asking the participants to respond to the following questions.

3. Write these three questions on the board:

   What would our team be like if it were the way you wanted it to be? Can you think of what this new and improved team might look like? If you were a coach, how would you like your team to be?

4. Allow the participants to write down their responses to these questions (5 minutes). Remind the group that they are to approach these questions in a positive manner by writing down what they would like, not things that they don't like.

5. After everyone is finished writing, it is time to share.

6. Each person takes a turn reading his or her ideas. After each person shares his or her ideas, the other members of the team may respond in the form of "What I agree with," "What I don't understand," and so on. Remind the group that only one person is allowed to speak at a time.

7. After all ideas have been heard, the ideas should be broken down into two categories: qualities (how we would like the team to be), and actions (what the team needs to do in order to be that way).

   Examples of qualities are closeness, respect, and cooperation. Examples of actions are listening to someone's concern, being on time to practice, and maintaining good study habits.

8. Since the team goal serves as a guideline or ideal to be striven for, it should be a statement of qualities. See Chapter 16 for examples of team goals.

9. Once the team goal has been established, the next step is to put the action statements into practice. Each team member is asked to think about what he or she could do to reach the team goal.

Suggested Discussion Questions:

1. What were you feeling during the activity?

2. What were you thinking as the activity progressed?

3. What did you learn from this activity?

4. What about the activity surprised you?

5. What did you learn about others from the activity?

Index

Abuse
  player, 7, 54
  of team privileges, 163
Acceptance
  of athletes for who they are, 51
  and caring, demonstrating, 51–54
  messages of, 50–51
  need for, 38–39, 49–50, 54–55, 56
  personal biases affecting, 55
  and significance, listening reflecting,
    101–102
  unconditional, 50, 51
Accidents, 92, 93, 97
Accomplishment, 85
Accountability, 63, 120
  in problem solving, 174
Actions
  effective, after firm messages, 116
  ineffective, after soft messages, 117
Affiliation, emotional, see Acceptance;
    Belonging
African American, acceptance of term, 52
Alienation, 61, 62
American Coaching Effectiveness
    Program (ACEP), 3
American Indians, 53
Anger, 22
  controlling, 154
  effect of, on constructive communi-
    cation, 125–126
  effect of, on players, 154
  progression from unexpressed, to
    resentment and hostility, 94–95
  uncontrolled, and discipline, 146
Anxiety, 23
  about emotional safety, 91–92, 95
  about physical safety, 91–92
  recognizing symptoms of, 95–96
Arguing, 155
Artificial charmer, 137
Asian American, acceptance of term,
    52–53
Assaults, effects of emotional, 94–95
  See also Safety
Assumed inadequacy behavior, 138,
    139, 140
  prescription for, 142
Assumptions, making, 76–77

Athlete, new reality of emerging, 12–13
Attention-seeking behavior, 136–137,
    139,140
  prescription for, 141
Autocratic coach, 21
  player response to, 22

Barriers, 70
  condemning athletes to failure, 71–77
Basic-level change, 43
Beck Anxiety Inventory, 96
Behavior, helping athletes to learn from
    their, 163–164
  See also Mistaken goal(s) of behavior
Belonging
  finding sense of, 135, 136
  need for, 38–39, 49, 54–55
  See also Acceptance
Benefits, emotional, through sports
    participation, 3, 8
Bernard, B., 61–62
Bettner, Betty Lou, *Raising Kids Who
    Can* (with A. Lew), 188, 190
Biases
  personal, affecting acceptance, 55
  testing for, 56–58
Birthdays, remembering players', 56
Body language, 104, 129
Brainstorming, 132, 173–174
Brown, Eugene, 3
Browner, Paul, 43
Brownell, W., 96
Bryant, Paul "Bear," 60–61

California Task Force to Promote Self-
    Esteem and Personal and Social
    Responsibility, 4, 34
Capability, need for, 39, 56
  and encouraging success, 83–90
  and structuring for success, 69–82
Carelessness, 161
Caring
  and acceptance, demonstrating, 51–54
  and respect, as foundations of
    negotiations, 171
Caucasian, *see* European American
Change(s)
  effect of social, on coaching, 8–10

evolution of, 13
levels of, 43
Cheating, 7
Chicano, acceptance of word, 53
Chinese American, acceptance of term, 53
Clarke, J. I., 50
Commitments, in problem solving, 174
Communication
    of coach's thoughts and feelings to players, 124–125
    destructive, 127
    effective, 101
    major barrier to, 110
    nonverbal, 115, 129
    normal everyday, 107
    skills test, 110–111
    See also Constructive communication; Empathy; Listening
Competent, need to feel, 39
    See also Capability, need for
Compliments, backhanded, 85–86
Confidence, 24
    displaying, 83–84
Conflict
    athlete/coach, 135
    operating assumptions for approaching, 171–172
    resolution, 170, 171, 174–176
    See also Mistaken goal(s) of behavior; Negotiations; Problem solving
Conklin, Robert, 37
Connecting with athletes, 56
Consequences, 159
    applying, 115, 120
    coaching beyond, 165–166
    difference between punishment and, 165
    rules to consider when applying, 168
    See also Logical consequence(s); Natural consequences
Constructive communication, 107, 124–125, 192
    completed message of, 128–129
    effect of anger on, 125–126
    four steps of, 127–128
    handling overbearing parents with, 129–131
    lack of response to, 132
    and nonverbal communication, 129
    other ways of using, 131
    sparingly used, 129
    See also Communication
Contemptuous athlete, 138
Content vs. process, 172

Contribution(s)
    for change, coaches', 10
    encouraging, 76
    providing opportunities for, 62–63, 84
    showing appreciation for, 90
Cooperativeness, 24
Criticism
    internal monologue of, 80, 81
    of players, 72–74, 84, 94
Cues, 119
    nonverbal, 102, 105
Culturally diverse populations, 13

Decision, questioning coach's, 8
Decision making
    encouraging participation in, 89
    limitations on athletes', 66
Declaration of Independence, 183
Defensive attitude, 22
Defiant athlete, 138
Democratic coach, *see* Empowering coach
Depressed athlete, 138
Destructive athlete, 137–138
Destructive patterns, replacing, with positive strategies, 9
Developmental Research and Programs, Inc., 188
Developmental tasks, accomplishing, 43–45
Dialogue, circular, 78
Dictatorial coach, *see* Autocratic coach
Dilemma, coach's, 4–5
Dinkmeyer, Don, 144
Directing, excessive, 75–76
Discipline
    empowering, 151–152
    hostile, 147–149, 152
    permissive, 149–151, 152
    problems, most common, 154–155
    problems, twelve helpful hints to reduce, 153–154
    purpose of, 146–147
    styles of, 147–152
Disrespect, coach's, 176–178
Disrespectful attitude, 22
Distance, keeping physical and emotional, 22
Downtime, rules about player, 119
Dreikurs, Rudolph, 73, 75, 135–136, 144, 145
Dropouts, school, 49
Drug abuse, 7
Dysfunctional behavior, 135, 136

See also Mistaken goal(s) of behavior
Dysfunctional teams, symptoms of, 40

Effort, recognizing, 84
Elkow, J., 92–93
Emotional safety, *see* Safety
Emotional well-being, effect of athlete's
    words or actions on coach's, 127–
    128
Empathy, 24, 102–103
    developing, 109–110
Empowered teams, 19–20, 28, 29
Empowering coach, 23–24, 30
    player response to, 24–25
Empowering discipline, 151–152
Encouragement, 74
    process of, 83, 90
    strategies for, 83–84, 89–90
Engh, Fred, 3
Enthusiasm, 24
Equality, 8, 9
Equipment
    lost or damaged, 161
    misuse of athletic, 162–163
    purposeful destruction of, 162
Ethnic terminology, sensitivity to, 52–53
European American, acceptance of
    term, 53
Evaluations
    as barrier to communication, 110
    postgame, 75
Excitement, 144
Expectations
    not yet achieved, 72
    successful teams with high, 61
    unrealistic, of athletes, 71–72
Explanations, allowing athletes to
    discover useful, 74–75
Eye contact, 104, 105, 115, 129

Failure, barriers condemning athletes to,
    71–77
Fair treatment, importance of, 136
Faith, displaying, 83–84
Favoritism, coach's, 191–192
Fear
    of coach, 30
    for emotional safety, 91–92, 94, 95
    for physical safety, 91–93
    symptoms of, 95–96
Feelings
    and constructive communication,
        124–125, 127–128, 131
    listening for, 103–104
    validating, 77, 79, 103, 107, 108–109

Fighting, 118, 155, 161
Firm messages, 107, 113–116
Firmness, and empowering discipline,
    151, 152
Fisher, R., 174
Focused attention, providing, 53–54
Forgetting, 155, 160
Foundation
    of positive coaching, 33–34
    team forum, of mutual respect and
        emotional honesty, 184–185
Framework, construction of inner, 33–34
Frustration, 23

Gerstein, A., 170, 171
Glenn, H. Stephen, 71, 75, 165
Goal(s)
    emotional, of coaches, 3–4
    leaders helping to reach, 60–61
    setting, 59–60, 84
    team, 189–190
    of young people vs. goals of sports
        education, 43–45
Goode Vick, Candace, 27
Gordon, Thomas, 86, 87, 127
Greenberg, Herbert, 109
Guilt, 167

Hahn, D., *Understanding Your Health*
    (with W. Payne), 43–44
Hand gestures, using simple, 52
Handshake, 52
Handwritten notes, 56
Happiness, 24
Hart, L., 21
Helpfulness, 24
Helpless athlete, 137
Hispanic American, acceptance of term,
    53
Honesty, team forum foundation of
    emotional, 184–185
Hostile discipline, 147–149, 152
Hostility, progression from unexpressed
    anger to, 94–95
Humiliation, 148

Images, building positive, within
    athletes, 69
I-messages, *see* Positive I-messages
Improvement, recognizing, 84
Independence, establishing sense of
    relative, 43, 45
Indignation, 148
Injury, fear of, 92, 93

Instructors vs. leaders, 27
Insults, 155
    mixing praise with, 85–86
Intrinsic worth, 51
Involvement
    athletic participation and, 61–62
    extent of meaningful, 64–65
    list of activities for athletes', 62–63

Japanese American, acceptance of term,
    53
Job satisfaction, quiz about, 15–17

Katz, Lillian, 85
Katz, Robert, 14
Kelly, Eugene, 144
Kleinke, Chris, 96
"Know-it-all" role, coaches in, 74
Kurth-Schai, R., 62

Laissez-faire coach, *see* Permissive
    coach
Landor, Walter, 143
Latino, acceptance of word, 53
Lazy athlete, 137
Leaders
    coaches as, 27
    helping to reach goals, 60–61
    vs. instructors, 27
Leadership, 26
    empowering, 28–29
Lecturing, 74–75
Lew, Amy, *Raising Kids Who Can* (with
    B. L. Bettner), 188, 190
Listening, 51–52
    effective, 107
    for feelings, 103–104
    practicing art of, 104–105
    reflecting acceptance and signifi-
        cance, 101–102
    reflective, 104, 105–106, 107
Logical consequence(s), 123, 152, 159,
    161–163, 166, 168
    difference between punishment and,
        165
    time-out as, 164
Loneliness, 49
Lott, Lynn, 165, 175, 184
Lucas, John, 70–71
Lying, 7, 22

MacKenzie, Robert, 114
Manipulative tactics, 23
Marks, I., 95
Martens, Rainer, 3

Mayer, David, 109
McKay, Gary, 144
Mess, making, 162
Messages
    of acceptance, 50–51
    firm, 107, 113–116
    soft, 116–117
Mexican American, acceptance of term,
    53
Mistaken goal(s) of behavior, 136, 144
    four, 136–138
    identifying, 139–140, 143–144
    prescriptions for each, 140–142
    reasons for failure of, 138–139
Mistakes, learning from, 84, 90
Misuse, 161
    of athletic equipment, 162–163
    of team privileges, 163
Motivation, 56
    enhancement of, by athletes' input,
        63–64
Movement, rules about player, 119

Name-calling, by coaches, 79–80, 94
Names, sensitivity to pronunciation of,
    53
National Association for the Education
    of Young Children, 85
National Basketball Association, 70
National Youth Sports Coaches Associa-
    tion (NYSCA), Coaches' Code of
    Ethics of, 3–4
Native Alaskans, 53
Native American, acceptance of term, 53
Natural consequences, 152, 159, 160–
    161
    difference between punishment and,
        165
Needs, basic emotional, 44
    attending to your own, 40–42
    importance of understanding, 38–40
    nurturing athlete's, 37–38
    and operating assumptions for
        approaching conflict, 171
    vs. wants, 37
Negative qualities, 67–68
Negligence, law of, 97
Negotiations, 170, 172
    caring and respect as foundations of,
        171
Nelsen, Jane, 139, 162, 165, 175
    Positive Discipline, 184
Nurturing
    of athletes, 9–10, 37–38
    coaches, 10–12

Obnoxious athlete, 136, 137, 191
Opinions, asking players for, 89
Outbursts, frequent angry, 23
Overpraising, 86
Ownership, 63
    psychological, 29

Pacific Islanders, acceptance of term, 53
Parents, overbearing, 129–131
Participation, 29
    encouraging, 76
    and involvement, athletic, 61–62
Passive-aggressive behavior, 167–168
"Pat" on the shoulder, 52
Payne, W., *Understanding Your Health*
        (with D. Hahn), 43–44
Peer acceptance, 144
Perception, praise not matching
        athlete's, 86
    See also Self, perceptions of
Permissive coach, 22–23
    player response to, 23
Permissive discipline, 149–151, 152
Physical safety, *see* Safety
Piggybacking, avoiding, 166
Positive I-messages, 86–88, 90, 127
    practicing, 88–89
Positive qualities, 67
Potentials, discovering, of players, 66–68
Power behavior, 137, 139, 140
    prescription for, 141–142
Practices, motivation in, 63–64
Praise
    alternative to, 86–88
    craze, 84–85
    ulterior motives behind most, 85–86
Preconceived notions, 55
Prejudice, testing for, 56–58
Problems, in sports, 7–8
Problem solving, 132, 166, 172
    four steps to, 172–174
Procedures
    to prevent problems before they
        occur, 119–120
    team rules and, 117–123
    violation of, 120
Process vs. content, 172
Program for Athletic Coaches' Educa-
        tion (PACE), 3
Psychological ownership, 29
Punishment
    difference between consequences
        and, 165
    and hostile discipline, 147–149

    for motivation, 64
    threats of, 75–76
Purpose, sense of, 59
    See also Significance
Put-downs
    by coaches, 79–80
    among teammates, 155

Questions
    closed, 106
    open-ended, 106

Racial terminology, sensitivity to, 52–53
Racism, 7
Rage, 94–95, 125
    See also Anger
Reagan, J., 170, 171
Rebellious athlete, 137
Recognition, 74, 175, 177
Reconciliation, 176, 177
Recovery, Four R's of, 175–176, 177
Reflective listening, 104, 105–106, 107
Reminding, 167–168
Repeating, 167–168
Resentment, 148
    progression from unexpressed anger
        to, 94–95
Resolution, 176, 177
Resourcefulness, 24
Respect, 34
    and caring as foundations of
        negotiations, 171
    and emotional safety, 93, 94
    and empowering discipline, 151, 152
    importance of, 28
    lack of, 23
    team forum foundation of mutual,
        184–185
Responsibility, 24, 62, 176, 177
    assuming increasing levels of, 43, 45
    delegating, 65–66
    failure to live up to, 155, 160–161
    giving, 84, 89
    lack of, 161
Retaliation, 148
Revenge behavior, 137–138, 139, 140
    prescription for, 142
Richardson, Peggy A., 111
Ridiculing, by coaches, 94
Robinson, Jackie, 54
Roethlisberger, F. J., 110
Rogers, Carl, 110
Rosenberg, Morris, *Society and Adoles-
        cent Self-Image*, 47

Rules
  challenging, 121–122
  characteristics of good, 118
  consequences to support, 159
  to consider when applying conse-
      quences, 168
  flexibility of, 120–121, 122
  ground, for team forums, 188
  keeping within spirit of, 120–121
  limited choices of, 122–123
  player input in making, 122
  and procedures, team, 117–123
  violation of, 120
Rutter, M., 61

Safety, 163
  and coach's negligence, 97
  and effects of emotional assaults, 94–
      95
  emotional, 93–94
  importance of physical and emo-
      tional, 91–92
  need for, 39, 56, 91
  physical, 92–93
  rules, 118, 119
  and underprotection vs. overprotec-
      tion, 96
Sarason, Seymour, 62
Sarcasm, by coaches, 94
Self, perceptions of, 35, 42–43, 69, 172–
    173
Self-discipline, 146
Self-esteem, 4, 34, 35, 42, 47
  attacks on, 126
  building healthy, 37–38
  and need for acceptance, 49, 50
  and praise, 85
Self-identity, forming initial, 43, 44–45
Self-image, 34, 35, 69, 70
  contribution of criticism to lowered,
      71–73
  scale to assist in understanding, 46–47
Self-imposed inadequacy, *see* Assumed
    inadequacy behavior
Self-perception, 35, 42–43, 69, 172–173
Self-worth, 34, 35, 85
Sexism, 7
Significance
  and acceptance, listening reflecting,
      101–102
  need for, 39, 56, 59–68, 135, 136
Simple-level change, 43
Sincere encounters, providing, 53–54
Skill(s)

conceptual, 14–15
for effective coaching, 13–15
human, 14
professional, 14
Smiling, 52
Smith, Dean, 42
Social behavior, evaluating athletes',
    according to adult standards, 72
Social changes, effect of, on coaching,
    8–10
Social interaction, developing social
    skills needed for, 43–44, 45
Socially inept athlete, 138
Soft messages, 116–117
Solutions, 172
  involving athletes in, 166
  vs. logical consequences, 162, 165
Sports education
  at crossroads, 5
  goals of, vs. goals of young people,
      43–45
Standards, maintaining low, 77
Stereotypes, 55, 56
Strengths
  athlete's, 83
  rating team's, 195–196
Stressful and frightening situations,
    avoiding, 138
Stroking, internal, 80–81
Stubborn athlete, 137
Stubbornness, 22
Styles, coaching, 20–21, 25–26
  autocratic, 21–22
  empowering, 23–25, 30
  permissive, 22–23
Success, structuring team for, 80
Suggestions, asking players for, 89
Suicide, 61
Superiority, 144–145
Surler, C., 85
Swearing, 118
Sympathy, 102
Synergy, concept of human, 171

Talking
  by coach, 106–107
  excessive, 74–75, 101–102
  rules about player, 119–120
Talking back, 22, 122
Team clown, 136
Team forum(s), 166, 167, 183, 191, 192,
    196–197
  agenda items at, 195
  blank agendas at, 193–194

broken agreements at, 194–195
common administrative mistakes in, 193
consequences at, 194
definition of, 183–184
foundation of mutual respect and emotional honesty, 184–185
getting started, 188–190
griping at, 193
ground rules for, 188
how to have effective, 186–188
issues inappropriate for, 192–193
with large groups, 193
receptivity of athletes to concept of, 194
structure, 185–186
waiting for next, 194
Team rules and procedures, 117–123
violation of, 120
Thai American, acceptance of term, 53
Threatening, 94
Tiedemann, Russ, 30
Time-out, as logical consequence, 164
Tolerant coach, testing of, 155–158
Touching, appropriate, 52
Trust, 28–29, 93
Tutko, T. A., 56

Unconditional acceptance, 50, 51
See also Acceptance
Uncooperativeness, 22
Ury, W., 174

Validating feelings, 77, 79, 103, 107, 108–109
Van Ekeren, Glenn, 55, 61
Verbal attacks, by coaches, 79–80
Violence, 7
threat of, 92
Vulgar language or gestures, 155

Wants vs. needs, 37
Warning, 94
Warren, William, *Coaching and Motivation*, 42
Wehlage, Gary, 61
Weinberg, Robert S., 111
White, *see* European American
Winning, attitudes toward, 3, 4, 42
Withdrawal, 23, 142, 148
Words, power of, 70

Yelling, for motivation, 64
You-messages, 88–89, 127
Youngs, Bettie, 38